FOREWORD BY JOHN BEVERE

HOW TO KEEP YOUR HEAD ON STRAIGHT IN A WORLD GONE CRAZY

DEVELOPING DISCERNMENT FOR THESE LAST DAYS

RICK RENNER

Harrison House

How To Keep Your Head on Straight in a World Gone Crazy: Developing Discernment in These Last Days

ISBN: 978-1-68031-290-4
Ebook: 978-1-68031-291-1
LP: 978-1-68031-292-8
HC: 978-1-68031-293-5

8316 E. 73rd St.
Tulsa, OK 74133

Published by Harrison House
Shippensburg, PA 17257
www.harrisonhouse.com

2 3 4 5 / 23 22 21 20 19

Editorial Consultants: Cynthia D. Hansen and Rebecca L. Gilbert
Text Design: Lisa Simpson, www.SimpsonProductions.net
Cover and Graphic Design: Debbie Pullman, Zoe Life Creative Media
Design@ZoeLifeCreative.com, www.ZoeLifeCreative.com

ENDORSEMENTS

My friend Rick Renner is a gifted teacher who makes the Bible come alive by explaining key Greek phrases in a way people can understand. In *How To Keep Your Head on Straight in a World Gone Crazy*, Rick admonishes spiritual leaders to stay focused on the authority of the Bible and sound doctrine, and he encourages believers to "shine the light of God's glory to those who sit in darkness."

Like Rick, I believe this can be the greatest moment for the Church. I pray we will make a Kingdom impact as we boldly proclaim transforming truth in the pulpit and public square.

James Robison
Founder and President
LIFE Outreach International
Fort Worth, Texas

"How do we live for Christ in a world that has gone crazy?" Rick answers the question by delivering a crushing blow to the raging cultural deceptions. He exposes the lies that Satan uses to weaken the Church.

But Rick does not stop there. After slaying the lies, he breathes life back into a forgotten key to power — a key that will not let us settle for survival but demands total victory. God has given Rick a reliable map through the maze of our wicked age — a living training manual for amazing victory in the end of days and a long overdue conviction of the Holy Spirit to jolt us into an unbreakable bond with Christ.

Mario Murillo
Mario Murillo Ministries

Rick Renner is right on time with *How To Keep Your Head on Straight in a World Gone Crazy.* It will help you navigate the challenging new moral landscape that has many believers frustrated and confused. Instead of keeping you on the defense, it will equip you to be more than a conqueror as you represent Jesus well in a lost and dying world.

Daniel Kolenda
President and CEO
Christ for All Nations

Almost 50 years ago, God raised me up to influence the generation of my three oldest children. I began as a children's minister, and when they became teenagers, I developed a cutting-edge youth ministry. Their generation is now taking its place as leaders of Christ's Church. My greatest concern for them is the same as it was 50 years ago: Will they build their lives on the words of Jesus Christ or conform to the ever-changing norms of modern culture? Rick Renner has gifted this generation with a thoroughly researched, eye-opening guidebook that I wholeheartedly endorse!

Willie George
Founding Pastor
Church on the Move
Tulsa, Oklahoma

Rick Renner has done it again in his new book *How To Keep Your Head on Straight in a World Gone Crazy!* In his trademark style, Rick shares a powerful "now" word to the Body of Christ, with a strong call to return to the basics of the Word of God. I could not agree more! The Church's greatest days are ahead and in his book, Rick Renner skillfully and compassionately shows leaders and believers how to navigate perilous times while holding fast to the word of life.

Beth Jones
Author/Pastor
Host of "The Basics With Beth" TV Program

In this book, Rick makes the case for a world gone wrong in so many ways. He also shows a pattern of the enemy's agenda to deceive throughout history that repeats itself but can be confronted and defeated. Chapter after chapter, *How To Keep Your Head on Straight in a World Gone Crazy* walks through the stages of historical cycles of decline while also offering biblical perspective and a strategic plan to counter the madness with the hope we have in Christ. One of the most powerful lines from the book says, "We must not ignore alarming events transpiring in the world around us just because those events are not directly affecting us at the present moment." He is 100-percent right, and with each chapter you read, you will see your place in the fight and a plan for victory.

Jentezen Franklin
Senior Pastor, Free Chapel
New York Times Best-Selling Author

In the present age, an entire generation is at risk of embracing error and rejecting truth. Romans chapter one, verses 22 and 25, remind us, "Professing themselves to be wise, they became fools.... They exchanged the truth of God for a lie." But it hasn't always been like this. And I've got just enough faith to believe we can get our head on straight again.

In the face of a culture that's convinced itself that good men are monsters, life is bad, killing is a virtue, and children and adults should trade places, Rick Renner brings a message of hope for our nation. He sees this alarming situation clearly, and is determined to do all he can to awaken a somnolent church and a sleeping clergy. He lays out a convincing case for acknowledging, adhering to, and advocating the truth of the Word of God. We can know it; we can defend it; and we can enlist others in our campaign to rescue a generation from deception, decline, and eventual death, which is the inevitable result of believing a lie. I am gratified that Rick Renner wrote *How To Keep Your Head on Straight in a World Gone Crazy*, and I am pleased to recommend it to you.

Dr. Rod Parsley
Pastor and Founder
World Harvest Church
Columbus, Ohio

In this book, Rick Renner does a masterful job laying out the enemy's plan to deceive, if possible, the very elect. With the last-days invasion of seducing spirits and doctrines of demons, there is a cry to be relevant, and many compromise God's Word to fit in. The signs of the times encompass a departure from the faith. It will take courageous men and women to stand up in these delusional times. Love warns that leaders must speak boldly, bringing correction to end-time error. We cannot allow popular culture to influence us, nor can we allow a Gnostic invasion of the Church. Rick spells out the solution — a mighty move of the Holy Spirit and the establishment of sound doctrine, the foundation of the Church.

We cannot be quiet; we must speak up. I highly recommend *How To Keep Your Head on Straight in a World Gone Crazy*. Thank you, Rick, for laying out the blueprint for the last-days Church to get back on track. If not, judgment will be the result.

Dr. Rodney Howard-Browne
Pastor/Author
Revival Ministries International
Tampa, Florida

We are living in a time when people are drifting away from the teachings of the Bible. I believe it's vital for every believer, pastor, and spiritual leader to know what the Bible teaches and to stand firm, regardless of the ever-changing trends of society. That's why Rick Renner's timely new book *How To Keep Your Head on Straight in a World Gone Crazy* is so important for every believer to read. Using his extensive knowledge of New Testament Greek, Rick skillfully explains biblical prophecies given to us for these times and how we must respond.

Robert Morris
Founding Lead Senior Pastor, Gateway Church
Best-selling Author of *The Blessed Life*, *Frequency*, and *Beyond Blessed*

Rick Renner is known internationally as a Bible scholar and teacher of God's Word, but his newest book *How To Keep Your Head on Straight in a World Gone Crazy* is truly "next level" — poignant, powerful, and practical. Renner has crafted each chapter with keen insights for the Church amidst a world that prefers sound bites over substance. A book this timely could only be written from a voice with decades of experience who has ministered the world over and has a strong grip on the Scriptures. This voice now not only calls every Christian to a "revival of the Bible," but also shows how to live with Spirit-guided and Jesus-initiated discernment in a world lost in confusion with competing voices. I heartily commend Rick Renner's book. I hear his voice and sense his heart on each page, calling us to greater devotion for Jesus Christ and inspiring us to maximize God's Word in our lives.

Jeremiah J. Johnston, Ph.D.
President, Christian Thinkers Society

How To Keep Your Head on Straight in a World Gone Crazy by Rick Renner is a book that every spiritual leader and believer must read. Whether you pastor a megachurch, lead a small group, or are simply a believer who loves God's Word, the information Rick lays out can only be described as alarming and extremely sobering. Rick's book addresses issues that are so vital to today's Church that, as a pastor, I am going to include it as a must-read for anyone involved in any form of spiritual leadership in our ministry.

Gary Keesee
Pastor/Author/Broadcaster
Gary Keesee Ministries
Faith Life Church
Columbus, Ohio

This book is not only a masterpiece — it is also severe medicine for a severe last-days disease. I have always had a great respect for what I call intelligent boldness, and in this book, Rick not only intelligently and boldly diagnoses the plague of our times, but he also supplies the healing and the formula for future resistance. *How To Keep Your Head on Straight in a World Gone Crazy* is an extremely bold message with intelligent proof and should be read by the entire Body of Christ — especially all those in leadership. I only wish I had written it, because this book is a life-changer.

Mark T. Barclay
Preacher of Righteousness
Mark Barclay Ministries

Rick Renner's book *How To Keep Your Head on Straight in a World Gone Crazy* tells the unvarnished truth about where society currently is and its future. It points out what Jesus said in Matthew 24 about deception being utilized by Satan to accomplish his goal. Frankly, there are many books out there to read, but *this* one is a must-read book for every Christian. I highly recommend it.

Keith Butler, Bishop
Pastor, Author
Word of Faith International Christian Center
Keith Butler Ministries
Southfield, Michigan

Since the 1960s, revelation of the Word and the restoration of the things of the Spirit have come to every denomination and reached into all the unchurched quarters of society. People are hungry to know more about God and to experience the reality of His presence. But with so many unchurched and scripturally untaught Christians, the Church has become a fiasco of one "revelation" after another.

In a world where self is exalted above all else, scriptural truths are too often added to and twisted into flesh-gratifying permission to excuse any kind of behavior. The only way to be sure you are on the right side of biblical teaching is to be taught by those who have "studied to show themselves approved" and who live their own lives with the earmarks of Jesus: to say only what the Father has said and to love as the Father has loved. Rick Renner meets those qualifications — now, just as he has for the many decades he has been in ministry.

As Rick speaks the truth in love in *How To Keep Your Head on Straight in a World Gone Crazy*, real hope, real help, and real believing rise to reveal how weak, ungodly, and dangerous worldly thinking is. This is the kind of help we all need to walk in the power of holiness — for ourselves and for those around us who must be snatched out of the fire before the door of the age closes.

Terri Copeland Pearsons
Co-Pastor, Eagle Mountain International Church
President, Kenneth Copeland Bible College
Executive Officer, Kenneth Copeland Ministries

Rick Renner helps us understand what is happening in culture all around us today. He unpacks how the Bible predicts the foolish logic and reprobate mind that manifests in our current cultural realities. Rick stirs the Church to rise up, as the Church has done in history past, to be the salt of the earth, to contend for the faith, and to remind the world of holy sanity.

We must not sacrifice the potency of the Gospel for relevance. And since the younger generation is most affected, I encourage you to devour *How To Keep Your Head on Straight in a World Gone Crazy* and learn to reach out with grace and truth to the broken and deceived all around us!

Ron Luce
Speaker, Author, Director
Jesus Global Youth Day

This is more than just a timely and relevant word. This message is mission-critical for any Christian who would dare to live as a keeper of the faith.

Jeremy Pearsons
Pearsons Ministries International

Another masterpiece from Rick Renner that should be required reading for every believer, especially pastors and spiritual leaders. We are now living in "the time to come" that Paul warned Timothy about in his second epistle. However, too few spiritual leaders are willing to take responsibility for correcting and shaping the next generation. Silence and tolerance in the face of error are not acceptable. It is the knowledge of the truth that makes us free. *How To Keep Your Head on Straight in a World Gone Crazy* shows you how to recognize error and gives you the knowledge you need to preserve your generation.

Happy Caldwell
President, VTN Network
Little Rock, Arkansas

In this book, Rick Renner brings a clear message of truth to a chaotic fray. The issues addressed affect everyone. It is vitally important that we take a strong stance now on the forever-settled truths revealed to the Church. By reminding us of historic error, Rick reveals how insidiously over time the enemy has worked his way even into the lives of believers.

The enemy knows that many of us will not immediately embrace evil, so he takes the subtle approach of pressuring us to "just be tolerant." It's no wonder that "tolerance" is one of the most heralded concepts of the hour, because the enemy knows that tolerance is the first step to conformity.

Romans 12:2 has commanded us to "...be not conformed to this world...." Although pressure to conform can be intense, we must identify with Christ. Jesus said that the world hated Him because "...I testify of it, that the works thereof are evil." Even if we must endure slander and being ostracized and hated, this is what it means to be His witness. We have the duty and honor of being light and salt in a dark, decaying world.

As you read this very well-prepared book, you'll find the Holy Spirit revealing and reminding you of the unchanging Truth we must not compromise. When we choose to hold fast to what has been given us, our hearts will be guarded and the enemy will have no place in us. And when this is our stance, it will be said of us, even as the Master said, "...The prince of this world cometh, and hath nothing in me" (John 14:30).

Keith Moore
Pastor, Teacher, Author
Faith Life Church/Moore Life Ministries
Branson, Missouri and Sarasota, Florida

After reading through Rick Renner's book *How To Keep Your Head on Straight in a World Gone Crazy*, I am taken by his boldness to take on the issues of today's world and the present condition of many of the churches in our own country. He takes up each issue scripturally and historically, showing much of the instability we see and have wondered about. Yet he addresses no problem without giving solutions. This book is a must for all ministers and believers in these last days we are all living in.

Bob Yandian
Pastor, Teacher, Author, Broadcaster
Bob Yandian Ministries

The apostle Paul spoke of certain elders who exerted themselves, laboring in word and in doctrine. Rick Renner is certainly at the top of the list of such ministers in modern times. If you have never read after Rick before, he communicates with utmost respect for the authority of Scripture, with intense focus, and with surgical precision.

How To Keep Your Head on Straight in a World Gone Crazy presents a sobering and challenging look at rapidly shifting societal trends and challenges the Church to respond appropriately. The very issues Rick tackles will determine whether believers will be conformed to the world or whether they will be true light and salt in the earth. I especially appreciate Chapter Seven of Rick's new book — "Could You Pass a Doctrine Test?" It is absolutely imperative that Christians be solidly grounded in the historic and foundational truths of Scripture. This book is a great contribution to the Body of Christ, and believers will be well-served to absorb and apply its contents.

Tony Cooke
Bible Teacher and Author
Tony Cooke Ministries

How To Keep Your Head on Straight in a World Gone Crazy is a common-sense, biblical approach to critical issues facing the Church. In this book, Rick is adamant about the Church's need to anchor her beliefs and practices upon the unchanging truth of Scripture. Many in the Body of Christ have unwittingly embraced a watered-down version of the Gospel, and it is an hour when strong voices are needed to move the Church back to the bedrock of scriptural truth we were founded upon.

Rick Renner is one of those voices that God has raised up for such a time as this to help believers embrace the current move of the Holy Spirit while clinging tightly to the never-changing truth of Scripture. This book is an invaluable resource for Christian leaders and will prove to be immeasurably helpful to any believer who desires to have a broader understanding of God's work in the world as well as a deeper, more fruitful, personal walk with the Lord. We need to heed the clarion call that rings so clearly in *How To Keep Your Head on Straight in a World Gone Crazy.*

Bayless Conley
Pastor, Author, Broadcaster
Cottonwood Church
Los Alamitos, California
Host, "Answers with Bayless Conley"

It seems obvious to me that Rick Renner is called and anointed not only to help us understand and rightly divide specific texts, but to help us remain properly oriented to the larger context of challenges and solutions unique to the Church of our day. I'm sure we can all agree that America's departure from the standard of God's Word in just a few decades is staggering. Even more troubling, however, is the silent acquiescence of many church leaders in the apparent desire to remain "relevant" to the general population. Deception is obviously widespread. Thank you, Rick, for the wake-up call — and for the doctrine test.

Mac Hammond
Senior Pastor, Living Word Christian Center
Brooklyn Park, Minnesota

Few people have inspired me to dig as deep into the Scriptures as has Rick Renner. For almost three decades, I've read his writings, listened to his teachings, and have grown in my love for Jesus, His Word, and His Church. Rick's latest offering, *How To Keep Your Head on Straight in a World Gone Crazy*, is precisely what we have come to expect from him. He writes with the heart of a shepherd, the insight of a prophet, and the wisdom of a teacher. This book will strengthen your faith to stand firm in these crazy times.

Dr. Terry M. Crist
Lead Pastor, Hillsong Church
Phoenix, Tucson, Las Vegas
Host, "Café Theology," Hillsong Channel

This book is a must for the end-time Church to know where she stands — and don't take this book lightly. We are right in the middle of the greatest spiritual war. It's time for the Church to *wake* up and *get* up and fight the good fight of faith! This prophetic teaching is a warning to many not to move away from the foundations of God's Word and for the Church to be a voice of Righteousness, Truth, and Justice!

Rev. Margaret Court AO, MBE
Senior Pastor, Victory Life Centre
Perth, Western Australia

AO (Order of Australia is an order of chivalry established by Elizabeth II, Queen of Australia, to recognize Australian citizens and other persons for achievement or meritorious service)
MBE (Most Excellent Order of the British Empire is a British order of chivalry rewarding contributions to the arts and sciences, work with charitable and welfare organizations, and public service outside the civil service)

I have to agree that sometimes it seems as if the world has gone totally *insane*! Society tries to tell us that God's not fashionable and the Bible is no longer relevant. Rick Renner's timely new book *How To Keep Your Head on Straight in a World Gone Crazy* teaches us how to recognize these "end times" and understand the prophecy that's ultimately being fulfilled. Satan's unrelenting mental bombardment has the world completely *deceived* and spiraling out of control! We have to stand firm and stop apologizing for God's Word! Society may change — but Christ will always remain the *same*!

David Crank
Senior Pastor
FaithChurch.com
St. Louis, Royal Palm, and West Palm Beach

In the contemporary world, it has become common for facts to be twisted in support of various positions. Because of that, mutual trust has been largely undermined, but it has also ignited a desire for reliable facts with firsthand sources. The book you are about to read has a profound approach toward fact scrutiny, so you may find a footnote with a firsthand source to almost all of the facts cited in the book.

What really fascinates me as a lawyer is that the undertaken research is both factually and legally correct, especially in regard to the WWII and the Nuremberg proceedings, so you can trust the facts and conclusions drawn in this book. When the world goes crazy, we have to stand for our values based on a genuine and everlasting source of truth — *the Holy Bible.*

Michael Sondor

- Head of Project Group, Legal Department, LLC VTB DC
- LLB and LLM in International Law and Russian Corporate Law (graduated with distinction and diplomas signed by Chief Justice of the Russian Supreme Court)
- Privileged to argue cases before the Supreme Court of the Russian Federation

---

In *How To Keep Your Head on Straight in a World Gone Crazy*, Rick Renner helps each of us remember how imperative the infallibility of the Bible is and what devastation results if we depart from what once and for all has been given to us through the Scriptures. With solid, Bible-anchored arguments, Rick shows the consequences of today's liberalism in the Church, while at the same time pointing to what each of us can do to make necessary changes happen.

Matts-Ola Ishoel
Senior Pastor and Author
Word of Life Church
Moscow, Russia

In this book, Rick Renner provides scriptural insight, as well as current and historical context, regarding the times we are privileged to live in. First Chronicles 12:32 (*NIV*) says that the men from Issachar "...understood the times and knew what Israel should do...." Rick does a masterful job warning the Church of demonic attacks and the deceptions at work in these last days.

How To Keep Your Head on Straight in a World Gone Crazy is a great tool to help Christians get a bird's-eye view of the age in which they live. I encourage you to read this book and "...contend for the faith which was once delivered unto the saints" (Jude 3).

Duane Vander Klok
Senior Pastor and Author
Resurrection Life Church
Grandville, Michigan

How To Keep Your Head on Straight in a World Gone Crazy is a clarion call to the Church in this hour that challenges the Church to do everything possible to reach people — *EXCEPT compromise*! In a culture and Church that is departing from the Word of the living God, Rick challenges us with his expertise from the Greek language like no one else can. In this hour of rampant deception, I believe this book is a vital part of God's standard of truth that we need to hear in these last days!

Jim Frease
Senior Pastor and Author, Joy Church
President, World Changers Bible Institute
Mt. Juliet, Tennessee

How To Keep Your Head on Straight in a World Gone Crazy is a masterpiece written by one of the leading prophetic voices in the Body of Christ. Written at just the right time, this book documents with clarity the chaotic attack of the enemy against God's good creation and the overwhelming hope and victory that is available to us in Christ.

I believe this book should be on the top of every believer's reading list and probably needs to be read more than once. It will sober you and motivate you to "...live righteously in the midst of a crooked and twisted generation, among whom you shine as lights in the world, holding fast to the word of life..." (Philippians 2:15,16 *ESV*).

Lee M. Cummings
Senior Pastor for Radiant Church
Richland, Michigan
Overseer of Radiant Network of Churches
Author of *Be Radiant* and *Flourish: Planting Your Life Where God Designed It To Thrive*

What a privilege it is to live in the last of the last days with the opportunity of participating in the great final harvest of souls of the Church Age! But we also face great spiritual dangers with the world descending into ever-increasing darkness, just as Scripture predicted! As one of God's generals, Rick Renner calls us to wake up and see that the spirit of the world is trying to infiltrate the Church with false doctrines.

Our only hope to stand uncompromised for God in these times is to be firmly established upon God's Word as our final authority. Through Rick's vivid word pictures, he brings the New Testament warnings to life, stirring our hearts out of passivity so we can take our place in God's army.

Derek Walker
Senior Pastor
Oxford Bible Church
Oxford, England, United Kingdom

DEDICATION

Acts 1:1 tells us that Luke wrote the book of Acts for an individual he referred to as *Theophilos*, a name constructed from the Greek words *theos* and *philos*. The first word means *God*, and the second word means *love*. However, when combined into one word, as Luke did in Acts 1:1, the name *Theophilos* is formed, which is a name that depicts anyone who is a *God-lover*. A number of Bible scholars suggest that Luke coined this name as his special way of addressing every *God-lover* who would read the book of Acts throughout the ages to come.

IN A SIMILAR FASHION...
I DEDICATE THIS BOOK TO *DIDACHOPHILOS*.

As Luke perhaps coined the name *Theophilos* to address all *God-lovers* who would eventually read the book of Acts, I have coined the name *Didachophilos* from two New Testament Greek words to describe my audience of readers.

The name *Didachophilos* is constructed from the words *didache* and *philos* — the first word meaning *doctrine* and the second meaning *love*. But when compounded, the name *Didachophilos* is formed, which figuratively depicts *any person who loves Bible doctrine and is committed to its purity*. In other words, the name *Didachophilos* denotes any person who is a *doctrine-lover.*

If you count yourself among those who refuse to loosen their hold on the eternal truth of God's Word and have chosen never to move from those immutable realities, then you are part of the *Didachophilos* to whom I dedicate this book. My prayer is that this book will fortify your faith in the veracity of Scripture and that it will help you know how to keep your head on straight as you victoriously navigate the stormy seas of this prophetic end-time season that God has called us to live in by the power of the Holy Spirit.

CONTENTS

ACKNOWLEDGMENTS

As usual, I want to acknowledge those who worked with me in this writing project. To produce a quality book requires multiple minds, hands, and eyes — and I am appreciative of all who used their God-given skills in helping me refine what I believe the Holy Spirit has instructed me to write.

I first want to say thank you to Denise for her constant support and valuable advice as I wrote these pages. As I always do, I asked her to read the manuscript and to give me her view of what I had written. Besides Denise, Paul Renner and Joel Renner played a major role in reading and providing comments that were so very helpful in my writing process.

Cindy Hansen, my long-time editor, did a marvelous job as always on editing the manuscript. I am thankful for her writing partnership on many book projects over many years.

Becky Gilbert, the head editor of our ministry, provided not only her fine-tuning editorial skills to this project, but also many thoughtful spiritual insights that are so valuable to me — all while ably overseeing the vast array of ministry editorial projects that are continually "in the works." I'm so grateful.

Likewise, I want to acknowledge Maxim Myasnikov (my assistant in Moscow), who worked endless hours to verify information about the Nazi atrocities of World War II that are held in the archives of the Lenin State Library in central Moscow. I am so thankful to him for his commitment to help me provide accurate historical information. In addition, I am very thankful to Moscow attorney Michael Sondor both for offering his insightful assistance and for securing access to remarkable historical documents that hold riveting and truly sobering accounts of the Nazi activity I write about in Chapter One. In addition, I want to thank Jon Blume and Dan Beirute for their historical and legal perspectives regarding the issues covered in this book.

I wish to also thank the many Christian leaders who took time to review this book and to provide their thoughtful comments and endorsements. The quick responses by a host of these leaders and their willingness to help me in this regard were very impacting to me personally. These are men and women who hold such great responsibility in the Kingdom and manage such busy schedules. I am grateful for their brilliant minds and eyes on this book project. Wow, I am just so thankful to you all.

I also want to express what an honor it is to work with Don Nori and Brad Herman and the rest of the team at Harrison House. I am thankful for your partnership in getting the message to hungry hearts.

Last, I want to express my profound thankfulness for the team God has assembled as coworkers in the Kingdom of God. Together — with the help of the Holy Spirit — we are impacting multitudes as we pray for a genuine revival of the Bible in the Body of Christ. I am eternally thankful for the faithful participation of each of you in this great and holy venture.

FOREWORD

Dear reader, I'm quite happy you hold this book in your hand. I'll share why in a moment. But first, I want to thank Rick Renner for several things: First, for being a man of God who never compromises truth for personal gain. Second, for being an excellent husband, father, and grandfather. Third, for faithfully birthing and pastoring the Moscow Good News Church in Moscow, Russia. Fourth, for traveling globally to make disciples of nations. And finally, for being a dear friend to Lisa, me, and our sons.

Now allow me to expound on the importance of this message. Experts in propaganda understand that a cleverly presented lie repeated often enough will eventually become accepted as truth. Numerous political campaigns thrive on presenting misinformation motivated by a hidden agenda. Satan is no different. As "the prince of the power of the air" (Ephesians 2:2), his plan has always been to control people through deception. Unfortunately, the problem with deception is...well, it's deceiving.

Deception poses a major problem because people who are deceived believe wholeheartedly that they are correct, accurate, and on the side of truth — but in reality, they are not. That's why deception is so scary.

Paul warned that in the last days, many "...will not endure sound doctrine, but according to their own desires, because they have itching ears, they will heap up for themselves teachers; and they will turn their ears away from the truth and be turned aside to fables" (2 Timothy 4:3,4 *NKJV*).

It's a gradual progression. This deceptive spiral begins by not enduring sound doctrine. Another way to say this is that those deceived don't stay committed to foundational biblical teaching.

Because of their own desires, they will turn their attention away from the truth and will embrace fables. Another word for fables is "myths," which means *a widely held but false belief or idea.*

So in essence, Paul was saying that many in our time will gravitate toward doctrine that is culturally acceptable — whether it aligns with God's Word or not. With selective hearing, these individuals will hold to the status quo and gravitate toward those who will tell them what they want to hear at the neglect of what they *need* to hear. They will drift from truth and become lost in a sea of confusion because they are not anchored in the Word of God. This seduction is so twisted that it has resulted now in many calling "good" *evil* and "evil" *good* — thus fulfilling Isaiah's prophecy (*see* Isaiah 5:20).

The concerns Paul had to address are the same concerns we are having to address. Along with this solemn warning, Paul also noted how subtle this deception will be. He wrote, "But I fear, lest somehow, as the serpent *deceived* Eve by his craftiness, so *your minds may be corrupted* from the simplicity that is in Christ. For if he who comes preaches another Jesus whom we have not preached, or . . . a different gospel which you have not accepted — *you may well put up with it*!" (2 Corinthians 11:3,4 *NKJV*).

Satan deceived Eve by causing her to question the validity of God's Word and, in the process, perverted God's character in her eyes. This same deception can and has crept into the Church through the avenue of incorrect preaching and teaching that have been cleverly packaged to appeal to the desires of the flesh — much like the way Eve embraced the devil's twisted truth.

Unfortunately, many believers have done the same — leaving the door wide open for the enemy to wreak havoc! With this access, not only are these spirits of deception attempting to lure the secular world under their influence, but they are also attempting to do so with the Church. This is why the apostle Jude vehemently wrote, "I have to write insisting — begging! — that you fight with everything you have in you for this faith entrusted to us as a gift to guard and cherish" (Jude 3 *MSG*).

If we leave this problem unaddressed, it will continue to weaken Christians and position them to fall prey to the snare of the devil's insidious schemes. This is why Jude begged that we fight with everything we have for the faith that was entrusted to us.

Please grasp the severity and urgency of this issue!

More than ever, we need discernment — which will keep us from mixing up good and evil, especially in a day when deception runs rampant. So how do we develop and exercise discernment? Through godly fear, which gives us a love for truth. The degree of our ability to discern is proportional to our level of the fear of the Lord and our understanding of God's Word. Simply stated: The more we fear God, the more we'll esteem and tremble at His Word — and, thus, we'll be able to discern correctly.

Again, when a lie is repeated often enough and left unchecked, it will eventually become accepted as truth. The question is, *why have we put up with it?* Have we forgotten that what we tolerate, we empower? Silence is communication! Silence communicates agreement and grants permission. We enable deception when we refuse to confront the lies.

Silence is not an option!

This is why Paul prefaced his prophetic statement with, "Herald and preach the Word! Keep your sense of urgency [stand by, be at hand and ready], whether the opportunity seems to be favorable or unfavorable. [Whether it is convenient or inconvenient, whether it is welcome or unwelcome, you as preacher of the Word are to show people in what way their lives are wrong.] And convince them, rebuking and correcting, warning and urging and encouraging them, being unflagging and inexhaustible in patience and teaching" (2 Timothy 4:2 *AMPC*).

Christ followers, especially leaders, if you are holding this book, please heed its exhortation to preach the whole counsel of God. My dear friend, Rick Renner, has not kept silent about this crucial matter. I'm so thrilled you're holding this message in your hands, because Rick not only demystifies the cloud of confusion, exposing the enemy's traps — he provides the solution to overcome them. Rick does a remarkable job of calling the Church back to the authoritative voice of the Scriptures so that we can experience what Rick has coined — *a revival of the Bible*!

Sincerely,
John Bevere
Best-selling Author and Minister
Cofounder of Messenger International
June 2019

A 'MUST-READ' INTRODUCTION

This is a "must-read" introduction — because it is important for me personally that you read it before you start the first chapter of this book. This book is very different from anything I've written before, so I want you to first hear my heart about the words I penned in this book before you turn to Chapter One and begin reading.

We are living in messy times. I'm sure you would agree that it seems the world has gone crazy on many fronts. For those whose thinking is biblically based, it is shocking to see how far society is drifting from what was once held precious in terms of morality and faith. But 2,000 years ago at the very beginning of the Church Age, the Holy Spirit foretold that a very strange season would emerge both in society and in the Church as we approached the end of the age. We are living in that season.

It was prophesied that seducing spirits with doctrines of demons would lead masses into deception in the last of the last days. That is the time frame we find ourselves in, and we are indeed observing society throwing off the voice of Scripture to create a new world with a new moral code that is both messy and chaotic. I'm sure you would agree that we are living in a mind-boggling period of deceived thinking that most of us wouldn't have imagined possible a generation ago.

In the first chapter of this book, I deal with issues that demonstrate how far the pendulum had already swung in the not-so-distant past, as well as how vastly far it is swinging in the present hour. Focusing on those issues is not my purpose. I have simply pointed out these developments to demonstrate the challenges facing our times and the need for believers to keep their wits about them and their eyes fixed on Jesus. As we sail further into the end-time seas, grasping and maintaining our hold on His eternal truth is a *must.*

The good news is that the Scriptures also prophesied that a mighty outpouring of the Holy Spirit would come upon the Church at the end of the age — that is, a visitation of God's power, resulting in a massive last-days harvest of souls. So in addition to seeing widespread deception, we are destined to be a part of the greatest harvest of souls to ever occur in the entire 2,000-year history of the Church. The fact is, we are in the midst of that end-time visitation right now, and the Holy Spirit is being mightily poured out on every part of the globe.

We are living in both the greatest of days and in the most troublesome of times. More and more, society as a whole is rejecting the authoritative voice of the Bible and seems bent on embracing self-destructive and ungodly ways of thinking and behaving. Many believers, pastors, and spiritual leaders do not know how to respond to the moral mess and doctrinal errors emerging all around them. Not wanting to be perceived as being judgmental or condemning, they often choose to remain silent on issues where the voice of the Bible needs to be spoken to a world that is going astray.

That is why it is so important for us to learn how to think right, use our sound minds, stay sensitive to the Lord in our hearts, and keep our heads on straight in this world that is going crazy as we approach the end of this age. You see, the Bible prophesied that seducing spirits would invade society, and it is occurring exactly as the Holy Spirit said that it would. This deception is so sophisticated and insidious in its seduction that it has even taken hold of some believers and spiritual leaders in various quarters of the Church. But that is what the Holy Spirit prophesied some 2,000 years ago — and that is the theme of the book you hold in your hands, along with instruction on what we as believers must do about it.

Most Christians will never be theologians. Even many pastors and solid spiritual leaders who know the power of the Holy Spirit and who believe in the authority of the Bible will never teach at that level. But because we are living in a last-days season when seducing spirits are luring people away from the core teachings of the Bible, it is vital that every believer, pastor, and spiritual leader knows the non-negotiable tenets of the faith and makes the decision to dig his or her heels into the bedrock of Scripture and to never budge from its authoritative voice. Every believer needs to know what the Bible teaches about these basic doctrines and to *hold fast to the truth*, regardless of the ever-changing trends of a wandering society.

The devil fully understands that the Word of God alone has the power to open blind eyes and set men free. This is why he seeks to nullify the Bible's voice and to relegate it as an antiquated document from the past that has no relevance for the present hour. That is also why we must take this rock-solid stance on the absolute authority of the Bible and learn to partner with the Holy Spirit to see the power of God drive back the forces of darkness.

The prophet Isaiah foretold a day would come when gross darkness would come upon the peoples of the earth. But he also triumphantly declared that this day would be the golden moment for God's people to rise and shine with His glory (*see* Isaiah 60:1).

We are living in that prophesied time. But even as gross darkness is coming upon the world, so also is this God-ordained, long-awaited, prophesied moment for the Church to rise and shine the light of His glory to those who sit in darkness! This is the greatest hour of opportunity the Church has ever faced — and you and I have been chosen by God to be participants in these significant days before Jesus returns.

I also want to state how important it is that we do not sit around and casually criticize those who are in spiritual trouble because they have veered away from sound doctrine or right living. Although it's necessary for each of us to be awakened to the challenges, it is essential that we find a positive way to contribute to the solution. For this reason, in the final chapters of this book, I address the role we must assume to prayerfully intercede for all wayward believers and errant spiritual leaders who have been duped and seduced by the spirit of this delinquent age.

My prayer is that this book will help gear you mentally and spiritually for this present day and for the days ahead. I sincerely pray that you find it a valuable tool to help you think right when the world around you seems to be doing the very opposite.

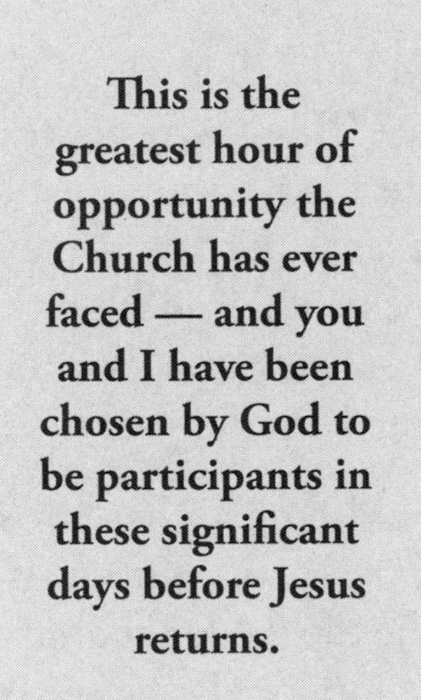

This is the greatest hour of opportunity the Church has ever faced — and you and I have been chosen by God to be participants in these significant days before Jesus returns.

I say again that this is our greatest moment. But as such, we must be aware of the devil's desire to derail us, and we must proceed into this prophetic season with careful thoughtfulness. These are days to exercise great caution and to learn how to block any inroads the devil would try to use to find access into our lives personally and into the lives of all God's people at this crucial hour.

I ask you to invite the Holy Spirit to speak to you through the pages that follow. Turn to Chapter One, and let's get started discovering what the Holy Spirit prophesied about the end of the age and how we as God's people must respond.

Rick Renner
Moscow, Russia, 2019

Arise, shine; for thy light is come,

and the glory of the Lord is risen upon thee.

For, behold, the darkness shall cover the earth,

and gross darkness the people:

but the Lord shall arise upon thee,

and his glory shall be seen upon thee.

— Isaiah 60:1,2

CHAPTER ONE

A WORLD GONE CRAZY

You and I are living in *strange times*!

We are actually living at the very end of the age — and as a result, we are going to see and experience things that no other generation has ever witnessed. Some things will be so far-fetched and bizarre that as rational, thinking people, we will find it incomprehensible. Indeed, to many of us, it already seems that common sense has been thrown to the wind on various fronts, replaced with irrational beliefs that are cheered on by a morally delinquent culture. But as those born to live in this hour, we must simply accept it as fact. You and I *will* be witnesses to strange developments as we near the end of this last-days time frame.

The Scriptures long ago foretold that the last days would be strange. But because you and I were born in this time, we will inevitably be thrust into the face of some of the "weird" that goes along with living in this end-times territory. The challenge before us as God's people is to keep the lunacy *outside* the Church and our families, refusing to allow our thinking to be muddied by the spirit of this age. We must dig our heels into the long-established truths of Scripture and determine to keep our heads on straight in a world that seems to have gone crazy. This book will show us how to do it.

Approximately 2,000 years ago, the Scriptures prophesied of this end-time delusion: "Now the Spirit speaketh expressly, that in the latter times some shall depart from the faith, giving heed to seducing spirits, and doctrines of devils" (1 Timothy 4:1). In this verse, the Holy Spirit alerted us that there would be an invasion of seducing spirits that would attempt to lead society off track into unthinkable levels of delusion at the very end of the age. In the years ahead of us before this age ends, we will witness advances of delusion beyond what any of us could have imagined.

We're going to study prophetic utterances in the New Testament that describe the ever-expanding influence of seducing spirits and doctrines of devils that will mark the very last of the last days. As you read on, you will see what the Bible explicitly foretold — that a worldwide mutiny against God would eventually come. By observing cultural changes that are developing all around us, we get an unmistakable feeling that surely we are already in the middle of this creeping rebellion.

In this first chapter, I will give some concrete examples of the lunacy that has been worming its way into the culture over this past century. I give these examples not as a focal point or even as a point of contention, but simply as evidence of how far delusion and a widespread mutiny against God and His Word have already advanced in modern society.

Society today seems to be like a ship lost at sea that is drifting farther and farther off course. Over the passage of seafaring history, countless ships have been lost at sea because no course correction was put into place to get them back on track when they began to lose their bearings. Many Christian leaders believe that "lost at sea" describes exactly where the world is right now.

As people of faith, we want to present the belief that God has good things in store for us and for mankind. However, we can't ignore the evidence that a moral anchor has been lost and "the ship" is veering way off course.

There is no doubt that we are witnessing a society gone morally adrift at the end of the age — lured into depths of degeneracy and depravity over this past century that have not been seen since the days when paganism ruled the earth. In fact, we may be witnesses to a pandemic of reprobate thinking on a level that no generation of any epoch in history has witnessed before.

As believers, it's so important for us to recognize the dangerous reefs that lie hidden from common view and threaten to shipwreck this last-days society, causing it to sink to depths of evil our minds don't want to accept that man could ever go again.

We'll spend much time in the chapters that follow getting well acquainted with God's perspective and the Church's role in these tumultuous times. The rest of the chapters in this book will be filled with Bible exposition that will thrill your heart! But before we get there, I believe the following discussion is a needed wakeup call for us as believers. It serves as a stark reminder that we *must not* ignore alarming events transpiring in the world around us just because those events are not directly affecting us personally at the present moment. Society is dangerously adrift in a sea of deception and moral confusion, and its present course, unaltered, will ultimately lead to destruction.

Two World Views

Before we continue, I need to say that if you are committed to a biblical worldview, you will agree with much of what you are about to read in this chapter and throughout the rest of the book. But if you believe that the Bible is simply a philosophical option rather than the immutable voice of God's authority, it is possible you may not appreciate the position that I take in the pages that follow.

We *must not* ignore alarming events transpiring in the world around us just because those events are not directly affecting us personally at the present moment. Society is dangerously adrift in a sea of deception and moral confusion, and its present course, unaltered, will ultimately lead to destruction.

A biblical worldview is based on the infallible Word of God, and when a person adheres to the view that the Bible is entirely true, he consequently allows it to be the foundation of everything he says and does. This is my position, and from this I will never deviate. Decades from now, I will continue holding to this position because my faith is deeply rooted in the unchanging voice of Scripture.

My life task is to know Scripture better, to grow in my understanding of it, and to never depart from the eternal truths contained in it. Those who do not hold this view may perceive people who believe like this as being contrary, intolerant, narrow-minded, inflexible, and obstinate because they remain fixed to unchanging biblical truth.

But those who have a non-biblical view will fluctuate on many issues that are already answered for those who have a biblical worldview. Even the most basic issues for this group may shift because their beliefs are affected by the ever-changing current thought and by the most recently accepted norms, whatever they may be.

A non-biblical worldview is primarily fashioned and informed by the fields of science, medicine, and education, as well as by societal norms. These factors are constantly in the state of flux created by the variant drifts of societal currents and the newest theories. Therefore, those who adopt this view will likely change what they inherently believe multiple times in the years to come. This is an unstable and unreliable path that floats on trends rather than on faith that is fixed in absolute truth.

My life task is to know Scripture better, to grow in my understanding of it, and to never depart from the eternal truths contained in it.

Because of these very vastly different worldviews, people on both sides rarely coincide, especially on issues of morality and doctrine. In cases of disagreement, we should respectfully disagree and maintain civility.

In Ephesians 2:2, Paul wrote that unbelievers walk "according to the course of this world." In that verse, Paul used a series of Greek words to picture people who live by the ever-fluctuating whims of a constantly changing culture. Even in early New Testament times, believers lived by fixed scriptural truth as opposed to those who lived by the fleeting and ever-shifting cultural norms of the day.

As is the case in today's society, many pagans in the First Century perceived Christians to be narrow-minded because they adhered to a fixed standard from which they would not budge. Consequently, many pagans harbored ill feelings about Christians and widely believed them to be *antisocial*, *contrary*, *incompliant*, *intolerant*, *narrow-minded*, *nonconformist*, *inflexible*, *obstinate*, and *uncompromising*. That means if many Christians today feel like they take the brunt of hostility from an unbelieving world, they can rest assured that this has been felt by myriads of believers in times past.

As believers, we need to keep the anchor of the Word in place and not drift off course with the madness that is luring so many into this state of confusion in these last days.

In light of all this, I want to say that what you read about later in this chapter is not a personal assault on anyone. I will mention the plight of certain people whom I believe are living in a state of deep-seated confusion. It is simply my biblical perspective of what is happening in our modern society.

My purpose is to help those who hold to a biblical worldview understand how to stay true to the truths of God's Word in a society that is becoming morally adrift. The Bible prophesied that this would occur at the end of the age, and as believers, we need to keep the anchor of the Word in place and not drift off course with the madness that is luring so many into this state of confusion in these last days.

How To Frame the Discussion Ahead

Keep all this in mind to help frame the enormity of what you are about to read. We're about to navigate a painful glimpse into what mankind is capable of when demons are given far too much sway to facilitate hell's limitlessly evil imagination. The shocking atrocities I'm about to briefly mention were fully sanctioned by a government that was elected into power (by "the will of the people") through deception at an opportune time in history. That's important to understand, for we are living in a society that has been groomed for some time to be caught in a similar way in an ever-tightening snare of demonic deception.

Also, don't lose sight of our divine mandate as you read the rest of this chapter. Through the sacrifice of His Son, God established the Church on this earth with the intention that evil would *never* be left unchecked. We represent the highest authority in all creation, and we've been given weapons of warfare that are *mighty* for the tearing down of the enemy's strongholds (*see* 2 Corinthians 10:3-5). We have the name of Jesus, the blood of Jesus, and the mighty sword of God's Word. And through the power of prayer by the Spirit of God, we are called to diligently keep watch and faithfully do our part to *thwart* Satan's ability to carry out his evil strategies!

Through the sacrifice of His Son, God established the Church on this earth with the intention that evil would *never* be left unchecked. We represent the highest authority in all creation, and we've been given weapons of warfare that are *mighty* for the tearing down of the enemy's strongholds.

Let that perspective undergird you as you proceed to read this next section. Let the horror of what you're about to learn *fire you up* to do your part in the days ahead to ensure that the Church takes her rightful place and steadfastly shines forth the eternal Word of truth to combat darkness.

This wakeup call is not intended to hurt you. My prayer is that it will help you see more clearly what demonic deception can look like when left unchecked to follow all the way to the inevitable end of the devil's agenda. I also pray that this new measure of clarity becomes part of your arsenal to help you become a more effective "watchman on the wall" for God's Kingdom in your community and in your nation as the tumultuous days that lie ahead continue to unfold.

A Real-Life Horror Story Exposed

In 1945 at the end of World War II, the victorious Allied troops entered Nazi concentration camps and were *aghast* at the human suffering they discovered there. As the full scope of the atrocities committed inside the camps was uncovered in the months and years that followed, the world came to know how Nazi forces had systematically murdered millions of people they considered to be inferior in the regime's efforts to create a "superior" race.

But one of the hidden horrors uncovered as Allied troops liberated the concentration camps was what remained of the sadistic experiments performed on human beings on a wide scale in the name of producing and preserving that pure master race. The scope of these unthinkable experiments is staggering to the human mind, and all of them were conducted away from public scrutiny until discovered by Allied troops.

When Allied troops entered the concentration camps at the end of the war, they discovered the atrocities committed by Nazi doctors, and they exposed their crimes in the media. The international community was rightly outraged, and the worldwide response was to call for those who had carried out these deeds to be arrested, sentenced, and sent to prison or even executed for their monstrous, despicable, and unspeakable crimes against humanity.

Before vast numbers of prisoners in those concentration camps met their final fate, whether in gas chambers or by other means, vile and abhorrent experiments were performed on them at the orders of Nazi doctors. The list of horrors these demented physicians committed is so extensive and grotesque that I will not attempt to list them all or describe them fully. The experiments performed were enormous in scope, and many are still unknown. However, I believe it's needful to open a small window into what deception can look like — and the extent of manifested evil that is possible on this earth — when evil is left unchecked because a large part of the Church within a society ignores its civic responsibilities, as well as its divine mandate to always "watch and pray" (*see* Matthew 26:41).

Behind locked gates of concentration camps, Nazi doctors carried out gruesome experiments on human captives — often under the guise of "helping the war effort"— who had been sent to concentration camps by Nazi forces. For instance, chemical attacks had become a new risk since World War I, so Nazi doctors used their access to the vast supply of helpless human subjects in the concentration camps to develop coinciding research. They would expose innocent prisoners to the unspeakable torment of mustard gas and other lethal chemicals to learn about their effects on the human body.[1]

I believe it's needful to open a small window into what deception can look like — and the extent of manifested evil that is possible on this earth — when evil is left unchecked because a large part of the Church within a society ignores its civic responsibilities, as well as its divine mandate to always "watch and pray."

The "war effort" rationale would also be used to ascertain how quickly infection spread in battle wounds.[2] Prisoners' legs, arms, and torsos were cut open with no anesthesia and intentionally flooded with bacteria as doctors scattered dirt, glass, and splinters into the wounds to make the infection spread faster. Then they agonizingly scraped the wounds — again, with no anesthesia — to learn how effective newly created experimental drugs were in fighting infection.

[1]Joshua A. Perper and Stephen J. Cina, *When Doctors Kill: Who, Why, and How* (Springer Science & Business Media 2010-06-14), p. 72.
[2]Professor Volker Roelke, "Nazi Medicine and Research on Human Beings," *The Lancet* (December 2004).

Women were not spared in these World War II hellholes called Nazi concentration camps. Along with the men, women were also worked to death, starved, beaten, hanged, shot, gassed, poisoned, and even burnt alive in the crematoriums. And women were often the subjects of the heinous Nazi medical research going on inside the camps. For instance, in the buildings where the top-secret medical research was conducted, unspeakable experiments were often performed on non-pregnant women to discover more efficient ways to sterilize, and on pregnant women to find new ways to abort babies in the womb — all toward the Nazis' long-term goal of eliminating "undesirable" populations.[3]

Concentration-camp doctors also worked intensely at validating their Nazi philosophy that Jews and Gypsies were genetically inferior in a variety of ways. One experiment conducted to this end was to contaminate these categories of prisoners with excruciating and dreadful diseases to see if they would die more quickly than other races that they considered to be superior.[4]

As for the fate of the subjects if they survived these unimaginable procedures, it was of no concern to the Nazi doctors, as they considered the prisoners "useless eaters" who were less than human and therefore were "lives not worth living."[5] These doctors were well aware that the victims' next stop would likely be the gas chamber for extermination.

Widespread Evil Always Has Its Roots in Widespread Deception

How could the depths of such horror ever have come about? A deadly deception dubbed "racial hygiene" had taken root in

[3]Laurence Reese, *Auschwitz: A New History* (New York: Public Affairs, 2005), pp. 178-179.
[4]Holocaust Encyclopedia, "Nazi Medical Experiments," https://encyclopedia.ushmm.org/content/en/article/nazi-medical-experiments.
[5]"Lives Not Worth Living: The Nazi Eugenics Dream in Our Own Time," https://aleteia.org/2014/09/12/lives-not-worth-living-the-nazi-eugenic-dream-in-our-own-time/.

the psyche of the German medical profession in the post-WWI years. Those in the field of medicine who embraced the concept in the early days largely had little concept of the future nightmare they were helping to lay the groundwork to facilitate — for a society was being groomed for something more evil and insidious to come.

The science of *eugenics*, an offshoot of Darwin's theory of evolution promoting the idea of "the survival of the fittest," had actually been growing in acceptance in several civilized nations — including America — ever since the late Nineteenth Century. Proponents of eugenics pursued this policy of racial improvement through controlled breeding, providing justification for such policies as forced sterilization, segregation laws, marriage restrictions — and, later, abortion.

The eugenics deception would befoul the moral underpinnings of Western society at large and the medical profession in particular in the decades leading up to and following World War I. One historian noted, "The concept [of eugenics] expanded on Social Darwinism to include a more proactive approach to improving the species, manipulating the natural selection process to purify a nation's bloodlines. To do so, eliminating undesirables was portrayed as *healing* the nation."[6]

Nowhere was the poisonous philosophy of racial hygiene more firmly embraced to a more devastating effect than in post-WWI Germany. Its malignant approach fit perfectly in the Nazi mindset, fueling Hitler's obsession to cleanse German society of all "unfit" elements in pursuit of the pure Aryan race. By the time World War II broke out, racial hygiene had been an active policy within Germany under Nazi leadership, and a large portion of the medical profession had gotten caught in its web.[7]

[6]Naomi Baumslag, M.D., *Murderous Medicine: Nazi Doctors, Human Experimentation, and Typhus* (Washington, D.C.: Baumslag, 2005), p. 36.
[7]Ibid., pp. 35-42.

In those early days of the Nazi regime, many medical professionals initially joined the Party amidst promises of better financial benefits and greater opportunities for advancement during an economically difficult and chaotic time. But toxic seeds of deception had been planted in these doctors and nurses on the premise that producing a pure master race of people justified any means necessary to obtain it.

Over the decade of the 1930s, those seeds would grow into the governing philosophy in the German medical community. In the years preceding WWII, this belief paved the way for doctors and nurses to justify the sterilization, and later the "mass euthanasia," of hundreds of thousands of the "unfit" — mentally ill, genetically diseased, alcoholics, etc.[8] Having "sown the wind" in the devising of evil means to achieve a desired goal, Nazi doctors were setting the stage to "reap the whirlwind" (*see* Hosea 8:7).

Having "sown the wind" in the devising of evil means to achieve a desired goal, Nazi doctors were setting the stage to "reap the whirlwind."

Tracing the Seeds of Present-Day Deception

After World War II, documentation was also found for a host of inhumane experiments in which Nazi doctors systematically amputated limbs of concentration-camp prisoners without anesthesia, using their scalpels to cut away at victims as part of ongoing, so-called studies to test new medicines and observe how the human body would adapt to various disfigurements.

As a result of these horrific procedures, the prisoners used for these experiments underwent unimaginable terror, agony,

[8]Ibid., pp. 22-25.

mutilation — and, very often, death. If they survived, they were permanently disabled. When this hideous maiming and mutilation was exposed in 1945, the international community raised their voices in condemnation and called these practices sick, sadistic, and inhumane.

But these Nazi doctors didn't stop with those unspeakably cruel surgical procedures. They descended into the lowest levels of depravity as they surgically attempted to alter the gender of men and women.[9] Behind the walls of concentration camps, doctors used their scalpels to remove male organs and mutilate female organs in an attempt to see if a person's gender could be surgically changed.

The first primitive sex-change operations were being performed in Germany in the late 1920s and early 1930s and were met with a variety of responses. Historical documents have revealed that when the Nazis came to power, they attempted to destroy all medical records of these earlier sex-change operations.[10] The Nazi position regarding such surgical procedures was that such practices might potentially promote homosexuality, a lifestyle that Nazis held to be repulsive. Later, however, behind the walls of concentration camps, Nazi doctors reengaged these procedures by performing experimental sex-change operations — this time under inhuman conditions on helpless concentration-camp victims who had no choice in the matter.

Most of the WWII sex-change operations were carried out under the supervision of Dr. Josef Mengele at Auschwitz. The

[9]Josef Mengele, "The Angel of Death" (HolocaustOnline.org, 2014) http:/holocaustonline.org/josef-mengele *and* N.V. Sapoznikova, M.U. Balabanova, A.A. Beibulatova, V.I. Cherkasov, M.V. Zaburdyaeva, A.A. Mazur, E.S. Parshikova, Y.A. Perevalova, L.R. Punga, V.A. Yaschenko, R.R. Kalimullina, V.V. Umnova, V.A. Chapurina, *Echoes of an Unfulfilled Childhood* (Nizhnevartovsk State Humanitarian University: Russia, 2010), p. 190.
[10]Asher Kohn, "The Nazis Delayed Medical Advances in Sexual Reassignment Surgery for Decades," *Business Insider* (June 11, 2016) https://www.businessinsider.com/nazis-delayed-medical-advances-2016-6.

majority of Mengele's victims who underwent these barbaric surgeries — often without anesthesia — died on the operating table or soon after. Almost all evidence of these procedures was destroyed before the arrival of the Allied Forces — which in the case of Auschwitz was the Red Army. For this reason, when the atrocities of Nazi doctors were examined at the Nuremberg trials, sex-change operations were not brought before the tribunal.

In fact, much of what is known about these gruesome sex-change experiments came to light *after* the Nuremberg trials concluded. It also appears that this specific category of experimental surgery was relatively rare compared to the established experimental programs such as those created to determine the effects of high altitudes and freezing temperatures on the human body. But regardless of the frequency or infrequency of sex-change surgeries, concentration-camp survivors did eventually give heart-wrenching testimony that Nazi doctors indeed attempted these procedures on victims, along with other dreadful medical experiments.[11]

There is no evidence to suggest the Nazis' objective was to produce transgendered people. Nazi doctors performed these sex-reassignment experiments as a part of the Nazis' larger push to produce possible scientific legitimacy for the regime through a variety of their sadistic experiments — and they had no moral issue with utilizing their huge reservoir of "disposable" human subjects who were crammed in the concentration-camp barracks.

This was a horrific, real-life scenario, worse even than the fictional depiction of Dr. Frankenstein, who produced his living creature from non-living elements. In stark contrast, the Nazi doctors used living, feeling human beings — each born with a divine destiny to fulfill — on whom to perform their sadistic

[11]Jeffrey Daniel Mucha, *Child Victims of Nazi Medical Experimentation: A Child's Lamentation* (Master's Thesis: University of Amsterdam, 2017), p. 53, *and* Simon Wiesenthal, *The Murderers Among Us: The Simon Wiesenthal Memoirs* (New York: McGraw-Hill, 1967), p. 155.

experiments. The Nazi doctors who engaged in these practices claimed they did so in the name of scientific advancement. But more likely, these demonically inspired doctors were pursuing their own self-advancement in the hierarchy of the Nazi medical profession while satisfying their personal hatred and disdain for those deemed unworthy of life.

Among a host of other atrocities too numerous to mention, the gruesome Nazi medical procedures briefly mentioned in this chapter tell us what happens when deception is allowed to run its course with no resistance against it. *We need to take heed* — because what goes around comes around. There really is nothing new under the sun. If not restrained, evil in any generation will become more and more bold, brazen, and aggressive.

And as has always been true, it's easier to *keep* the enemy out than it is to try to *get* him out once access has been granted through an open door. In today's society, the Church is truly in the "pushback" season of the latter option. The door to deception was again swung wide open through ignorance and passivity, and the thief is in the house.

It's easier to keep the enemy out than it is to try to get him out once access has been granted through an open door. In today's society, the Church is truly in the "pushback" season of the latter option. The door to deception was again swung wide open through ignorance and passivity, and the thief is in the house.

From 'Mad Science' to 'Scientific Breakthrough'

What was the root deception that led a modern society such as Germany down this demonic path to conclude that a human being could be placed in the category of "useless eater" and "a life not worth living"? We can find that root in Darwin's theory of evolution, which promoted a concept of man as an evolutionary being scientifically categorized with other mammals and subject to the process of "survival of the fittest." This theory was widely promoted in Germany in the years leading up to WWII.

As a result of the growing influence of Darwinism, many in the German medical field began to conclude that the weaker of the human species were disposable. The biblical belief that humans are made in the image of God and that every person has intrinsic value was put aside.

When the fundamental belief that man is made in God's image is replaced with the notion that man is merely a part of the evolutionary process, the dignity God gave man by creating him in His own image is seriously undermined.

A study of the dangerous trajectory established in the German medical field in the years following World War I reveals the serious ramifications of such a belief system. When the fundamental belief that man is made in God's image is replaced with the notion that man is merely a part of the evolutionary process, the dignity God gave man by creating him in His own image is seriously undermined. Human beings begin to be viewed as mere objects in an evolutionary process who can be altered scientifically or medically without moral considerations or consequence.

But this latter view of man isn't just the stuff of history. It reflects the perspective of many, if not most, in the scientific and medical fields today. It is an inevitable outcome when society rejects biblical knowledge to embrace the belief that humans are nothing more than objects of the evolutionary process. As more and more reject the premise that man is made in God's image, a growing number find it easier than in the past to promote surgical altering of the gender identity He has given to each person born on the earth.

What is being widely promoted today in terms of gender-reassignment surgeries doesn't fit in the same category of the torturous medical experiments performed in Nazi concentration camps on unwilling victims under barbaric conditions. Nonetheless, these modern procedures are based on the same premise — that man is not an immortal being, uniquely created in the image of God. Those who support and promote this practice fundamentally do not believe that God, man's Creator, has defined his gender identity. Such a perspective then makes it acceptable to experiment with or to alter the image and gender that human beings were born with.

These experiments performed by Nazis were *all* condemned by the international community of that time when they were publicly exposed. Yet in these strange times in which we live, the one procedure that has reemerged as acceptable, even normal, is *gender reassignment* — otherwise known as sex-change operations.

Some may argue that sex-reassignment surgeries would have eventually come about over a period of time, regardless of the Nazi doctors' participation. This may be true; yet the point of this discussion remains the same. What was once deemed to be one of the universally rejected medical experiments conducted by Dr. Mengele and his team of Nazi doctors is now being carried out in hospitals and clinics all over the planet as doctors attempt to surgically change people's genders. What was once generally viewed as sickening and repulsive is now being heralded by progressive thinkers as a great scientific breakthrough of human advancement.

Some correctly assert that the sex-change operations performed by Nazi doctors were war crimes because they were carried out on prisoners against their will — and that what doctors are performing today is different because it accommodates those who *wish* to submit themselves to the scalpel. Of course, it is certainly not a war crime by any standard for people to modify their bodies in whatever way they wish. People freely use plastic surgery to alter their appearance all the time.

However, for a person to willfully undergo a procedure to alter his or her gender is a completely different question, as it is an assault on their very identity. Furthermore, these modern procedures are being performed on those who are most certainly in an extreme case of confusion both mentally and emotionally. For one to willfully have such an irreversible, maiming procedure performed on one's own body is itself a symptom of inner chaos and spiritual sickness. Yet society as a whole has veered so far from biblical truth and is so affected by delusional thinking that more and more people are embracing the notion that gender is not determined at birth by the Creator and may be electively changed by surgery.

None of this happens overnight. Sin and deception follow progressive steps along the way that only a discerning heart, firmly founded in God's Word, will recognize (*see* James 1:14,15).

As we continue to explore the downward spiral of widespread deception within modern society, keep foremost in your mind our vital role as the Church. It's our responsibility to take an uncompromising stance on God's Word and to serve as the restraining force that impedes deception's forward progress in society so it cannot take hold and entrench itself in people's minds as "just the way things are."

When the Church isn't doing its part, people are more likely to accept a lie and keep making bad choices that sink them deeper into deception until the lie becomes their paradigm or mindset — "just the way things are" — in their thinking. This demonic paradigm establishes itself as a stronghold in their minds that exalts itself against the knowledge of God and ultimately leads to destruction (*see* 2 Corinthians 10:3-5). This dangerous progression perfectly fits the case of gender-reassignment surgery.

Just as a small group of elites at the time of WWII bought into a lie about a superior race that was being popularized in their day, today there is a growing number of people who are buying into the lie that gender is a choice and not determined at birth. This is part of a new wave of deception that is spreading across the planet to indoctrinate people *en masse* with the demonic lie that a new day has arrived and the mindset of only two traditional genders is a thing of the past.

It's our responsibility to take an uncompromising stance on God's Word and to serve as the restraining force that impedes deception's forward progress in society so it cannot take hold and entrench itself in people's minds as "just the way things are."

In today's society, this preposterous notion that a person's gender can be changed is a recurrent message that continually bombards modern society through its educational institutions and many forms of media. The intention is to wear people down until the shock factor wears off and they begin to adjust to the idea that changing a person's gender isn't so bad or so physically and emotionally damaging after all.

All of this is a blaring signal that delusion is oozing into the mainstream of society at an ever-increasing rate. In this hour when it seems the world has gone morally crazy, it is vital that we as believers keep our heads on straight.

Delusionary Times

As we've seen, First Timothy 4:1 warns, "Now the Spirit speaketh expressly, that in the latter times some shall depart from the faith, giving heed to seducing spirits, and doctrines of devils...."

The word "seducing" in this verse is translated from a form of the Greek word *planao* and describes *a deception*, *a moral wandering*, or *a person or nation that has veered morally from a solid path and is now adrift*. However, it is also very important for you to understand that this word *planao* can also be translated as the word *delusion*, and that is probably the best translation in this context.

First Timothy 4:1 could be therefore taken to mean, *"Now the Spirit speaketh expressly, that in the latter times some shall depart from the faith, giving heed to spirits of delusion...."* In this pivotal verse, the Holy Spirit prophesied that at the very end of the age, spirits of delusion would stealthily, methodically, and seductively entice people away from long-held established truths into doctrines or new concepts that are advanced by demon spirits.

In the following chapters, you will see how these spirits attract people and lead them astray. At this point, however, I want you to understand that the Bible forecasts a time when *spirits of delusion* will be rampant in the earth and will lead society into a condition of delusionary reasoning and believing.

For instance, many thought they would never see the day when society would be so confused that it would question whether a man is a man or a woman is a woman. Yet people are bombarded from every direction with the notion that changing one's sex, or gender, is perfectly normal.

In recent years, if you were to add up all the genders being offered as options on leading social-media websites and various applications for jobs and education, you would be shocked to find literally *dozens of genders* that a person can claim other than the one on his or her birth certificate! This issue of gender confusion, I believe, is one of the greatest signs that these delusional spirits are already full steam at work in the culture.

As I said in my "Must-Read Introduction," this subject of transgenderism is not the focal point of this book. But it is important to emphasize that these issues about gender fly in the face of God's original intent concerning creation, marriage, procreation, life, creativity, and fruitfulness according to His will, plan, and design. This deviance from what Scripture clearly teaches is a demonic attempt to overthrow these God-given institutions and the model of His crowning creation.

But let's face it. When people don't know if they are male or female, or when they actually embrace the belief that there are *dozens* of genders from which to choose — this is indicative of a deeply delusional state. Those who have embraced this lie will not appreciate this next statement, but I believe it to be very true: *Only seducing spirits and doctrines of demons could convince intelligent people to embrace such absurdity.*

Let me remind you that not so long ago, such thinking would have been labeled a symptom of a mental illness. But this deceptive form of "progressive thinking" is finding such widespread acceptance today that some are now even alleging that it is inappropriate to record a child's gender at birth! They assert that birth certificates should no longer indicate whether an infant is a boy or a girl at birth — *only that he or she is an infant.*

What a burden it is, these progressive thinkers contend, to tell a little boy that he is a boy or to tell a little girl that she is a girl. Why burden children with gender identification? Instead, these thinkers claim, identification of gender should be *deferred* until later when the child becomes old enough to determine if he or she "feels" more male or female!

To a rational thinker who still believes that science — anatomy and DNA — dictates our gender at birth, all of this sounds like insanity and nonsense. But this delusional line of thinking, not long ago considered preposterous, is rapidly spreading across the stratum of society in an end-time bid to become "the norm."

'It's All About Feelings'

The madness of this thinking was recently demonstrated to me again in a TV interview I saw that was conducted with another self-styled, progressive thinker who was the parent of a little boy. The interviewer asked the parent, who is well-known for her progressive outlook on sexuality: "As a progressive parent who wants to help her little boy find whether he's more boy or more girl as he gets older, how do you greet him each morning?"

The parent answered, "Every morning, the first thing I do is go into my son's bedroom, sit on the side of his bed to greet him, and I ask, 'Tell me, sweetheart, what do you feel like today? Do you feel more like a little boy or a little girl today?'

"However my little boy answers me determines how I will treat him that day," the woman continued. "If he wakes up feeling more like a girl, then on that day I'll treat him like a girl. If he wakes up on a particular morning feeling more like a boy, then on that day I'll treat him like a boy. It can change each day, depending on how he feels when he wakes up."

The parent told the interviewer, "The last thing I want to do is put pressure on my little boy to think and act like he's a boy simply because he was anatomically born a boy. As a good parent, I want to give him the option to think and act like a girl if that is what he feels. As a responsible parent, I consider it my job to help him 'feel his way into his gender.' It has nothing to do with anatomy; it's all about feelings."

All about feelings. Friend, this way of thinking is *delusionary.* A parent like this is setting up a child for gender confusion, identity confusion — *life* confusion — and rampant insecurity on many levels. Children need affirmation of who they are from the outset of their young lives; they do *not* need to be questioning their sexual identity. Instead, they need parents who tell them, "You are a wonderful young boy, and you will grow up to be a great man," or, "You are an amazing young girl, and you will grow up to be a great woman."

How destructive it is to start children out in life with the message, "We can't figure out who you are, and we're not sure who you will be when you get older."

The Holy Spirit warned us that spirits of delusion will be loosed in society at the end of the age (*see* 1 Timothy 4:1). Today delusion is *pervasive*. Many who have wavered on such basic issues now conclude that we who believe anatomy determines our gender are antiquated and behind the times — relics of a past way of thinking that they believe is no longer relevant.

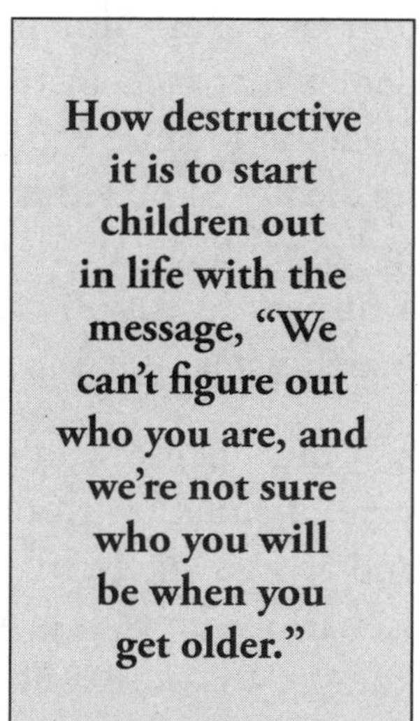
How destructive it is to start children out in life with the message, "We can't figure out who you are, and we're not sure who you will be when you get older."

But let's consider the word "delusion" and see what medical books have said about it up until now. According to science's most recently stated definitions:

- A delusional person has *a belief* or *feeling* that is based on *an incorrect interpretation of reality.*
- A delusional person clings to *a false belief* even if he is confronted with *evidence, facts, or proof that refutes his false belief.*
- A delusional person is difficult to help because he rarely admits that he is delusional. He often refuses psychiatric treatment, instead searching for ways to *affirm*, *support*, and *sustain* his delusion.

A One-Sided, 'One-Armed' Lie

Let me give you a hypothetical example of a delusional person who refuses to acknowledge reality when confronted with facts but instead seeks to support his delusional perception. Imagine a man with two normal arms who has the delusion that he has only one arm. Although he has two fully formed arms, this man denies that fact. Instead, he actually goes to a surgeon and says, "Doctor, I realize you're going to tell me that I have two arms, and medically I know this is true. But in spite of the provable facts, I *feel* more like a one-armed person. I would like you to schedule a surgery to cut off one of my arms so that my body will finally match what I *feel* is true about me."

Any doctor who agreed to schedule an amputation in this type of situation would be considered unfit for medical practice and would likely be sentenced to prison. Yet as absurd as this scenario sounds, it is precisely what happens when a man says, "I know I was born a man, but I *feel* like I am a woman trapped in a male body" — and vice versa when a woman says she feels like she is a man trapped in the body of a female!

This type of delusional thinking is on the increase. It is simply a fact that growing numbers of *males* are claiming to feel like they are actually *females* that are trapped in *male bodies* — and growing numbers of *females* are claiming to feel like they are actually *males* that are trapped in *female bodies*. If you don't know anyone in this category, it's likely you will at some point, because this deceptive craze is growing exponentially — and it's especially on the rise among younger people who are the main targets of gender confusion.

Until recently, such confusion was regarded in the medical field and throughout society as a mental disorder that should be treated under the care of a psychiatrist or counselor. But today this is being repackaged as a birth defect that some medical professionals suggest can be fixed with a surgical procedure.

As nonsensical as this argument is on its merits, this is precisely what some in the medical world are suggesting with increasing regularity. Of course, this is not the way those medical professionals would describe it. But in essence, this is what they are doing by performing these surgical procedures to address a mental-health issue! The current trend seems to say, *Just go with your feelings; there's nothing wrong with you that a surgical procedure will not cure.*

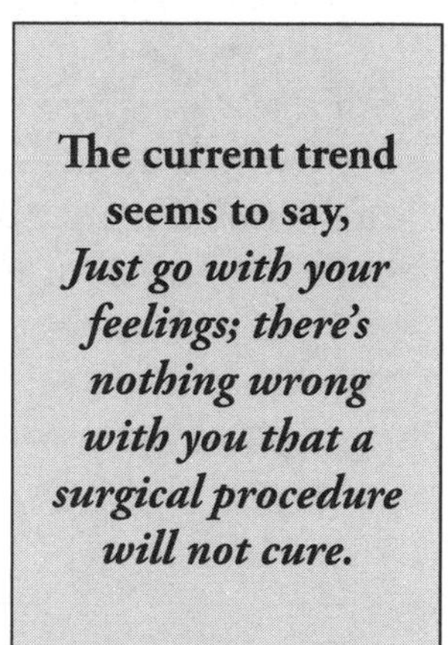

This confusion has hit such a high that now people are claiming to be neither male *nor* female! The new rage is to be *bigender*, *trigender*, *polygender*, *pangender*, or even *gender-fluid*. People who put themselves in this last category claim that their gender is so *fluid* that they can switch back and forth — male to female, female to male — from moment to moment, depending on what is *felt* in a given situation. In other words, in one moment, a person can claim to be male, but in the next moment, claim to be a female. Yet "*gender fluidity*" is just another delusional tenet in the devolving, amoral system of a world gone mad.

It is okay for us to recognize that this is all last-days nonsense!

In spite of the ever-growing list of celebrities and other voices that endorse these ideas, we who believe God created man as *male* and *female* are on the right side. We are standing on the authority of the Bible.

And even beyond the ultimate authority of God's Word, consider the uncompromising reality of scientific data when the remains of a human body are exhumed. Every skeleton will tell the truth. A DNA test will reveal whether that skeleton holds an XY or XX chromosome. And except in extremely rare cases of chromosomal anomalies, *that* is what determines whether the person was a male or a female — no matter *what* kind of operation the person might have had while alive!

In spite of the ever-growing list of celebrities and other voices that endorse these ideas, we who believe God created man as male and female are on the right side. We are standing on the authority of the Bible.

It is unthinkable that many parents are encouraging their children to decide their gender from a very young age. If the child decides differently than their birth gender, the process of "social transitioning" begins. Later on, "stage two" is introduced — hormone treatment to promote physical symptoms of the child's preferred gender.

Then in a recent court decision in a major Western nation, the court decided it had no role in the decision between child, parents, and physician for the child to advance to stage three — the irreversible step of gender-reassignment surgery.[12] Thus, before an adolescent's brain is fully developed and before he or she is legally allowed to vote, drink, or sometimes even drive, that young person is being allowed to choose to be transported into an operating room to be surgically and irreversibly altered and "reassigned" a new gender.

How I wish that someone could justly accuse me of exaggerating, but in Western society this travesty is being perpetuated against children more and more frequently, often with the endorsement of their parents and physicians. How can this not be considered child abuse? A mental and emotional vacuum has been created in children by authority figures and parents who have become delusional themselves or who have abdicated their responsibility to train their children in line with biblical standards.

I am not stating that every parent of those who are confused about gender or who have undergone sex-reassignment surgery has abdicated his or her parental responsibilities. Scores of parents have done everything they knew to do to raise their children correctly, but seducing spirits working through society have targeted younger people, and many children and young adults have fallen victim to this outrageous scheme.

Punishment for Independent Thought

It is clear that the enemy is targeting our very youngest. Satan has been well aware that to reach children *en masse*, the educational system had to be brought under the sway of his deception.

[12]Michelle Brown, "Children with gender dysphoria no longer have to seek court approval to undergo surgery," https://www.abc.net.au/news/2018-03-16/children-wanting-surgical-gender-change-no-longer-need-court/9557444.

In the Western world, the devil's strategy has been largely successful. The education system is public for the most part and, as such, is federally funded. Educators are mandated to indoctrinate teachers in training and to write curricula for the classroom that undermines biblical authority (and *all* godly authority), as well as respect for God. This humanistic curriculum blurs the lines of truth, incites confusion, obliterates common sense, and punishes independent thinking. Any thinking that is outside the box of the "kinder, gentler" world of progressive humanism is not only frowned on, but is often met with violent, punitive resistance.

It is clear that the enemy is targeting our very youngest. Satan has been well aware that to reach children *en masse*, the educational system had to be brought under the sway of his deception.

We need to establish it in our own minds that it is absolutely right for us to hold to the belief that the attempt to surgically change a man into a woman or a woman into a man *was* and *still is* a perverted and twisted business.

In fact, it's not only *okay* to recognize and acknowledge that such assertions belong in a world gone mad, but to do so is a healthy sign! It means we haven't become numbed and desensitized to the subtle changes in the moral tide that we've experienced over the last 50 years. It also means we recognize that of late, there has been a sweeping downward shift in that moral trend.

Are our memories so short that we have forgotten that the international community condemned Nazi doctors for doing these very things? Yet the "Frankenstein-type" activity of Nazi doctors is back in the operating room. However, this time these actions aren't occurring behind the walls of concentration camps.

Now "Dr. Frankenstein" is working in sophisticated hospitals and is being cheered on by liberal progressive thinkers.

Besides this subject of gender confusion, consider the 2015 Supreme Court decision legalizing gay marriage. Even though it has now been ruled to be in agreement with the U.S. Constitution, it is in direct contradiction to the Word of God. And beyond that — perhaps as one of the most dramatic modern instances of this downward moral trend — consider the 2019 New York and Illinois bills that legalized late-term abortion *right up to the birth pangs of delivery and possibly beyond!*

Let me put it another way to emphasize this crucial point: It's not only okay to recognize that such deceived ways of thinking are wrong, but it's actually our *responsibility* as the Church of Jesus Christ to "come out from among them" (*see* 2 Corinthians 6:17). We are called to come out from the catacombs of intimidation, as well as from the defilement of the world — and to stand as beacons of God's truth, regardless of opposition or backlash.

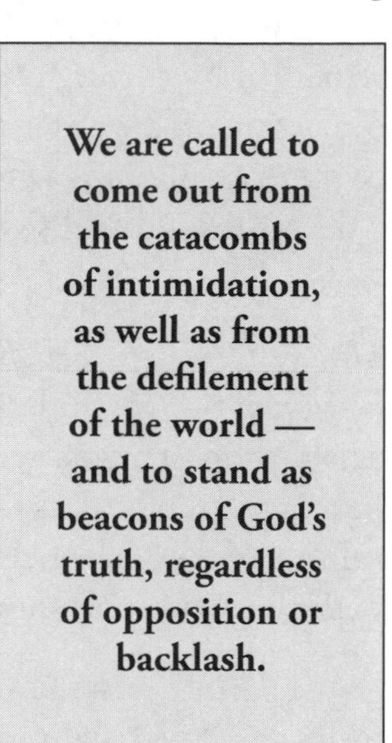

What can the Church do? That is the subject of the rest of this book, and in the following pages, I will unfold to you answers from Scripture that have the power to change your life and the lives of those around you.

Compassion, Not Judgment

It is imperative that we have compassion for people who struggle with any type of disorder. Gender confusion is a serious condition, and God calls us to be compassionate toward those who are struggling and hurting.

That's true even when people don't want to hear anything to the contrary of their own conclusions about their sexual identity. Our compassion must be extended, especially when we *know* that the actions someone has taken are to his or her own lasting detriment. These precious souls need answers from the Word of God. They need the Holy Spirit to heal their souls. They need the compassionate touch of Christ to be transmitted to them through non-condemning believers who themselves have been forgiven, delivered, and restored by the redemptive power of the Cross.

But let's keep our heads on straight. Gender confusion is a complicated spiritual and psychological problem that *cannot* be remedied by cutting off a man's penis to create an artificial vagina or cutting off a woman's breasts and surgically altering her urethra to try to turn it into a penis. This is not a reasonable answer to such a deep spiritual and psychological issue. In fact, it is *delusionary.*

Remember, one definition of "delusion" is, in effect, *maintaining fixed false beliefs that are contradicted by reality or rational argument* — which describes well this reprobate way of thinking. Those who struggle with the serious issue of gender confusion need a mental healing — not a surgery to try to make their physical makeup match their mental confusion. We need to help them with the *right* tools, not a surgeon's scalpel.

Make no mistake — we live in a world that is increasingly losing its collective moral mind on many levels. Many rational thinkers have difficulty comprehending how deception and depravity have caused society to descend so far and at such a fast rate into moral confusion.

But this is only the tip of the iceberg. What we will see develop in society between now and the ultimate end of this last-days time frame is beyond our current ability to fathom. Bizarre notions once considered the stuff of science fiction and horror movies will move from the mental, imaginary realm into our physical realm as manifested realities.

For a moment, let me speak prophetically about the future. In the years to come, we will see science venture into unthinkable realms that would have been considered blasphemous in a past time when society was more Bible-based. But as society increasingly rejects the Bible as its measure of truth and morality, it will open itself to possibilities that were considered abnormal and deviant to Bible-minded people.

The lid has already been removed from reason, and commonsense thinking has been thrown to the wind, replaced with the whims of the ever-fluctuating times. We can therefore soundly forecast that in the not-so-distant future, society will begin implementing ideas and actions that would have been inconceivable abominations to previous generations.

Futurists are predicting developments that may sound mind-boggling and deeply disturbing to us as believers, but they are not far-fetched concepts to the modern mind that is no longer rooted in a moral foundation. Remember, the idea of widespread transgenderism sounded far-fetched a mere generation ago, but today it is a reality that is confronting our world with force.

The lid has already been removed from reason, and commonsense thinking has been thrown to the wind, replaced with the whims of the ever-fluctuating times.

Over these past decades, the horrors of the Holocaust have faded from the collective mindset of post-WWII generations. Most younger people alive today are not educated about what happened then. They are not able to fathom

God is calling His Church to take its place as His restraining force to enforce Christ's victory, slow down the advance of the enemy's evil agenda, and make way for the great end-time harvest of souls.

the depths to which the devil can take human beings who have become fertile ground for his seeds of demonic deception to grow — and inspire them to do unthinkable evil to their fellow man.

God is calling His Church to take its place as His restraining force to enforce Christ's victory, slow down the advance of the enemy's evil agenda, and make way for the great end-time harvest of souls. However, some things must come to pass according to the immutable word of the Lord, who declares the end from the beginning (*see* Isaiah 46:10). It's not a stretch to say that a host of unthinkable manifestations of evil lie ahead that will make the horrific atrocities of the Nazi regime pale in comparison.

Ancient History's Rendezvous With Deception

It is important for you to know that much earlier in history, there was another demonically dark period when society interfaced with evil, causing a descent into the lowest levels of depravity and eliciting divine judgment. This nefarious period occurred in Genesis chapter 6, when the earth was infiltrated by seducing spirits that came to lure mankind off track and to influence society with deceptive ways of thinking and repulsive behaviors. One could rightly say it was early history's rendezvous with seducing spirits and doctrines of demons.

During those ancient times, the thinking of man became distorted and twisted, and his behavior became perverted. Genesis 6:5 says, "And God saw that the wickedness of man was great in the earth, and that every imagination of the thoughts of his heart was only evil continually."

At that early moment in history, man became so seduced by evil influences that "...*every* imagination of the thoughts of his heart was *only* evil continually"! Society in that era of time was entrapped by a seducing influence, yielding to the enemy's diabolical plan to lead mankind off track through mutinous acts against God. Eventually mankind became so twisted that God could find only a few individuals who remained untainted — *Noah and his family.*

Noah remarkably adhered to the truth and refused to become infected by the vile influences that surrounded him. As a result, God was able to use Noah's family to start the human race over again after He had sent the flood to wipe out that utterly contaminated generation.

Noah, with his family, stood against the opinions perpetuated in society at that time. They were at odds with a world filled with evil that raged against them. Even in the face of ridicule, they followed what they knew to be true. As a result, they were delivered from destruction and became the inheritors of the earth and progenitors of the current world population.

What Satan did at the beginning of time — seducing society with evil spiritual influences — is precisely what he is attempting to do again at the very end of this current era. Once again, a worldwide mutinous attitude is developing toward God and His Word — and as before, it will eventually be met with a harvest of judgment.

Satan knows full well his time is short. In the brief time he has left, he is attempting to assault and disfigure man — the very one who is made in the image of God. It is truly the ultimate insult against God to mar His prized creation, whom He created to be only male or female, and to undermine and tear down every institution He so skillfully created, including the institution of marriage.

Because we live at the end of this prophetic period called the last days, we must recognize that we will see bizarre and nonsensical acts become more and more commonplace and embraced as normal. We can be sure that as time progresses, it will seem that all restraints have been thrown off and that, as a culture, we're galloping at an ever-increasing speed toward lunacy on many fronts.

It is truly the ultimate insult against God to mar His prized creation, whom He created to be only male or female, and to undermine and tear down every institution He so skillfully created, including the institution of marriage.

The closer we get to the end, society will sink deeper into depravity and deception. Isaiah prophesied that a day would come when evil would be called good, good would be called evil, and darkness would be substituted for light (*see* Isaiah 5:20). That day is here — and we are witnessing *firsthand* things that were once considered evil, dark, and *unthinkable*.

According to the prophetic teaching of Scripture, seducing spirits with doctrines of demons will invade society as we approach the end of this age (*see* 1 Timothy 4:1). As a result, new versions of deviant thinking will become entrenched in society as this "ship" sails further and further off course.

The last-days assault has already begun. The seeds of deception have long been planted, and an evil harvest awaits. As representatives of Almighty God, we have a responsibility to raise the standard of His truth in every situation. We must be willing to stand at odds with every law that is opposed to Scripture. We must dig our heels into scriptural truth and *refuse* to bend with the times, no matter what everyone else around us is doing. *This* is how we keep our heads on straight in a world gone crazy! We'll study that in greater detail in the pages that follow.

No One Excluded — Freedom for *All*

The stronghold of deceived thinking that I've described in this chapter is growing like a wildfire out of control. As the earth was assaulted by evil influences in Genesis chapter 6, evil spiritual beings with diabolical ideas presented as "new" are again attempting to pervert and distort society and to lead it away from God. What happened in the beginning is occurring again at the end of this age. The Holy Spirit prophesied this would happen, and it is transpiring just as He forewarned in First Timothy 4:1.

Many Christians are baffled about how to respond to the moral changes confronting them through every arena of society, such as science, medicine, media, entertainment, and education. They see the deception that is trying to influence their children and grandchildren. If they are being sensitive to what they see, their spirits are on full alert.

Many pastors and spiritual leaders are deeply troubled by these events and are earnestly seeking for God's wisdom about how to navigate these times. On one hand, they feel the utmost need to project hope that common sense will return. On the other hand, these same leaders feel compelled by the Spirit to help their followers stay on track in a world that is morally drifting further and further from shore.

Like it or not, this is where we find ourselves.

Society is changing. The moral climate is devolving while progressives assert it is upwardly evolving to new and previously unknown levels of sophistication. Even 20 years ago, you would have shaken your head in disbelief to hear that such developments could happen. But as crazy as it is, this is the state of our modern world. And as demonically inspired changes continue to cut their way through society, it will leave hurting, shattered lives in their wake.

We will be given the opportunity to minister to people who are confused and struggle with depression, addiction, thoughts of suicide, and other destructive behaviors. The wide-scale nature of such destructive behaviors is evidence that end-time demonic activity is attempting to ravage the earth's population before the age closes. When seducing spirits — or spirits of delusion — come with "newfangled ideas" that are, in reality, thinly cloaked doctrines of demons, they indeed come to steal, kill, and destroy on every possible level (*see* John 10:10).

We must seek the face of God to know how to respond to this confusion and help people find peace, healing, and restoration. Those who are wayward, confused, and bound in sin are not to be rejected because of their deception, and certainly that includes those who have already made modifications to their bodies. All need the forgiveness, deliverance, and freedom offered through the Cross of Calvary.

The Early Church also had to seek God to know how to confront the moral dilemmas and consequences of sin in their own generation. Only the Holy Spirit could provide the wisdom and help that those converted pagans needed as they sought to live free from their past lives when they were outside of Christ.

In the same way, it is imperative that we seek the Holy Spirit's assistance to help those who come to us shattered and broken by the effects of sin and regretful decisions. Every person needs the message of Christ, salvation, and the redemption that is offered to him or her in the great plan of God. No one is excluded from the salvation and freedom that Christ gave so freely when He laid down His life *for all.*

Think About It

1. The challenge before us as God's people is to refuse to allow our thinking to be muddied by the spirit of this age.

   Monitor your own progress concerning that divine challenge. How well are you keeping the streams of your own thought life clear and pure from the world's way of thinking and perceiving? How successfully are you withstanding the many external voices that can bombard your mind and threaten to "muddy the waters"?

   Ask the Holy Spirit for help to identify any contaminant. He will be faithful to do that and then to lovingly lead you to a strategic "washing of water by the Word" to help you renew your mind and change your way of thinking in that area (*see* Ephesians 5:26).

2. Modern society is in serious need of a course correction back to alignment with the foundational truths of God's Word. Dare to ask yourself, *What's my part?*

   You have a voice within your sphere of influence and perhaps beyond what you have yet conceived. What are your gifts, abilities, and opportunities that the Lord has placed within you and at your disposal that may be part of His answer? Let Him show you how to help establish His truth as the eternal compass in people's hearts in this day — even if it is in one heart at a time.

3. It is evident that Satan has a distinct strategy to groom society over a period of time to accept his lies as reality. It's important to be aware of the enemy's strategies in order to effectively thwart them with the wisdom and power of God. Identify specific ways the devil has been working in different arenas — such

as education, entertainment, politics, and even religion — to dismantle people's belief in God's eternal truths in an ever-tightening snare of demonic deception.

4. It's easier to keep the enemy out than it is to try to get him out once access has been granted through an open door. What are the different ways the door to deception was swung wide open in Western society over the past decades? What specific ways can the Church "rise and shine" to fulfill its role in society in the days ahead now that "the thief is in the house"?

Chapter Two

SWIMMING UPSTREAM IN A DOWNSTREAM WORLD

As we consider the steep plummet into moral decadence that we are witnessing in the world today, I believe it is important to turn to the words of Jesus when He stood at a spot overlooking the Temple Mount and spoke with His disciples about the days leading up to His return. They asked Jesus for specific "signs" that would indicate that it was the end of the age. (For a thorough discussion on this subject, I recommend that you read my book, *Signs You'll See Just Before Jesus Comes.*) One crystal-clear sign Christ gave was that "iniquity would abound" just before the consummation of this age (*see* Matthew 24:12).

That word "iniquity" in Greek is *anomia.* It is actually a form of the word *nomos*, which is the Greek word for *law*, used to depict *the standard of what is legally or morally correct.* But when an *"a"* is attached to the front of this word (the plural form in this case), it becomes *anomia.* That *a* has a *canceling* effect. So rather than depict *law* or *a correct moral standard*, the word *anomia* holds the opposite meaning — that is, *without law*, *lawless*, or *no moral standard* — and it pictures *people who possess no fixed moral standards.*

Those who live this way are *void of standards*, *without law*, and *living in a state of lawlessness.* By using this word in Matthew

24:12, Jesus told us that society will throw out all previously agreed-upon moral standards and will depart from God's well-established laws at the very end of the age.

As we have already seen, First Timothy 4:1 tells us that seducing spirits — *spirits of delusion* — will be in full operation worldwide at the end of the age to entice society to stray from established truths and moral standards. For those who resist being carried away by the force of that demonic current, the world system will attempt to throw them off and set them aside. There will even be an attempt to sequester and quarantine individuals or groups who adhere to godly moral standards that an end-time society considers to be outdated and no longer pertinent or applicable to life. We can see a modern-day example of this type of societal rejection and ostracization in the banning of a popular fast-food chain from the food courts and campuses of some universities, airports, and other places because of its pro-family, pro-life stance.

As a part of this last-days scheme, society will be seduced by demonic influences to construct a new world order that has few, if any, hard-and-fast rules of what is morally right and wrong. In essence, this will be *a lawless world* — that is, a world free from the "outdated" voice of the Bible. Society will attempt to disconnect from most moral standards that were once held to be the common rule and view of society. That is what *lawlessness* means in an end-time context.

Doesn't this sound exactly like the world you and I are living in today? The Holy Spirit was absolutely accurate when He forecast that a time would come when long-established standards based on ageless Bible truths would not only be cast off and rejected, but they would also be vilified as bigoted, hateful, narrow-minded, prejudiced, intolerant, and no longer applicable in the "real" world. Friend, you and I are living witnesses of such a bizarre time. Time-tested truths, long-held moral standards, and even scientific evidence are being tossed aside by a last-days generation who possess almost no fixed principles — especially when it comes to the issues of human sexuality.

According to Jesus, this lawlessness "will abound" just before the wrap-up of this age. The Greek word translated "abound" is *plethuno*, which depicts something *abundant*, *excessive*, or *over the top*. It refers to *anything that abounds in an extraordinary measure*. You could even say it pictures something so *profuse* that it can be likened to *a river overflowing and flooding its banks*.

This word emphatically means that just before the curtains close on this age, lawlessness will *profusely proliferate* around the globe. Society at large will disregard formerly well-established paths of morality and absolute truth and throw off all restraint as people forge an unrecognizable path of man's own making — one that is *apart from* and even *opposite to* the law of God.

Paul's Statement About a Society That Rejects God

In Romans 1:21, Paul brilliantly explained what happens when society turns from God. The apostle wrote, "Because that when they knew God, they glorified him not as God, neither were thankful; but became vain in their imaginations, and their foolish heart was darkened."

The word "knew" depicts *acquaintance* or *general knowledge*, not personal knowledge, such as the knowledge possessed by a person who knows Jesus Christ as his Lord and Savior. In this verse, the word "knew" pictures a society that previously possessed *a general acquaintance*, *a general knowledge*, or *a God-fearing attitude*. This lets us know that even if society was not comprised of authentic Christians, at least the people *recognized* and *acknowledged* God and His blessings upon them.

Paul used the word "knew" in the past tense, which tells us he was depicting a society that had *lost* its acknowledgment and sense of dependence upon the Almighty. The first part of this verse could actually be translated, *"Although they once had a general acquaintance with and knowledge about God and about things related to God...."*

In Romans 1:21, Paul depicted a society that has arrived at the conclusion that the acknowledgment of God is out of fashion with the times. As a result, people have progressively put God off to the side and out of sight, ceasing to give Him the recognition that is due Him. This divergent path leading away from man's dependence upon God triggers a state of spiritual and moral wandering that becomes more and more pronounced over time.

Paul went on to describe the consequence of this destitute spiritual condition. When society decides that the acknowledgement of God is no longer intellectually fashionable, people eventually become "vain in their imaginations."

The word "vain" is the Greek word *mataioo*, which means *ruined* and, in this case, depicts something that is *error-filled*. The "something" that is filled with error is the people's "imaginations." The word "imaginations" is from the Greek word *dialogismos*, a word that unmistakably refers to *mental activity* — a person's *reasonings*, *deliberations*, *calculations*, or *thinking processes*.

When these various Greek words are used together in the phrase "vain in their imaginations," a specific meaning is produced. Paul was explaining that when society sets God aside, *error* is released, eventually leading to *ruin* on multiple levels. It is like an inevitable "chemical reaction" that will always occur if the right elements are mixed together.

Scripture tells us that wisdom begins with the fear and knowledge of God (*see* Proverbs 1:7). So if society respects, recognizes, and acknowledges God, it results in enlightenment. But the opposite is also true. When the fear and knowledge of God is diminished and society begins to move away from Him, this is a spiritual "chemical mix" that will always produce an environment where *intellectual nonsense* — conclusions that don't make either rational or spiritual sense — become the inevitable consequence.

Eventually error begins to proliferate and spill into every sphere of society — courts, education, families, entertainment, business, government, and religion. The deceptive process continues until man's intellectual reasonings taint all the deliberations, calculations, and thinking processes of the general population.

We each need to face this reality of what man is without God. When the knowledge and fear of God is removed, a vacuum is formed, causing intellectual and spiritual darkness to flood in and fill the void.

I'm not saying unbelievers are unintelligent — because there are many intelligent unbelievers. But Paul stated that although people may be intellectually brilliant, when such people drift far from the truth, they eventually cast off intellectual restraint and pass into the realm of foolishness and deception. They see themselves as highly intelligent progressive thinkers — but because of the conclusions they embrace, God says they actually become fools (*see* Romans 1:22). In fact, in verse 21, Paul wrote

We each need to face this reality of what man is without God. When the knowledge and fear of God is removed, a vacuum is formed, causing intellectual and spiritual darkness to flood in and fill the void.

that "their *foolish* heart was darkened" as a result of turning away from God and His standards.

This word "foolish" is translated from a form of the Greek word *asunetos.* In actuality, it is the word *sunetos* with an *a* attached to the front of it. The word *sunetos* describes *supreme intelligence* or *conclusions and understandings supported with correlating evidence or facts.* It pictures *a person so mature in his thinking that he has the ability to accurately see a full picture.* But in Romans 1:21, this word *sunetos* has an *a* attached to the front of it, which has a reversing effect. Rather than portray *intelligence,* this word portrays a person who has *lost his intelligence* or who has *a lack of intelligence.*

Paul used this word *asunetos* to tell us what happens when people turn away from God: Rather than getting smarter, they regress and become more and more *preposterous* in their reasoning, deliberations, calculations, and thinking processes. According to Paul's brilliant argument, inspired by the Holy Spirit, a society that moves *away from* God always moves *toward* ludicrous and defective believing and reasoning processes that are dominated by spiritual darkness.

Paul went on to say that a society that moves away from God acquires a "foolish *heart.*" The word "heart" in Greek is *kardia,* which is the word for *the physical heart.* The usage of this word at this juncture is very important, as you will see.

As you are well aware, the heart pumps blood throughout the circulatory system of the human body. Its pumping action is so powerful that virtually every part of the body has blood in it. But in Romans 1:21, Paul didn't refer to the physical heart; rather, he used the word *kardia* to depict the "heart" of a lost society. Paul revealed that when society moves away from God, its heart fills with *foolishness.* Then just as the human heart pumps blood into the various parts of the physical body, the heart of a wayward society will begin to pump *foolishness* and *flawed thinking* throughout its "circulatory system." Eventually every stratum of that society is touched with the destructive effects of the foolishness produced when man separates himself from his Creator.

Paul says such a society will eventually become "darkened." That word "darkened" is a translation of the Greek word *skotidzo*, which denotes *physical* or *spiritual darkness.* But metaphorically it is used here to depict a world or society flooded with darkness that eventually spawns depravity, immorality, and *many* ungodly behaviors.

As these God-rejecting societies sink deeper and deeper in depravity, immorality, and other ungodly behaviors, Romans 1:22 says the so-called leaders of a godless world will claim to be on the cutting edge of a new future and a new order, free of past moral restraints. But that verse also reveals *God's* perspective of this baseless claim: "Professing themselves to be wise, they became fools."

When a society moves away from God, its heart fills with *foolishness.* Eventually every stratum of that society is touched with the destructive effects of the foolishness produced when man separates himself from his Creator.

The word "professing" and the tense used in this verse tells us that these alleged progressive thinkers *continually assert* that they are wise. This constancy of assertion portrays people who are putting themselves forward as leading the way for the rest of the pack.

They assert to be "wise," which is the Greek word *sophos*. This was the same word often used to portray *highly educated people*, such as scientists, philosophers, doctors, teachers, and others who were considered to be the super-intelligentsia of society. It depicts a class of individuals who believe themselves to be *clever*, *astute*, *brilliant*, *intellectually sharp*, or *especially enlightened.*

Paul again referred to this same category of so-called progressive thinkers in Second Timothy 3:2. In that verse, he called them "proud." This is a translation of the word *huperephanos*, a word that pictures a person or group of people who see themselves above the rest of the crowd. It portrays *uppity, arrogant, haughty, high-and-mighty, impudent people who carry an attitude of insolence*. It depicts those who claim to be intellectually advantaged above the rest of the crowd with the right to decide what is right or wrong or what should be viewed as antiquated and out of fashion. This is a person or a group of people who could accurately be called *intellectual snobs*.

In Romans 1:22, Paul stated the reality — that these people are "fools." Forgive the bluntness of this statement, but the Greek word for "fools" is *moraino* — which is the word for one who is *mentally ill* or *mentally deranged.* It is the same word from which we derive the word "moron." This means that in Romans 1:22, when Paul wrote that these alleged intellectuals are "fools," he minced no words and made no apologies as he declared that such people are, in reality, intellectual *morons.*

With all this in mind, I'd like to share a wider interpretation of Romans 1:21,22:

> *"Although society once had a general acquaintance of God, a general knowledge of God, and a reverence for things related to God, a time came when people found it no longer fashionable to give God His due reverence. Rather than be grateful to God for their blessings, they forgot who blessed them and ceased to be thankful. They turned from God, and as a result, they began to veer morally, which resulted in their thinking becoming laced with error that affected how they reasoned about everything. They alleged it was all right to believe things*

that are not supported by correlating facts and evidence, and eventually their conclusions became totally out of touch with reality.

"A normal heart pumps blood, but the heart of a God-rejecting society pumps and proliferates foolishness until it is filled with darkness that eventually spawns depravity, immorality, and godless behaviors. The so-called leaders of a God-rejecting society constantly assert that they are brilliant intellectuals of a new way of thinking, even though it is difficult to fathom how they could claim such a thing. Regardless of what they assert, their words and their ways of thinking make them sound like those who are mentally ill or mentally deranged. How could anyone think what they propose is normal? Make no mistake about it — those who think this way are clearly morons."

As Paul continued, he stated in Romans 1:28 that a God-rejecting society does not "like to *retain* God in their knowledge." Unlike the situation in Romans 1:21, this isn't a case of being only generally acquainted with God or His standards. These people really knew Him; they simply no longer wanted to *retain* that knowledge.

This is a depiction of a person or a group of people who were once familiar with God and His standard but who found that standard inconvenient for the new morality they wanted to construct. Because they no longer wanted to retain God in their minds and lives, Paul informed us in Romans 1:28 that "God gave them over."

Does this phrase mean that God abandoned them or pushed them away, as some suggest? Scripture reveals that God holds out hope for everyone and He is not in the habit of giving up on or abandoning anyone. *So what does this phrase mean?*

This is another case in which the Greek clears up the confusion. The Greek words used in Romans 1:28 would be better translated, *"God released them."* God did not give them up or abandon them; He simply released them to follow their wayward inclinations because that is what they wanted to do.

God's Spirit will plead with people not to abandon truth and go another direction. But if society chooses to do so, He will *release* the people to follow their inclinations. That is precisely what the words of Paul mean in Romans 1:28.

What Is a 'Reprobate' Mind?

In Romans 1:28, Paul described a God-rejecting society that ultimately develops a "reprobate mind." When we think of a "reprobate," we usually think of a person who is sick, disgusting, twisted, or perverted in some way. But in this verse, Paul used this word to describe an entire society that has become *reprobate.* In Romans 1:28, he wrote, "…Even as they (society) did not like to retain God in their knowledge, *God gave them over to a reprobate mind…."*

I want to make it very clear from this verse what God did *not* do. This verse does not say God gave them a reprobate mind; it says He "gave them *over*" to a reprobate mind. The difference is very significant. The words "gave them over" is translated from the Greek word *paradidomi*, which means *to hand over* — or, in this case, *to release* or *to transfer.*

Let me give you a simple illustration to help you understand what Paul was communicating in this verse. Let's say you are walking near a muddy pond with slippery banks that you should avoid in order to keep from falling in and getting covered with mud. Because I know the pond is nearby and that you'll get filthy if you fall in, I may try to alert you and thus protect you from experiencing that mishap.

However, if you know that muddy pond is there, yet you choose to walk over to it and deliberately dip into that filthy mess, who am I to stop you? It wouldn't be a wise thing for you to do, but if you really wanted to act like a pig and wallow in the mud, you could do that!

In the same way, God chose not to hold society hostage against its will. Instead, He honors people's choices and *releases* them to follow the path of their choosing — even if they choose to follow their wayward instincts that He knows could have seriously damaging effects. When people do not want to retain God in their knowledge, He simply *releases* them to do as they wish. And as they walk away from God's spiritual laws and His well-established biblical principles, they put themselves in a position to become "reprobate."

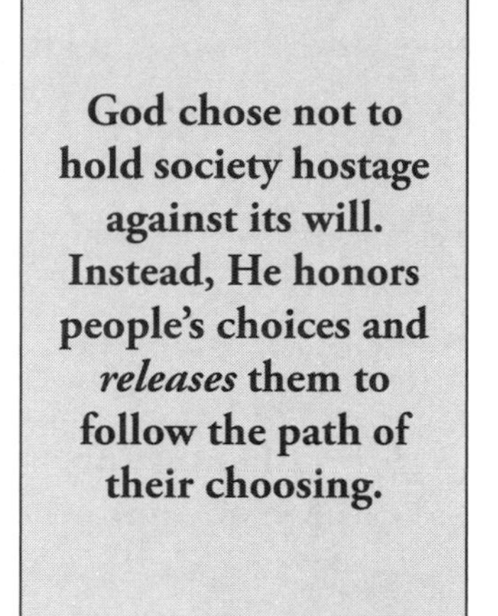

The word "reprobate" is translated from the Greek word *adokimos*. The word *dokimos* means *approved*, *fit*, *reliable*, and *trustworthy*. However, when an *a* is attached to the front of this word, making it *adokimos*, it reverses the meaning and instead depicts one who is *disapproved*, *unfit*, *unreliable*, and *untrustworthy*.

This depicts a society that has been exposed to a negative spiritual influence for so long — and in such heavy doses — that it has become *compromised*, *impaired*, *ruined*, and *no longer trustworthy*. This is the meaning of the word *reprobate* as used in the New Testament. And in Romans 1:28, it specifically depicts the collective mind of a society — or even the mind of an individual — that has become so tarnished, tainted, hardened, and both spiritually and mentally compromised that it loses its ability to arrive at sensible, godly conclusions. (Just think back to Chapter One, where you caught a horrific glimpse of what a society turning reprobate looks like. That process was on full display in Nazi Germany in the years leading up to and during World War II.)

Although God gives people marvelous minds worthy of great esteem, the word translated "reprobate" speaks of minds that have been damaged by continuous exposure to evil influences and by being bombarded over and over again with wrong thinking. Consider the sobering implications revealed in Romans 1:28. A person's mind, created by God to gloriously function, can become *unfit* if it is regularly exposed to toxic environments and wrong types of thinking. It can lose its ability to discern what is morally right and wrong.

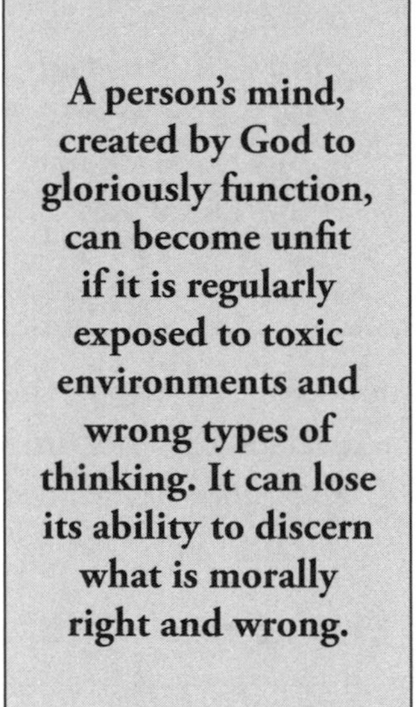

That same mind may remain brilliant in many respects, and the person who possesses that mind may be a marvelously talented individual. Nonetheless, if that person's mind has become reprobate, it is now morally debased, unfit, and twisted in its thinking. In God's view, such a person — or even an entire society — has lost the ability to think correctly, to separate good from evil, or to judge what is right and wrong.

This is why it is so important to guard what you expose your mind to. You must also help your children and grandchildren understand the need to guard their minds against immoral or negative influences. Teach them that this type of destructive exposure will dull people's conscience and adversely affect their minds, which God intended from the start to work wonderfully.

What's Wrong With Wrong?

This is sadly the state of affairs in the day we're living in — the very end of the last days. People's minds are being inundated with false information and a celebration of various forms of immorality, including a deluge of false propaganda about human sexuality. This is a last-days attack of seducing spirits bent on modifying the collective mind of society and creating a way of thinking that is free of moral restraint. This modification process is spreading its tentacles into every sector of society. Even people who grew up in church are now becoming affected and changed in how they view issues that *should* be set in stone in their lives.

How did this happen? It is the result of an unrelenting mental bombardment by wrong people, wrong sources, wrong information, and wrong spiritual influences. It's all part of a demonic strategy that is being waged against the human race (including believers) to adversely affect people's thinking, damage them mentally, and distort their minds until they can no longer see what is *wrong* about *wrong*. Ultimately, this process results in people choosing sides that are opposed to those who adhere to long-held biblical truths.

A demonic strategy is being waged against the human race (including believers) to adversely affect people's thinking, damage them mentally, and distort their minds until they can no longer see what is *wrong* about *wrong.*

As a result of the collective mind of society being mentally modified — that is, becoming seriously ill-affected and sin-damaged — that society will eventually end up "...do[ing] those things which are not convenient" (Romans 1:28). The words "not convenient" simply mean people will do things that are *not morally right or fitting.*

Proverbs 23:7 reveals an important principle: "...As he thinketh in his heart, so is he...." *Never forget that a person's actions follow his thinking.* The devil knows he just needs to find an inroad of access into the mind of a person or into the collective mind of a society. If he can do that, it won't be long until that person's or society's overall behavior will conform to a new and deceptively appealing way of thinking that is far from the well-established, time-tested standards that God clearly states in the Bible.

As God's people, we must be alert to the fact that Satan is loosing hordes of seducing spirits with doctrines of demons in these last days to lead an entire generation into delusion. Satan has launched a covert operation to seize minds — *especially young minds* — to lead them off track. The enemy is using the voices of influential people in entertainment and the media — those who already have been beguiled and seduced to believe a lie. His goal is to victimize a last-days generation and lead them into ways of thinking and behaviors that damage their minds and steal, kill, and destroy on as many levels as possible.

We have seen that Isaiah 5:20 (*NASB*) speaks of a day when people "...call evil good, and good evil; who substitute darkness for light and light for darkness...." This forecasts a day when society at large will become reprobate and lose its ability to discern the difference from right and wrong — even to the point of justifying bad as good and good as bad. This is the day in which you and I live — an end-time moment that the Holy Spirit specifically warned us about in First Timothy 4:1.

The current trend toward lawlessness — that is, the construction of a new world order with morals contrary to those stated in God's Word — will eventually produce a collective mindset in society that no longer feels the pain or conviction of sin and is numb to its consequences. When this phase is fully developed, people's immoral behaviors that grieve God will be carried out without hurting the conscience whatsoever. It will indeed be a day when lawlessness — iniquity — will abound (*see* Matthew 24:12).

While I'm focusing primarily on society, we must not forget that society is made up of individuals who are negatively affected by the unrelenting mental bombardments of evil influences. This includes believers who have allowed themselves to drift so far from God's ways that they lie, steal, fornicate, live as couples outside of marriage, explore other types of sexuality outside the confines of God's Word, watch movies that once would have grieved their hearts — and the list goes on and on.

This continual bombardment of wrong spiritual influences, combined with a collective willingness within the Church world to endure that bombardment, causes Christians' minds to slowly become modified to tolerate more and more compromise. It is most unfortunate that in many cases, Christians no longer feel the pain in their souls of what God calls sin. They go to church and fellowship with others, all the while carrying on as if their actions are acceptable before God.

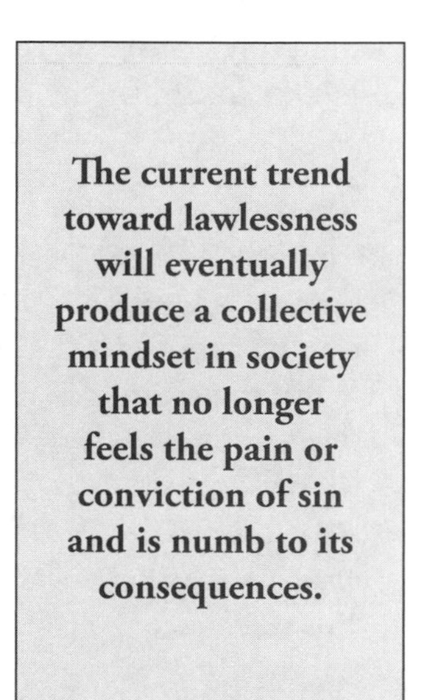

The current trend toward lawlessness will eventually produce a collective mindset in society that no longer feels the pain or conviction of sin and is numb to its consequences.

What has happened to these Christians' consciences, that they would experience no remorse about their sin? This is the toxic effect of ongoing mental modification. Very often their minds and consciences have become seared and hardened over a period of time in some areas of their lives. And, yes, it is likely that even these Christians have become *reprobate* in those compartmentalized areas of their minds.

Is There a Cure?

For believers who have made the egregious error of tolerating and yielding habitually to sinful behavior, there is *hope*. If they will acknowledge how far they've strayed and become willing to repent (*see* 1 John 1:9), the Holy Spirit will rise up like a mighty force from deep within to invade their thoughts and begin the process of renewing their minds once again to the truth.

This transformation of the mind will require a person to absolutely *submit* his or her mind to the Word of God and the work of the Holy Spirit (*see* Romans 12:1,2). It will require courage and sustained commitment, for once a person's mind has been this profoundly impacted by sin and deception, it can be restored to its previous condition only as that person submits his or her mind 100 percent to meditating on and obeying the truth of God's Word.

It is a fact that once a mind has become *debased*, it takes a great commitment to renew it. But the good news is that God offers hope for a believer who has strayed from the clear teaching of Scripture and is willing to do what is necessary to turn back to Him. The Holy Spirit will do the

God offers hope for a believer who has strayed from the clear teaching of Scripture and is willing to do what is necessary to turn back to Him.

miracle of taking his or her sin-damaged mind and renewing it to a right, holy, fit condition — a mind that is once again esteemed by God!

AN END-TIME MUTINY

Let's look again at First Timothy 4:1, which says, "Now the Spirit speaketh expressly, that in the latter times some shall depart from the faith, giving heed to seducing spirits, and doctrines of devils." In the next chapter, we will delve more deeply into this verse. But for now, I want to point out that it says the Holy Spirit "speaketh expressly" about these developments that will occur at the very end of the age.

Paul similarly wrote in Second Thessalonians 2:3 about a departure from the faith that would occur at the very end of the last days. In that verse, Paul said, "Let no man deceive you by any means: for that day shall not come, except there come a *falling away* first, and that man of sin be revealed, the son of perdition."

This phrase "falling away" comes from the Greek word *apostasia*, a word that is also used in the Old Testament Greek Septuagint to depict *mutiny against authority.* In Second Thessalonians 2:3, Paul used this word to depict a worldwide society engaged in an outright mutiny against the authority and the standards of God in the last of the last days. This agrees with Jesus' forewarning that "iniquity will abound" before the end of the age is reached (*see* Matthew 24:12).

This is precisely why we are seeing the nonsensical developments that we are witnessing in our world today. We are living on the cusp of the end of the age just before Jesus comes. Demon spirits have been released into the cultures of this world system in a last-days assault. They are charged with the satanic assignment to confuse, wear down, and unleash irreparable harm into the lives of as many people whom they can deceive as possible.

The Mystery of Iniquity

In Second Thessalonians 2:7, Paul prophesied that the "mystery of iniquity" was at work in the world, but that at the end of the age, it would become an aggressive force in society. Just as the Holy Spirit foretold it, we are witnessing this escalating mutiny against God and the voice of Scripture in our time. The "mystery of iniquity" has been released with a vengeance and is working full steam around the clock to seduce the world into mass deception.

Certainly it's true that believers of *every* generation have had to deal with issues of moral degradation and societal ills in the world around them. That the world is waxing worse and worse is certainly nothing new. But the *rapidity* and the *depth* of moral decline in modern culture over the last mere 100 years are significant. It seems as if all restraints have been thrown off, and we are galloping along on a collision course with the end of an era. The closer we get to the end, the deeper this lost world will sink into deception and depravity.

To "swim upstream" against the swift current of the world is not for the faint of heart. To sustain that forward press, it is imperative that we stand true to our Bible-based convictions. And we are also responsible for transferring that same strength of righteous conviction to the next generation, rearing our children to live as stalwart Christians filled with the Holy Spirit.

In the midst of it all, we can be assured that it will require supernatural strength to resist the pressure that will be mounted against Christians in the days to come. *But you and I are alive on earth at this time for a reason.* We are each called to fulfill a specific role as part of this strategic generation of believers at the end of the age.

In light of this fact, we should recognize that it's never been more crucial for us as believers to humbly seek God's face for wisdom, understanding, and insight concerning His path and His plan for us in this hour. Rather than succumb to fear, we must press into Christ and into the power of the Holy Spirit so that we can make a mark for eternity in as many lives as possible before the age ends. *The opportunity before us is remarkable and unprecedented.*

Because we live in the end times, we must be alert to the fact that the devil is attempting to groom and modify the world so that it will receive the man of lawlessness, who is, of course, the antichrist. A massive undertaking is being executed to lead the world into a state of epic lawlessness so that it will more readily embrace this Satan-inspired individual. The world is unaware of it, but it is being primed and prepared at this very moment for that time.

As this worldwide modification continues, we will witness things changing around us more and more. In the midst of this profound process of a worldwide shift, we will witness evil spiritual forces setting an entire spectrum of destructive fires designed to consume as many lives as possible. All of this and more is ahead of us as we approach the end of this age — which highlights with even greater force how crucial it is that we stick with the Bible and hold to the authority of Scripture in this late hour.

Overall, people in this last-days society do not know or revere the Bible as they once did. As Romans chapter 1 describes, society has gradually turned further and further away from God's truth because His ways and His wisdom do not conveniently fit into the world that liberal progressive thinkers want to construct. Because of this, people are largely ignorant of truth. They don't know they are pawns in the hands of seducing spirits that have been dispatched to lead them astray.

But this is not a time to cower in fear. It's a very strategic hour for us to press forward with the ever-relevant message of the Gospel and its delivering, life-saving, body-healing, mind-restoring message.

Watch Out for the Smoke!

It is also imperative that you and I never forget that the smoke of a fire is statistically deadlier than the fire itself. The facts show that 50 to 80 percent of people who die because of a fire do not die from burning — they die from *smoke inhalation*.

The Church may not be consumed with the blazing fires of moral destruction that the devil is trying to perpetuate in the world today. However, as those born into this end-times generation, we live in the midst of the destruction being wrought on society by seducing spirits. The lost world is going up in moral flames. These hellish fires are burning in our cities — in our schools, in the news media, in our courts, and, sadly, even in the lives of some people who attend our churches. It's essential that you and I do all we can to catch hold of people caught in the blaze and compassionately pull them out of the fires of destruction.

But we also must be ever aware of the smoke that is generated by these hell-inspired flames. We may not be in the midst of the fire itself, but we are not to forget the danger of breathing the smoke produced by these fires. The devil wants to bring the fatal influence of his "spiritual smoke" into our lives — into our churches, into our Christian communities, and even into our homes.

You and I are living in the end times — within close proximity to destructive moral fires that are sweeping across society. We must therefore wake up and stay alert regarding the dangers of *spiritual smoke inhalation* that could damage our lives or the life of our churches. As committed Christians, we are not among those who would embrace the moral delusions being perpetuated in society. We might even feel a repulsion to these delusions. Yet these fires are burning in close proximity to our lives, and the danger of inhaling their toxic smoke is real.

You and I are living in the end times — within close proximity to destructive moral fires that are sweeping across society. We must therefore wake up and stay alert regarding the dangers of *spiritual smoke inhalation* that could damage our lives or the life of our churches.

This insidious demonic smoke is trying to filter its way through every arena of modern society. Satan's goal is to poison our systems of education, entertainment, politics, science, medicine, the courts, and even our churches, using the world system and the morally deteriorating culture that surrounds us. His demonic hordes are tasked with bombarding people's minds with the goal of modifying their thinking and leading them through deception into destructive behaviors and regretful decisions. Only demon spirits could propagate evil on such a wide scale — which is precisely what the Holy Spirit prophesied in First Timothy 4:1.

It is essential that you and I, along with our friends, families, and communities, learn to recognize the enemy's deadly spiritual smoke when its poisonous fumes try to waft into our thought processes and create a haze of confusion.

- It's time to reinforce our minds with what the Bible teaches on vital subjects that are currently under assault.

- It's time to be courageous to challenge what we hear when it is diametrically opposed to biblical truth.
- It's time to learn to think rationally and soundly, even in the midst of a world that seems to be losing its collective mind.
- It's time to wisely use our minds to analyze what we hear.
- It's time for us to be discerning.
- It's time for us to be willing to be at odds with society if it has taken a position that is lawless and contrary to God's standards.
- It's time for us to aggressively pray for grace and wisdom to rescue those who are being victimized by this last-days ravaging of the human race.

All of this is what we must do if we are going to keep our heads on straight in these last days while living in a world that truly seems to be going crazy.

There are many believers who are somewhat aware of the severe shift in the political realm and in societal mindsets, but who have done nothing more than fold their hands and shake their heads in dismay. But that is *not* the answer. It is possible for Christians to be disgusted with society's downward moral trend and yet remain indifferent, void of the necessary compassion to persuade either sinner or saint.

We must draw near to God, pray, and live fully dependent on the Holy Spirit with a fierce, steadfast desire not to grieve, vex, or quench Him. A last-days sea of deception threatens to engulf and capsize our lives unless we are anchored in truth and allow the power of the Holy Spirit to help us stem the tide and stay the course.

Think About It

1. Western society has been on a calculated, demonic trajectory for some time now and is currently well on its way toward Satan's intended "bulls-eye" — a reprobate society that as a whole denies the absolute truth of God's Word.

   Have you thought through what this might require of you and your family in the days ahead? Have you made the firm decision to stand for the truth of God's Word, regardless the personal cost? What might that cost look like in practical, everyday living?

2. We already know from the Word of God that Satan's strategies will not prevail, and God will have His way in the end. There will be a last-days move that eclipses all others in the wrap-up of the age as the Body of Christ prepares for Jesus' return.

   In these greatest of days and most troublesome of times, your uncompromised stance for Jesus might put you on a roller coaster of opposites when it comes to man's acceptance of you. You might experience rejection and ridicule in one part of your day and then see someone's life changed forever by your godly influence in another part.

   How are you personally preparing in your walk with God today to navigate both sides of that spectrum — an increase both in persecution and in the harvest of souls — in the days to come?

3. Never forget — your actions follow your thinking. How you forge the inroads of your mind and to whom you allow access makes all the difference.

   Evaluate the "construction crew" you've allowed to build your own personal inroads. Are those roads built by the truths of

God's Word and the voice of the Holy Spirit in your own spirit and through your God-appointed leaders? Or do you entertain a mix that includes the voice of the world, the devil, and your own contrary flesh nature? Any kind of mix needs to be sorted out before you can effectively step in as God's representative of His time-tested standards to help others find their way to Him in a wayward society.

Chapter Three

AN END-TIME INVASION OF SEDUCING SPIRITS AND DOCTRINES OF DEMONS

We saw in Chapter One that Satan is conspiring to inoculate the world against truth with a deadly serum that will eventually mesmerize society with unprecedented delusion. In that chapter, I focused on ludicrous developments that are transpiring throughout modern society. But according to First Timothy 4:1, these same seducing spirits that are attempting to lure the world into deception will also try to infiltrate the Church with doctrines of demons at the end of the age. The Holy Spirit emphatically prophesied that this type of spiritual attack would occur *inside* the Church in the very last of the last days before Jesus returned.

Then in the last chapter, we talked about the fires of destruction that are burning throughout society, releasing toxic smoke into the surrounding environment. As previously stated, most people who die as a result of fire do not die because of the fire itself but because of *smoke inhalation*.

You are likely not in the middle of a personal moral fire, such as those raging throughout modern society. However, so many deadly blazes are burning in so many arenas of our modern culture — the business and entertainment worlds, the court system, our educational and governmental institutions, and even in our families — that you more than likely have to deal with the smoke in the air. And if you don't deliberately guard against that smoke wafting its way into your personal space and poisoning the atmosphere around you, you might very well breathe in the lie that the toxic fumes are a "normal" experience of modern life on this earth.

If you don't deliberately guard against the smoke wafting its way into your personal space and poisoning the atmosphere around you, you might very well breathe in the lie that the toxic fumes are a "normal" experience of modern life on this earth.

First Timothy 4:1 categorically forecasts that in the conclusion of the end times, a breeding ground for error will fester not only in the secular world, but also within the Church. For anyone with a discerning eye, it is unmistakably clear that these seductive spirits are already at work. One observing the absurd moral developments in various sectors of society can turn his focus on certain quarters of the Body of Christ and recognize the camouflaged error that is also trying to emerge in the Church in our times.

In the Christian world today, there are some spiritual leaders who seek a dangerous truce with the world under the guise of inclusiveness and compromise. Many of these leaders once held strong doctrinal positions. However, over time they began to shape their beliefs to meld with the changing moral climate of society — and in the process, they produced a Gospel message very different from the one presented in the Bible.

Although the world may change, Hebrews 13:8 teaches that Christ is the same yesterday, today, and forever. His truth does not change based on societal trends. Truth is truth, regardless of the particular brand of immorality that society has labeled "acceptable." Today, just as in the early days of the Church, whenever believers take a firm stand on absolute truth, they are viewed by the world as intolerant. But when it comes to truth, there *is* no room to mitigate it or blend it with other belief systems in order to "adapt."

The problem of worldly compromise continues to spread in the Church, and some even visible Christian leaders are promoting this trend. It is therefore vital for mature believers to be able to recognize this process of seduction that seeks to "repackage" the Gospel by adapting and diluting it in an attempt to make it more palatable.

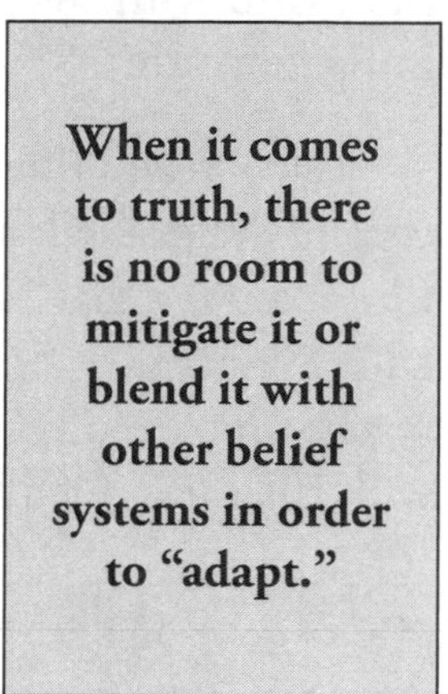

This is the destructive track that much of the Church is on as man's natural reasoning strives to reach a generation that is unfamiliar with the Bible and considers the dictates of the Word restrictive and out of date. Regrettably, we must call this what it is: *a departure from Scripture.*

The Pitfall of Pursuing 'Relevance' With a Last-Days Generation

I'm not talking about striving to remain relevant to the next generation in terms of using natural techniques, such as technology, lights, sound, or even new styles of music. I am certainly not against exploring new advances in technology or style. My own ministry is continually using new techniques that were not formerly available in order to help us be more effective.

Styles always change with the shift to a new generation. As part of the process of transitioning from one generation to the next, it is wise to utilize such means in order to stay current with what younger people relate to. Rather than stubbornly demand that we stick with older methods of communication that we're more accustomed to, our ministry has determined to continually keep learning how to use new techniques so we can keep reaching the world with the Word of God. But in the process, we do *not* mitigate truth!

That's really the dividing line we can never forget. This concept of "relevance" is almost impossible to define because it's an unstable idea that is constantly shifting, depending on the audience. Nonetheless, many on a quest to become relevant to today's generation are presenting a watered-down version of the Gospel with the misguided hope of impacting people on a broader scale.

We must never alter God's eternal, established, time-tested doctrinal truths to fit the preferences of a new generation.

But we must never alter God's eternal, established, time-tested doctrinal truths to fit the preferences of a new generation.

That last statement may seem self-evident to you. Yet the fact is, the Holy Spirit explicitly forewarned that a twisting of truth *would* come about as this age neared its end. We should not be surprised at the pursuit of many within the modern Church to modify and refashion age-old truth in an attempt to make it relevant to a world that is in the process of "going crazy."

God's Strategic Plan That Engaged the First-Century Generation of Believers

Let me give you an illustration of what God did in the First Century to make the Gospel message relevant and more communicable to the world at that time. Because language is the cornerstone of human understanding, God knew it would play an immense role in the spread and dispersal of the Christian faith. So He broke with traditional forms of communication and did something radical that enabled Him to speak to the widest audience possible.

God had historically communicated to His people in Hebrew. But instead of insisting on that same method of communication when He chose to speak to the entire world, God shifted to the Greek language.

When one considers the environment in which the First Century Church took root, the reason that Greek was God's choice as the language of the New Testament becomes clear. It was the common language of the day; it was, in fact, the first international language. A large swath of the civilized world spoke and read Greek, not Hebrew, because Greek was spoken as the primary working language in much of the Roman Empire.

In fact, if a person was fluent in Greek, he could freely communicate and carry on business in most towns or cities under Rome's authority. Even Jews who lived outside of Israel adopted and used Greek as their principal language. If they had stubbornly demanded to communicate with others only in Hebrew, it would have limited their audience and their business opportunities because Hebrew was not widely known.

Rather than force a pagan world to learn Hebrew in order to read the New Testament, God chose to make it easier for them to come to Christ by communicating in *their* language. By using the Greek language, which was known far and wide, the New Testament writers ensured that almost everyone in the far-flung empire could hear and understand the Gospel and then choose to accept or reject it.

The fact is, if the New Testament had been written in Hebrew, its message would likely have never penetrated the worldwide audience that Jesus came to redeem. The use of Hebrew would have limited the availability of the message, whereas Greek opened doors for the message to spread to the far reaches of the Roman Empire.

Furthermore, if the imagery used in the New Testament had been largely borrowed from the Old Testament, pagans would have missed the significance of most of the illustrations because they were simply unfamiliar with Hebrew culture. Therefore, God in His wisdom chose to utilize more of the imagery, symbolism, and figures of speech that the pagan world would understand. It's true that the New Testament does use images and concepts that were drawn directly from the Old Testament. However, the overwhelming majority of words and images in the New Testament are borrowed from the Greek world.

By choosing to use Greek, God demonstrated His willingness to do whatever was necessary to communicate using the language of man.

By choosing to use Greek, God demonstrated His willingness to do whatever was necessary to communicate using the language of man. Although Hebrew was God's language to communicate with His people under the Old Covenant, it was not the language that would reach the masses. So He chose to speak the truths of the New Testament in Greek, even as Hebrew retained its vital role in Israel. This is an example of planning strategically to reach more people.

Jesus Spoke Uncompromised Truth

But let's also consider this term "relevance" in the ministry of Jesus. In the Gospels, Jesus was constantly adapting His style of teaching to various audiences *without* mitigating the truth. He frequently addressed uncomfortable topics, such as His listeners' sinful behavior or the real place called hell — and He did it all unapologetically. Although the religious people often took offense at Jesus' blunt words of truth, the common folk were not offended by His message; in fact, they were *drawn* to Him. The people knew they could depend on Jesus to tell them the truth.

Jesus spoke to religious people in religious terms. He spoke to the upper crust and the wealthy of society in the language of finance that connected with their world. Jesus conversed using political overtones with bureaucrats, politicians, and government officials. He spoke in terms that farmers and fishermen could readily grasp when teaching those who made their living from the land or sea. When addressing the sick, needy, oppressed, or poor, Jesus spoke to them with words that gave hope and healing.

As you study the ministry of Jesus, you will find that He tailored His style of teaching to every audience without sacrificing truth.

As you study the ministry of Jesus, you will find that He tailored His style of teaching to every audience without sacrificing truth. Unlike Pharisees and Sadducees who spoke in lofty theological terms that the common man didn't understand, Jesus conversed in easy-to-understand terms, using vivid stories, illustrations, parables, and even humor to package truth for the ordinary man. He authoritatively spoke from scriptures in the Old Testament. However, by using up-to-date words, phrases, and illustrations, Jesus was able to frame those truths in a manner that the ordinary man could grasp. Yet no matter what method He used to communicate with His specific audience, He *never* altered, amended, compromised, diluted, or mitigated truth to make listeners more comfortable or to gain a following.

If we in our age want to follow the footsteps of Jesus, the Greatest Communicator of all time, we must also learn to speak in ways that the ordinary person can understand. In addition, we must make His standard *our* standard. Like Jesus, *we* must make the decision that we will *never* alter, amend, compromise, dilute, or mitigate truth to make our listeners more comfortable or to gain a following.

If we are faithful to speak and to hold fast to the truth of God's Word, all who hear our message can at least rest assured that they can depend on us to tell them the truth, even if it is uncomfortable to hear.

Hearing uncomfortable truth can be difficult for some people. But if we are faithful to speak and to hold fast to the truth of God's Word, all who hear our message can at least rest assured that they can depend on us to tell them the truth, even if it is uncomfortable to hear.

- Can people count on *us* to tell them the truth?
- When we get to Heaven, will we have the applause of God concerning our lives and ministries as a witness to the world (*see* 1 Corinthians 4:5)?

- Will He affirm that we always spoke the truth and didn't compromise?

As stated previously, styles come and go, and this will always be the case. Many of our methods and styles are cultural, not biblical, and can be changed if needed without sacrificing or mitigating truth. If a leader senses the Holy Spirit's leading to implement these practical types of changes that make a church feel more accommodating or relevant, the changes should be made, albeit with careful contemplation and consideration of long-term effects.

It is imperative to keep our heads on straight in this last-days season when so much is changing all around us. God is depending on the Church to be His voice to this generation. He is not against changing methods *if* it makes us more effective and relevant as we defend the faith and hold forth the Word of life.

Even God was willing to do this when He chose to use the Greek language. As we have seen, Jesus spoke in a language that the ordinary man could understand. But we must also remember that God will hold us accountable if we move away from eternal truths that He has established in His Word.

Do We Qualify To Be His Voice?

As part of God's Church, we are His voice to this end-time generation. We must understand what that really means and decide if we as believers in Christ qualify. To find out, let's turn our attention to the word "preach" for a moment.

The word "preach" used throughout the New Testament is a translation of the Greek word *kerusso*. This word means *to preach, proclaim, declare, announce*, or *to herald a message*. In that Early Church culture, it depicted the role of the official spokesman of a king. The job of this spokesman was to decree the desires, dictates, orders, or messages that a king wanted to communicate to his people. This position required the spokesman to deliver the message exactly as the king wanted it to be communicated. The spokesman had no right to alter, amend, or add to it in any way.

This Greek word *kerusso* and its meanings and implications provide the background for the word "preach" in the New Testament, which explains the role of one who is called upon to preach. This person's foremost job is to accurately represent God and to declare His message as He gave it with no alterations, modifications, or additions of his own. It is *God's* pulpit, not the pulpit of the spokesman.

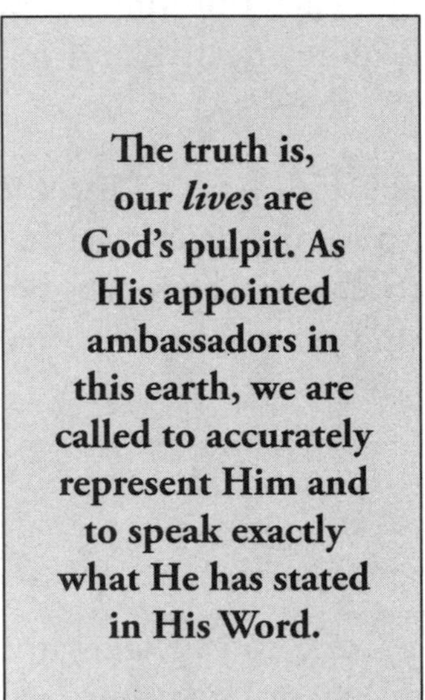

All who "preach" in any capacity must always keep this in mind — and that includes every one of us who are believers in Jesus Christ. The truth is, our *lives* are God's pulpit. We are *His* spokesmen, not the spokesmen of ourselves or other people, and we must never use this high and noble position to say or do what we wish. As His appointed ambassadors in this earth, we are called to accurately represent Him and to speak exactly what He has stated in His Word.

Everyone likes to be appreciated, but we must never forget that we are not here to be liked or to gain a following. We are called to be like Moses, who spoke on behalf of God and uncompromisingly represented Him and His message to the people. We are *not* to be like Aaron when he began to represent *the people* and pander to their carnal desires — even to the point of giving them a golden calf to worship when they demanded it.

For example, a modern-day trap of seeking popularity is the ever-broadening platform of social media in which success can be measured by how many "likes" a person receives. To garner more "likes," some use their pages to get attention, often making outrageous statements to create a buzz. Spokespeople for God may very well develop an audience and grow in popularity. But they must remember above everything else the One whose character and words they are to accurately represent at all times.

In our role as God's spokesmen, we must always keep in mind that everything we say and do is to represent Him, His holiness, and His character. We don't have the right to alter or modify His words to appease a world that is changing.

In our role as God's spokesmen, we must always keep in mind that everything we say and do is to represent Him, His holiness, and His character. We don't have the right to alter or modify His words to appease a world that is changing. He has called us to speak His message to the best of our ability just as He gave it and to convey it by the life-giving and transforming power of the Holy Spirit.

The Folly of Avoidance

Ministers are especially accountable before God to speak His message accurately and fully just as He has given it. Yet it is an undeniable fact that some who have highly visible pulpits or platforms have begun to diverge from long-held truths of the Bible. Careful observation of such instances reveals the sad truth that some ministers are pandering to the itching ears of a last-days generation. Instead of dealing with issues as Jesus did, these ministers now decline to address any issue of morality or deal with any sinful behaviors.

There are some ministers who won't even go near the unpopular subject of hell and who back away from labeling sin for what it is in case it might cause some of their listeners to feel discomfort. Such ministers often ignore current developments in the world that those under their spiritual care are genuinely concerned about. They publicly sidestep potentially controversial issues either because they don't know *how* to address them or because addressing them may risk putting their ministries in some type of legal jeopardy.

These ministers might argue that they are staying on the positive side of life — preaching *for* something instead of *against* something. Although it's true that the preaching of the true Gospel penetrates the darkness of this world with its light, this argument doesn't hit the mark when God has called His spokesmen to stand *against* the proliferation of evil. And often what they're preaching *for* presents a message that's too weak to withstand any onslaught of evil or to preserve and protect those under their care as the days grow even darker.

Anyone who takes this approach of avoiding vital but potentially controversial issues has backed away from his or her ministry to speak as God's voice in the earth.

Anyone who takes this approach of avoiding vital but potentially controversial issues has backed away from his or her ministry to speak as God's voice in the earth.

Dire consequences have resulted from this widespread retreat by many ministers from preaching God's Word on serious topics when His Word clearly *does* address those subjects. The modern Church has become populated with large numbers of people who live in sin, yet demonstrate no conviction of sin. These people carry on as if it is normal for a Christian to live in a backslidden state while expecting God to bless them.

I don't want to sound negative, but the situation I just described is very grave as it stands in this hour. To bring the Church back to where God wants it to be will require great courage on the part of God's leaders, His spokesmen. They must be willing to acknowledge the present sad condition of large portions of the Church. Then they must rise up and both publicly and privately refute every form of deception with a steadfast stance on God's truth — *regardless* of the consequences to them personally.

Having said that, I want to also stress that we can be thankful that everyone is *not* departing from truth. There is a huge number of spiritual leaders and Christian believers who are saying, "Enough is enough!" These faithful warriors are digging their heels into the bedrock of Scripture and *refusing* to bend with the times. They have determined that they will not be deceived into accepting a watered-down, diluted version of the Bible, and they are holding fast in prayer for a mighty outpouring of God's Spirit upon the Church.

We can be thankful that everyone is *not* departing from truth. There is a huge number of spiritual leaders and Christian believers who are saying, "Enough is enough!" These faithful warriors are digging their heels into the bedrock of Scripture and *refusing* to bend with the times.

We rejoice in the powerful witness of these faithful people of God. Nevertheless, we must not shut our eyes to what the Holy Spirit prophesied — for He clearly stated that many, *even inside the Church*, will be affected by seducing spirits and doctrines of demons at the end of the age. The fact that this is happening shouldn't surprise us because the Bible prophesied it. Since you and I live in the end of this prophetic season, it means *we* will see and experience some of the disturbing and even bizarre developments that will be a part of these latter days.

What the Holy Spirit Prophesied in First Timothy 4:1

This infiltration of seducing spirits and doctrines of demons was *not* prophesied in First Timothy 4:1 to scare us, but to *prepare us* and help us *prevent* those who are part of the Church from being beguiled. It's important to settle that within yourself. God is never interested in scaring His people, but He is *very* interested in warning us when danger is on the horizon. The Holy Spirit sounded this alarm to prevent this error from ever finding entrance into our churches, our personal lives, or the lives of our children and grandchildren.

Let's look carefully at the exact wording in First Timothy 4:1. Paul said, "Now the Spirit *speaketh expressly*, that in the latter times some shall depart from the faith, giving heed to seducing spirits and doctrines of demons."

Pay attention to the phrase "speaketh expressly," because this phrase is profoundly important in this verse. The word "expressly" is a translation of the Greek word *rhetos,* a word that describes something spoken *clearly, unmistakably, and vividly* or something that is *unquestionable, certain, and sure.*

By using this word *rhetos*, the Holy Spirit makes His point unequivocally clear. The events He is about to describe in this verse are *definite*; they will *surely* come to pass. Therefore, the Spirit speaks in *undeniable* terms.

In light of this, one could actually translate the verse:

- "Now the Spirit speaks in *absolutely clear words....*"
- "Now the Spirit speaks in *unmistakable terms....*"
- "Now the Spirit speaks in the *clearest of language....*"

This tells us there is no guesswork about this development. The Holy Spirit emphatically states it will definitely transpire in the latter days. The use of the Greek word *rhetos* makes it categorically plain that what the Spirit is saying is not optional or something that can be altered. He is clearly depicting something that *will* take place in the end of the age.

A Warning for the Last-Days Church

Paul went on to deliver the Holy Spirit's unmistakable message: "Now the Spirit speaketh expressly that in *the latter times*, some shall depart from the faith...."

The Holy Spirit is forewarning believers of a dangerous, demonic plot that the Church will have to contend with in these last of the last days. There have been many attacks against the Church throughout its 2,000 years of history. But in this verse, the Holy Spirit sounds the alarm that this end-time attack will be unlike previous ones and will be especially severe. This last-days assault against the Church will be so insidious that the Holy Spirit spoke in advance about it in absolutely clear, unmistakable, and definite words.

The verse states that this threatening attack will occur in the "latter times." The word translated "latter" in the *King James Version* is translated from the Greek word *husteros.* This word emphasizes the *ultimate end* or the *very last* of something. The word "times" is from the Greek word *kairos,* which in this case depicts *a season.* When taken together as one complete phrase, these words describe the *very last season* or the *very last period of time.*

There is no doubt that the combination of these Greek words describes the very end of the age, when nearly no time is left remaining in that last prophetic season. We can conclude, then, that when this invasion of seducing spirits and doctrines of demons occurs, it is a signal that the very end is upon us. In fact, Jesus made it very clear in His discourse about the end of the age in Matthew 24 that deception and delusion in society — and even in certain sectors of the Church — will be *the* primary sign that we are near the end of the age.

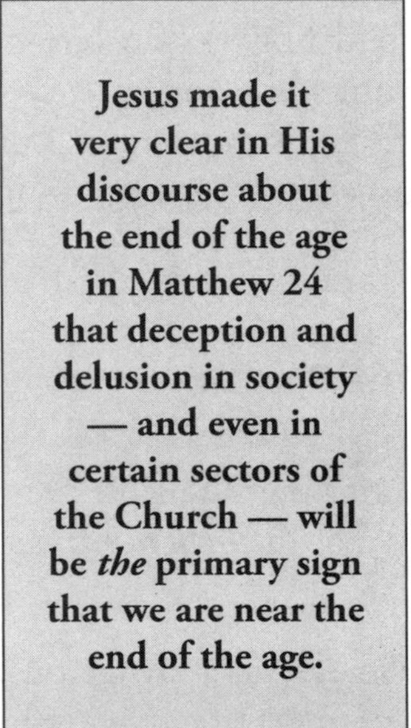

Jesus made it very clear in His discourse about the end of the age in Matthew 24 that deception and delusion in society — and even in certain sectors of the Church — will be *the* primary sign that we are near the end of the age.

I wrote about this extensively in my book *Signs You'll See Just Before Jesus Comes.* The following is a key portion of that discussion:

Jesus listed *many* signs that would indicate we were on the road to the end, but the *very first* sign He spoke to the disciples about contained a clear warning about wide-scale, world-wide deception that would emerge at the very end of this era. Jesus warned the disciples, *and us,* of the need to guard against that deception.

In Matthew 24:4, Jesus said, "...Take heed that no man deceive you." As Jesus began His discourse on the many end-time signs to watch for, He listed deception *first and*

foremost as a primary indicator that the conclusion of the age was upon us....

Let's see why Jesus placed such emphasis on this sign, even above other specific signs of the times.

Jesus warned believers that they must "take heed" to guard against the deception that would characterize the end of the period (*see* Matthew 24:4). The words "take heed" were intended to *jar* and *jolt* listeners to get their attention. As Jesus spoke the words "take heed," there is no doubt that the disciples perked up to *really listen* to what He was telling them. When He had their full attention, Jesus warned them that as the present age comes to a close, an end-times deception would attempt to infiltrate every part of society across the world.

The word "deceive" used in Matthew 24:4 is translated from a Greek word that means *to wander off course*. It could depict an individual who has wandered off course, or it could even describe a whole nation and even vast numbers of nations that have veered off course from a moral position they once held to be true. It suggests a moral wandering on a worldwide scale at the close of this period.

Let me try to help you more fully comprehend how this word "deceive" would have been used in Jesus' time. In the Greek, this word depicts the behavior of someone who once walked on a solid path, but who is now drifting and teetering on the edge of a treacherous route. This person has either already departed from his once-solid path and has lost his bearings as a result, or he is in the process of departing from it. The word "deceive" means he is going cross-grain against all that was once a part of his core belief system. Sadly, he is now deviating from his former solid moral position to a course that is unreliable, unpredictable, and even dangerous.

This word "deceive" tells us that there will be a mass divergence from time-tested biblical standards. By using this word in Matthew 24:4, Jesus was foretelling that a moment was coming when society would move away from the long-affirmed laws of Scripture. Although He specified *many* signs to indicate the conclusion of the age, Christ declared that this mass divergence from truth — and worldwide moral wandering — would be the *first*, *foremost*, and *primary* sign to alert us that the end was near. That is precisely why He named it first in His list of signs that would authenticate we have entered the wrap-up of the age.

The words of Matthew 24:4 are intended to let us know that those who live at the very end of the age will see *moral confusion* in society as deception attempts to engulf humanity with misinformation about what is morally right and wrong. I think you can see that Matthew 24:4 aptly describes what Christians are witnessing in contemporary history.

It is simply a fact that we are watching moral confusion rage among the civilized nations of the world as never before in our lifetimes. This confusion is perhaps no clearer anywhere than in the debate over gender identity — a manifestation of confusion so severe that it stuns most thinking minds. The culture most of us knew as we were growing up was established on Judeo-Christian values. But now, as the winds of change are blowing, we are watching as the world is rapidly departing from time-tested beliefs and traditions that are based on these biblical values.

As a result of this near abandonment of truth and throwing away of moral foundations, confusion abounds and society is teetering on a treacherous path — just as Jesus prophesied in Matthew 24:4. The spirit of this world is working furiously to eliminate all remnants of a godly foundation from society and to replace it with a last-days

deception that will ultimately usher in a time when the antichrist rules a lost world for a temporary period of time.

The fact that you are reading this book probably means you are spiritually sensitive to what is happening in the world today. So you know well that there is an onslaught of deception attacking our culture from every direction. There is a new propensity to rationalize away truth and replace it with politically "progressive" thinking. And unfortunately, like a sickness invades and sickens the human body, this end-times deception is seeping into every part of society. This "new" mindset can be found in our schools, our government, on television — and in virtually all forms of art and media....

Under the inspiration of the Holy Spirit, the apostle Paul also prophesied that a mass deception would occur at the end of the period as a precursor to Christ's return. In Second Thessalonians 2:11, Paul specifically stated that at the conclusion of this period, a vast percentage of the population of the world would be controlled by "delusion."

In this verse in Second Thessalonians, the Holy Spirit prophesied that a last-days society worldwide will become *beguiled*, *seduced*, and *duped*. All of these words are contained in this word "delusion." This prophesied period of deception will be so intense that people will believe what is false over what is obviously true, even denying facts and truths that are common sense and that nature itself teaches (*see* Romans 1:20).

According to Scripture, this period of worldwide deception will occur at the "outer rim" of the era — marking a time when delusion will attempt to pervade every realm of society. [13]

[13]Rick Renner, *Signs You'll See Just Before Jesus Comes* (Tulsa: Harrison House, 2018), pp. 39-43.

First Timothy 4:1 is the Holy Spirit's way of pointing His prophetic finger into the future to apprise you and me of this forecasted period of error that would emerge in the world and also in the Church in the *last season* of the Church Age. The Spirit was so serious and grave about what He saw happening in that season that He communicated it in absolutely undeniable, vivid, weighty, and definitive words.

A Departure From 'The Faith'

First Timothy 4:1 continues to say, "Now the Spirit speaketh expressly, that in the latter times *some shall depart from the faith....*"

The word "depart" is a translation of the Greek word *aphistemi,* which is a compound of two Greek words, *apo* and *istimi*. The word *apo* means *away*, and the word *istimi* means *to stand*. But when these two words are compounded, as in the word "depart," they form the word *aphestimi*, which means *to stand apart from*, *to distance one's self from*, *to step away from*, *to withdraw from*, or *to shrink away from*. It is from this very Greek word that we derive the word *apostate* or *apostasy.*

This "departing" depicts a departure that takes place *very slowly*, over a period of time, and it pictures a person who changes his position and withdraws from what he once believed. This departure occurs so gradually that those who are in the process of departing may not even realize they are in transition. But little by little, bit by bit, they are *backing away from* what they once believed and adhered to, and they are *moving toward* something very different.

This means that the "departing" the Holy Spirit prophesied about in this verse does not refer to a blatant, outright rejection of the faith, although it may eventually lead there. It describes something much more *subtle* than that. It portrays a gradual, step-by-step, almost undetectable departure over a period of time. It is a very slow withdrawal and shifting of position where the scriptures are concerned.

The verse goes on to say that "some shall depart from *the faith*" as we near the end of the age. In Greek, the words "the faith" has a definite article, which tells us that this is not talking about raw faith, such as faith for miracles.The definite article in the Greek text tells us that the words "the faith" refer to *doctrine* or to *the long-held, time-tested teaching of Scripture*. The verse categorically means that at the very end of the age, there will be some who will depart from the clear teaching of the Scripture — little by little distancing themselves from God's truth — to embrace something new that has captured their attention.

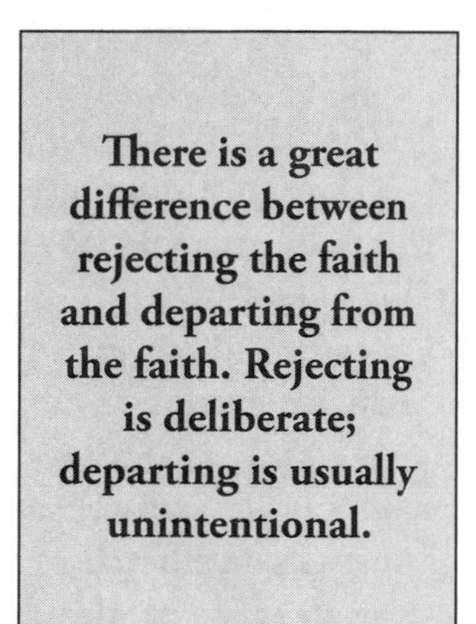

The verse doesn't say people will *reject* the faith; it says they will *depart from* the faith. There is a great difference between rejecting the faith and departing from the faith. Rejecting is deliberate; departing is usually unintentional.

Why the people are "departing from the faith" is not stated in the verse; however, the reason is implied. The verse says some shall depart from the faith, "...giving heed to seducing spirits and doctrines of demons."

The words "giving heed" are from the Greek word *prosecho*, a compound of the words *pros* and *echo*. In this case, the word *pros* means *toward*, and the word *echo* means *to embrace*. This word unequivocally pictures those who believed one thing for a long time. But now as a result of some influence, they are gradually releasing what they formerly believed and switching their focus toward something else. It pictures those who are slowly but surely releasing what has been familiar, precious, and dear — letting go of past firmly held beliefs — to embrace something new and different.

According to First Timothy 4:1, what is the external influence drawing people away from long-held beliefs and leading them in a new direction? By context, the "cause-and-effect" process taking place is revealed: There is a *step-up* in the activity of seducing spirits and doctrines of demons on the earth that is causing a society-wide *shift* from God's truth to deception.

What is the external influence drawing people away from long-held beliefs and leading them in a new direction? There is a *step-up* in the activity of seducing spirits and doctrines of demons on the earth that is causing a society-wide *shift* from God's truth to deception.

The Holy Spirit tells us in this verse that some at the end of the age will be seduced by a demonic influence that leads them into deception on many levels. As a result, these wandering end-time believers will open their minds to other possibilities and other avenues that lead to an embracing of other doctrines and systems of thought that represent a departure from what they previously attested to be truth.

There are many examples that demonstrate how society and even the Church has begun to depart from age-old truth. But as noted already, perhaps no example is more revealing than the current pressure to be inclusive and endorse all sexual lifestyles, even those that are clearly contrary to the teaching of Scripture.

The reason I refer to this example again is that I am convinced this issue will likely become the most problematic subject in the years to come. Gradually (and perhaps not so gradually), the moral framework of even those inside the Church will begin to be modified by the media and other societal institutions pressuring people from every side to change their thinking about this subject. Rather than stick with the scriptural truth that is so foundational to a godly society, even believers will begin to adapt to the new mindset.

I believe this subject will become a dividing line between those who steadfastly hold to the teaching of Scripture and those who say that we needn't be so strict — that in the name of tolerance, we should be more open-minded and meld into the new mindset. An ever-intensifying pressure will be brought to bear on believers to slack up on what they believe in order to become more relevant and to "reach" more people. However, to yield to that pressure and comply with society's expectations will require those believers to disregard significant portions of the Bible that address these issues.

This perfectly portrays how a careful, slow, almost unnoticeable, step-by-step departure is occurring over a period of time. Those of us who are committed to God's Word must determine that we will not budge from the Bible on key issues. We *must* keep our heads on straight on these issues even if the world seems to be going in another direction.

The Bible has never changed. Its teaching on these subjects has never been altered. But the authority and voice of Scripture is now being called into question by those who downgrade its authority and relegate it to the past, alleging that it is no longer entirely applicable in the current environment.

You may ask, "How did this transition in society happen? How is it possible that even notable Christians are changing their positions on such rock-solid biblical truths?"

At first, the shift of position on these and other key issues was very slow but steady. It was over an extended period of time that the departure from long-held and widely accepted moral positions took place. But now, in the very last days of these end times, this process of departure has accelerated until it is racing out of control, galloping forward in our culture at an ever-increasing pace.

As you are well aware, now even the courts, education, arts and entertainment, government, and a multitude of other arenas in society fanatically promote the new moral agenda. This seductive process has even stretched its long arms into religious circles where church leaders are encouraging people to throw off old mindsets and become more embracing of homosexual lifestyles and same-sex marriages.

In the midst of these society-altering changes, Christians who remain true to their time-tested beliefs and convictions on these subjects are being more and more subjected to harassment. This pressure of being bullied by a hostile world has caused many who once stood firm in their beliefs along these lines to modify their long-held beliefs and become more "politically correct" as they slowly depart from the faith.

An insidious shift in sexual morals has evolved over a number of decades. The shift has occurred so gradually and remained so well-disguised that those in transition were often not even aware that a transition was taking place. This departure from long-held beliefs and convictions is ongoing and under the guise of open-mindedness, fairness, equality, and even in the name of God's love. But this godless, immoral departure from Scripture is anything but loving and equitable. In reality, it has led us into the last-days territory of moral confusion and destruction as society has veered further and further off track.

Satan's agenda of deception has stepped up in scope and momentum in this end-time season we're living in, but his tactics are never new. He is always looking for an access point to insert his own wicked agenda in an effort to mutate and ultimately derail God's plan.

In the next chapter, we're going to see how early New Testament Church leaders dealt with early forms of demonic deception that threatened to take the Church off course almost from the outset of the Church Age. The Holy Spirit-inspired words those leaders used to warn believers of Satan's strategies back then have continued to instruct and warn believers against deception for more than 2,000 years — and they are especially vital to understand right now as we navigate the challenges of an end-time society gone adrift.

Satan's agenda of deception has stepped up in scope and momentum in this end-time season we're living in, but his tactics are never new. He is always looking for an access point to insert his own wicked agenda in an effort to mutate and ultimately derail God's plan.

Think About It

1. You are the bishop of your own soul, the watchman on the wall of your life. As you observe fires of destruction consuming so much of the moral fabric of modern society, what deliberate steps are you taking to make sure the toxic smoke of the world's way of thinking isn't sifting into your own personal space to poison your mental, emotional, and spiritual "atmosphere"?

2. Jesus is our Example in all things. The Bible says that as He is, so are we in the world (*see* 1 John 4:17). And when it comes to taking an immovable stance for God's truth, no one has done it better than Jesus Himself as He walked this earth. The religious people often took offense at Jesus' blunt words of truth, but the common folk were often drawn to Him. Even though He tailored His style of teaching to reach every audience, He never sacrificed truth, and the people knew it.

   Do the people in your life know that they can depend on you to tell them the truth, even if they don't like what they hear? And are you willing to stand for God's truth, no matter who is listening, even if the risk is real that they might choose to reject what you're saying and walk away from their relationship with you for good?

3. Our lives are God's pulpit, and we are His spokesmen. We don't have the option to say or do what we wish in any given situation.

   Consider situations you've been in where wrong was being exalted as right, and it was up to you to represent God's way of thinking and doing. How did you do in that moment? Did your words and your attitude accurately reflect His heart and thoughts? In what way could you adjust to be an even more effective representative for Him in similar situations that may arise in the future?

Chapter Four

EARNESTLY CONTENDING FOR THE FAITH

Even in the Early Church before the New Testament Scriptures were finished being written, a spiritual attack was already being waged against the Gospel. The purity of the Gospel message was in jeopardy of being twisted and distorted by leaders who were mishandling and modifying truth. The devil was attempting to invade the Church seductively through the influence of notable Christian personalities trafficking in spiritual error.

It had been only decades since Jesus had risen from the dead, and the seducing spirits Paul prophesied about were already trying to introduce error into the Church. In fact, the situation escalated so fast that Jude wrote, "Beloved, when I gave all diligence to write unto you of the common salvation, it was needful for me to write you, and exhort you that ye should earnestly contend for the faith which was once delivered unto the saints" (Jude 3).

According to these remarks from Jude, his prior plan had been to write an epistle about salvation. However, his plan was interrupted by news that error-filled teachings were attempting to infiltrate the Church. Jude was so disturbed about this development that he abandoned his plan to write a letter about salvation in order to write a letter about the encroaching danger instead.

As Jude began his letter, he explained, "...It was needful for me to write you...." The word "needful" is from the Greek word *anagke*, which denotes *an urgent necessity.* By using this word at this juncture, Jude let his readers know that the problem he saw was serious and needed to be addressed without delay.

Something was happening so underhanded that Jude felt pressed to urgently address the issue as quickly as possible. So without hesitation, Jude dropped his plans to write an epistle about salvation so he could alert the saints to the danger that was emerging and give instructions regarding how to confront the problem.

Take Courage and Run to the Fight!

Let's look again at what Jude wrote in verse 3: "Beloved, when I gave all diligence to write unto you of the common salvation, it was needful for me to write you, and exhort you that ye should earnestly contend for the faith which was once delivered unto the saints."

That word "exhort" is very important in this context. It is a translation of the Greek word *parakaleo*, which means *to urge*, *to beseech*, *to beg*, or even *to encourage*. It was a word often used by military leaders or by commanding officers before they sent their troops into battle.

Rather than hide from the reality of war, the commanding officer would summon together troops and speak straightforwardly with them about the potential dangers of the battlefield. The soldiers were soberly assured by their leader that bloodshed, injury, and even death could be encountered as they fought their battles.

A good commander wouldn't ignore these dangers or pretend they didn't exist; he knew it was his job to prepare the troops for war. So he would urge, exhort, encourage, and beseech his troops to stand tall, throw back their shoulders, look the enemy straight-on and eye-to-eye, and face their battle with steadfast courage.

Jude used this idea when he wrote to his readers. From the news he had received, Jude was aware that error was attempting to invade the Church. He knew that shutting his eyes and pretending the problem wasn't there wouldn't fix the problem. If no one raised his voice to stop the error, error would continue to spread its infection, and the message of the Gospel would be perverted. It was time for a mature Christian leader to stand up to refute what was happening. Jude was the man for that job.

If no one raised his voice to stop the error, error would continue to spread its infection, and the message of the Gospel would be perverted. It was time for a mature Christian leader to stand up to refute what was happening.

Refusing to allow the "enemies of the cross" (*see* Philippians 3:18) to promote their errant teachings without resistance, Jude stepped forward. Then like a commanding officer, he urged, exhorted, beseeched, and encouraged his troops to stand strong in the face of this assault. Like it or not, the enemy had invaded the ranks of the Early Church, and believers had only two options: They could either stand up for truth or surrender to the assault that was taking place. Jude exhorted his readers to stand strong and keep their heads on straight.

What Is Required To Contend for the Faith?

In verse 3, Jude exhorted his readers to "earnestly contend for the faith that was once delivered unto the saints." The words "earnestly contend" are a translation of the Greek word *epagonidzomai*, which is a compound of the words *ep* and *agonidzo*. The word *ep* simply means *for* or *over*. The word *agonidzo* denotes *an intense struggle*, and it is where we derive the word *agony*. In the First Century, the word *agonidzo* was exactly the word used to picture two wrestlers who agonized to win over the other in a wrestling match. Both wrestlers worked to gain the advantage and hurl their opponent to the ground, exerting every ounce of their strength and skill to win a very intense physical contest.

But when the words *ep* and *agonidzo* are compounded, they form the word *epagonidzomai*. Instead of referring to a general fight or a struggle, this word depicts *those who are fighting with all of their might to win a match* of some type. Jude's use of *epagonidzomai* means *to fight over an issue* or *to fight for a truth,* and it pictures *people who are wrestling between issues of truth and deception.*

The fact that Jude used the word *epagonidzomai* to describe the situation tells us that false teachers were already trying to "wrestle the faith to the ground" and subdue it so they could modify it to suit their own ends. Because deception was attempting to trounce truth, Jude used this word *epagonidzomai* to tell us that we have a responsibility to rise to such occasions and do all we must do to defend and guard the purity of the faith.

Even at that early moment in the history of the Church, seducing spirits with doctrines of demons were threatening to spread spiritual infection inside the Church. Thus, Jude commanded believers to "...earnestly contend for *the faith* which was delivered unto the saints." Especially notice the words "the faith" in this verse. As we saw in First Timothy 4:1, these words also have a definite article, which again tells us that this is not talking about raw faith, such as faith for the miraculous. Because the text has a definite article, we can know that the words "the faith" refer to *doctrine* or to *the time-tested, long-held teaching of Scripture*. We see here that even in the First Century, *the faith* was already under attack. That is why Jude found it urgently necessary to command Christians to defend and fight for the faith and to do all they could to retain its purity.

As is happening today, believers in the Early Church were being attacked *externally* by a godless society that surrounded them on all sides. Through the first few centuries of the Church's existence, believers successfully withstood wave after wave of intense pressure and persecution from the pagan world and a hostile government.

But Christians were also being attacked from *within* the Church as errant leaders introduced doctrines and new ideas that were diversions from truth. As a result of the destructive influence of these well-known, beloved brothers who had gotten off track doctrinally, a spiritual disease had begun to invade the Church. If it wasn't stopped, Jude knew it would produce an increasingly sick spiritual condition in the Church. So like a commanding officer, Jude raised his voice and called upon the saints to earnestly contend for the purity of the faith and to defeat error.

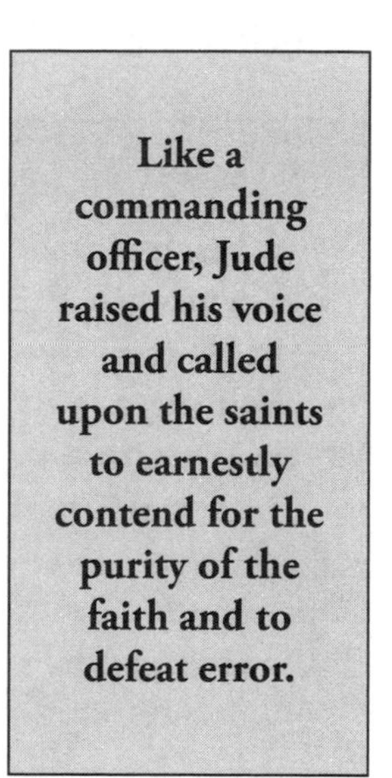

What was the corrosive spiritual disease that some leaders inside the Church were advocating? *Accommodation with the world around them in order to provide relief from persecution and from perpetual pressure to conform.* This errant doctrine promoted the idea, *Let's bend a little and become more willing to be more like the world so they won't have so many problems accepting us.*

Regrettably, the leaders who were making these spiritually toxic suggestions were beloved and well-known brothers within the Christian community. It was difficult for the church members to see them as evil. Yet despite the positions of responsibility and influence that these spiritual leaders held within the Church, they were in actuality encouraging people to embrace a philosophy of compromise — a path littered with dangerous eternal ramifications.

This doctrine of compromise promoted a watered-down version of truth to make it easier to comingle with the world around them. For believers who were under the assault of a society gone astray, it was a very real temptation to dilute what they knew to be truth and to become more accommodating to a lost world and its unredeemed manner of living so they would be less alienated in society.

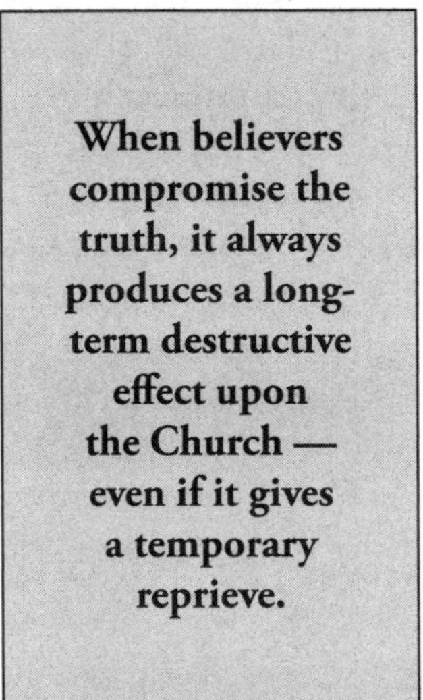

What these misguided leaders were suggesting was actually a demonic, stealth operation designed to compromise the truth. Satan is well aware that when believers compromise the truth, it always produces a long-term destructive effect upon the Church — even if it gives a temporary reprieve.

What is the destructive outcome produced by such a push for doctrinal and behavioral compromise? What happens when the Church ceases to stand for truth or to live holy lives separate from the world? When that type of wrong doctrine gains ascendancy, it produces a weak Church so contaminated with spiritual sickness that very little power remains in it.

For this reason, Jude raised his voice to sound the alarm to believers everywhere. His message was clear: They must *refuse to budge* from what they knew to be true and fully *commit* themselves to the defense of the truth.

Over a period of time, these well-esteemed, errant leaders had been led astray by seducing spirits. By turning their focus away from the hard-and-fast truths of Scripture to listen to new and enticing ideas, these leaders had become contaminated spiritually. That is why they were willing to barter truth for peace with a morally lost world. In that day and time, this was man's effort to be more "relevant" to the world.

It's important to understand that everyone in the Early Church did not depart from the faith. However, it only takes a few visible spiritual leaders getting off track to bring the infection of spiritual disease into the Church. Never forget that physical infections begin at the microscopic level with a relatively small number of contagions — and that many infections are often easily treatable if they are addressed in their early stages. However, if those same infections are left untreated, they can quickly grow out of control and lead to serious physical complications or even death.

Likewise, at the time of Jude's writing, this spiritual disease that was trying to infect the Church was still in its early stages. But Jude was aware that the error had the potential to become deadly for the spiritual progress of multitudes within the Church if left unchallenged. That spiritual infection seems to have entered through a few leaders whose influence provided a platform from which they could spread their message of diluted truth to fellow believers. Although the number of deceived believers was still small, that number was already in the process of multiplying inside the church — *exactly like an infectious disease.*

If this multiplication was not stopped by the power of the Spirit, it would spread from one believer to another until it finally affected not just a few, but the entire Church. Just as a physical infection can be stopped in its early stages from fully developing and causing serious or long-term harm, Jude was calling for the believers in the First Century to immediately *stop* the spread of this infectious teaching of compromise with the world.

Jude conveyed an unmistakable message: The Holy Spirit was calling upon his readers — and He's calling upon *us* in our day — to take a stand for truth. We are not called to engage in mud-slinging or to wage nasty attacks against individuals; that is *not* the behavior of the Spirit of God. But neither can we be timid when it comes to defending truth.

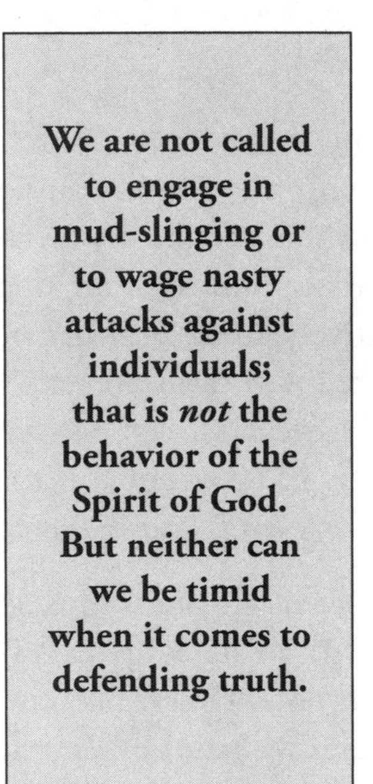
We are not called to engage in mud-slinging or to wage nasty attacks against individuals; that is *not* the behavior of the Spirit of God. But neither can we be timid when it comes to defending truth.

The devil knows the Gospel is the power of God (*see* Romans 1:16). Satan wants its truth to be watered down so that the full power of the Gospel will cease to be released. This is why Jude soberly urged us to agonize over and wrestle for the purity of the faith and to refuse to allow anyone — even leaders who are beloved and well known but have veered off course — to draw us away from it.

The words "earnestly contend" leave no room for misunderstanding what the Holy Spirit is instructing us to do. Dealing with error is not pleasant, but there is a time when it must be done bravely, lovingly, and in the power of the Holy Spirit.

A Special Challenge for Christians in the Last Days

Because of advances made in technology, the Christian world today is exposed to all kinds of Christian celebrities and personalities and a wide array of teaching. Through the avenues of Christian publishing houses, television and Internet programs, radio shows, and even entire Christian television networks, this generation has had the marvelous opportunity to access more information about the Gospel of Jesus Christ than any previous generation before us.

However, this unprecedented access to information also heightens the possibility of error creeping into our personal spaces. The continual influx of information requires us to use great discernment regarding whom we allow to speak into our lives.

I am thankful for the vast array of Christian television programs that are available today. After all, I am also a TV broadcaster who seeks to extend my voice through these various media outlets. However, I must tell you that I cautiously guard my home and am careful even about which Christian TV programs are allowed into our personal space. I agree with the old saying — everything that glitters is not gold.

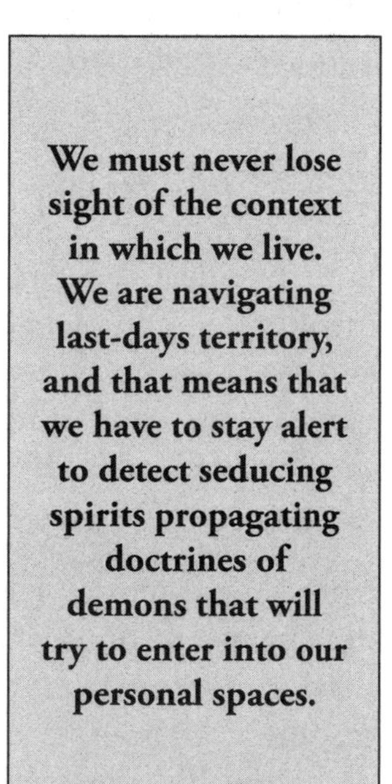

We must never lose sight of the context in which we live. We are navigating last-days territory, and that means that we have to stay alert to detect seducing spirits propagating doctrines of demons that will try to enter into our personal spaces. The Holy Spirit prophesied this would happen in our day. It's our responsibility to determine to use our sound minds, hold fast to the Scriptures, and refuse to budge from God's truth. In other words, *let's keep our heads on straight*!

No Improvements Needed

Jude emphatically wrote in verse 3 that we are to "earnestly contend for the faith that was *once* for all delivered unto the saints." The word "once" is the Greek word *apax,* and it means *once for all*. It carries the idea of *completion*, *finality*, or *something so complete that it needs nothing more to be added to it*.

By using this word *apax,* Jude stated that the Word of God needs no alterations, amendments, improvements, modifications, or revelations to be added to it. It was delivered "once for all" as *a finished, completed, perfect work*.

The fact that Jude used this word *apax* affirms again what kind of battle was raging at that time. Teachers infected with error were attempting to alter, amend, or "provide improvements" to the truth that had already "once and for all" been delivered to mankind — complete and perfect as it stood. Jude was strongly and clearly presenting his message: The Word of God was given to man with no need of modification or improvement. As it stands, the Word of God is *complete*, *final*, *authoritative*, and *life-changing*.

This is precisely why seducing spirits want to wrestle it away from us and replace it with seductive, newly styled doctrines of demons — to diminish the Scripture's ability to transform our lives. But no matter how appealing these "new" doctrines or so-called "progressive thinking" may seem to the natural mind, deception lurks beneath their camouflage. The Holy Spirit has made it clear that in the last of the last days, teachings and philosophies laced with error will lure people away from truth and into rampant confusion at the end of the age.

Entrusted Into Our Safekeeping

Jude firmly stated that this complete, final, and authoritative faith — which came with no need of any modification — was once "*delivered* unto the saints." The word "delivered" in Greek means *to deliver over to someone* or *to entrust to someone for their safekeeping*. It means to hand something down from one generation to the next, similar to traditions that are passed from one generation to the next in a family.

Traditions are easily lost. And if they're not lost altogether, long-held traditions can be altered and changed from one generation to the next over a period of time — *unless* someone cares enough to preserve them. Those who don't care too much about family traditions often view people who work hard at keeping family traditions the same year after year as being *picky*. But these meaningful traditions would be altogether forgotten if it weren't for those "picky" people who fight year after year to preserve them.

Jude uses the word "delivered" in this verse to set this very illustration before us. He confronted his readers — and he speaks to *us* — about our God-given responsibility to handle the Word carefully. God calls upon us to guard and defend it, doing all in our ability to present it in the purest form and as close as possible to the original message He intended to convey.

This is why we must read and study the Bible with a serious mind and with the commitment of a steadfast heart. To unlock the power that resides in the words it contains, we must delve deeply. It must be our lifetime aim to understand the Word

Speaking as God's spokesmen is one of the greatest responsibilities ever given to us as believers.

more comprehensively and to perceive ever more clearly what God is saying to us in it.

Speaking as God's spokesmen is one of the greatest responsibilities ever given to us as believers. We must handle His Word carefully and do our best to impart its powerful truth in its purest form to others.

The Highest Form of Revelation Available

When you truly come to an understanding of what the Bible is and the power it contains, you'll want to commit your life to sharing it in its fullest and purest form — nothing added, nothing modified. You see, besides the divine revelation that the Bible contains, *the power and presence of God Himself* is locked inside the Bible.

When a Christian drills deep and by faith taps into the divine power and presence contained in those Holy Spirit-inspired words, that power is released to change any situation in life. This is why Peter wrote that God's Word is filled with precious promises that pertain to every part of life.

> **According as his divine power hath given unto us all things that pertain unto life and godliness, through the knowledge of him that hath called us to glory and virtue: Whereby are given unto us exceeding great and precious promises: that by these ye might be partakers of the divine nature, having escaped the corruption that is in the world through lust.**
>
> **2 Peter 1:3,4**

Then in Second Timothy 3:16, Paul wrote these amazing words about the Bible: "All scripture is given by inspiration of God, and is profitable for doctrine, for reproof, for correction, for instruction in righteousness; that the man of God may be perfect, thoroughly furnished unto all good works."

The word "inspiration" in this verse is a translation of the Greek word *theopneustos*, which is a compound of the Greek words *theos* and *pneuma*. The word *theos* is the word for *God*, and the word *pneuma* is derived from the root *pneu*, which depicts *the dynamic movement of air*. But when the root *pneu* becomes *pneuma*, as in this verse, it also carries the meanings *life*, *force*, *energy*, *dynamism*, and *power*.

When *theos* and *pneuma* are compounded, the new word is *theopneustos*, which literally means *God-breathed*, and it is where we get the word "inspiration." Paul's use of this compound word tells us emphatically that the Bible contains the *life*, *essence*, *energy*, and *dynamic force* of God Himself and has the power to accomplish *whatever* needs to be done. As Ecclesiastes 8:4 so accurately states, "Where the word of a king is, there is *power*."

The Bible contains the *life, essence, energy,* and *dynamic force* of God Himself and has the power to accomplish *whatever* needs to be done.

Jude said this powerful Word was "delivered" to us for *safekeeping*. As stated earlier, it is our God-given responsibility to understand God's Word, fine-tune ourselves to what He has to say in His Word, and pass along His Word to others in the purest form possible. That emphatically means we are *not* to water it down to appease an ever-fluctuating end-times crowd.

At the time Jude wrote his epistle, the enemy was trying to insert error into the doctrine of the Early Church in an effort to defuse God's truth and divest it of its power. In the place of truth would be newly styled teachings that some were claiming to be "more fitting" for the society of their day. This was the serious challenge that those in leadership during the first centuries of the Church were up against. *Does this sound familiar to you today?*

Speaking Up in Delusionary Times

In early New Testament times and in the centuries following, apostles and early leaders spent a lot of time correcting false doctrines that were spreading like wildfire in the emerging Church. They didn't apologize for addressing doctrinal problems; in fact, at times, they even found it necessary to call out the names of those responsible for spreading false teachings in the Church.

Speaking up today has been made more difficult in modern society because, as mentioned earlier, the big issue is not truth, but *respect*. Truth has taken a back seat to the concept of honoring other people's beliefs — *even if those beliefs are diametrically opposed to the doctrines of the Bible.*

As a result, the Word of God has been "demoted" and relegated to a diminished position in the modern mindset as just one option among many. According to this inclusive mindset, everyone is right and no one is wrong. Unfortunately, in the Western world, this is not just the mindset of those outside the Church. This is the way many Christians are leaning as well.

Without a doubt, there is a culture of authentic, biblical honor that has been nearly lost in this last-days society. It has been redirected and redefined under the guise of inclusivism that "respects" everyone as being right — everyone *except* those who hold fast to and carefully guard biblical and moral absolutes. In fact, the new culture is a collective *refusal* to come under submission to God's absolutes as stated in His Word. This new "culture of honor" often excludes Bible-believing Christians and is, in fact, *dis*honoring of God and His holy, eternal, immutable, incontrovertible Word.

Without a doubt, there is a culture of authentic, biblical honor that has been nearly lost in this last-days society. It has been redirected and redefined under the guise of inclusivism that "respects" everyone as being right — everyone *except* those who hold fast to and carefully guard biblical and moral absolutes.

In this environment, much of God's Word is dismissed as being too restrictive or exclusive of other people's beliefs. Instead of being recognized as absolute truth, the Bible becomes used primarily for illustrations, motivational sermons, inspirational ideas and suggestions, principles to build a marriage or business, and so on. Meanwhile, it is generally suggested that no one has the right to imply that someone else is wrong in the way he or she applies Bible principles.

Even in the Church, the most basic tenets of faith are now largely not known by many churchgoers. Basic Bible doctrines such as the virgin birth, the sinlessness of Christ, man's sin, salvation, holiness, and eternal judgment are either unknown, seldom taught, or considered optional. In some churches, sound doctrine is replaced with social-justice messages in an attempt to appeal to mass audiences by making people feel better about themselves. True doctrinal teaching of the Bible is often diminished or replaced by variations of watered-down, "politically correct" instruction.

We are living in a time when people exalt their personal beliefs — founded on compromise, family of origin, environment, emotions, and so forth — over the truth of the Bible.

This "open-minded" approach to the Bible maintains that it is unfair to assert that Scriptures alone are the absolute foundation for truth. Even when it comes to the most basic beliefs, this mindset promotes the possibility that what we believe *could* be wrong or that others may be equally right but with a different approach. As a result, we are living in a time when people exalt their personal beliefs — founded on compromise, family of origin, environment, emotions, and so forth — over the truth of the Bible.

The Infection Has Already Begun To Spread

To what extent has this mindset already permeated the Church? Consider this statistic: It is a fact that approximately 40 percent of practicing Christians in America do not believe in absolute moral truth.[14] The trajectory of that statistic is changing at such an alarming rate that it will be out of date by the time this book reaches your hands.

To understand where this restyling of culture is headed, simply have an honest conversation with some young adults. You will learn firsthand that even many young Christian men and women hold a very negative view of people who adhere to absolute truth or absolute morality. "Narrow-minded" and "judgmental" are terms often used to describe such Christians who remain steadfast in their stance that God's truth doesn't change with the times.

[14]"The End of Absolutes: America's New Moral Code," Barna Research Group, 2016. https://www.barna.com/research/the-end-of-absolutes-americas-new-moral-code/.

When this is the prevailing mindset in a society — when the majority generally believes that everyone is right and no one is wrong — the act of correcting wrong beliefs becomes very difficult to do. In fact, in our day when many are moving away from the standard of absolute truth, large numbers of people — even in the Church — would consider it inappropriate to correct someone for what he or she believes, especially if that person *really believes it.*

The authority of the Bible has been greatly diminished, and it is now regularly viewed by many as one holy book among *many* holy books. Those who adhere to the Bible and believe in its absolute authority are widely deemed to be old-fashioned. More and more, societal opinion mocks those who claim that God's truth is the eternal standard. These defenders of the faith are viewed as being intolerant holdovers from a former age who are out of sync with present-day reality.

Modern society has become drunk on the self-gratifying "freedom" afforded those who accept this mad premise that everyone is right and no one is wrong in matters of faith, truth, and belief. The insanity of a world with no absolutes is quickly spreading its toxic poisons so far and wide into every sphere of society that, as we've seen, a growing number are not even sure of what gender they are!

Given this cataclysmic shift over the past few decades in the moral framework of modern society, we shouldn't be surprised that society at large is also confused about faith, truth, and belief. And as more and more people decide they don't believe in an absolute, fixed truth, we will continue to see fewer and fewer hearts open to be corrected in what they believe.

Once a person has concluded that there is no absolute truth, that person has also reached another conclusion by default: that no one has the moral authority to bring correction to someone else regarding faith, truth, and belief. This is just a refashioned camouflage for an ancient sin issue called *rebellion to authority* — one that enables people to escape correction, at least temporarily, in the name of open-mindedness.

But in the early centuries of the Church, the apostles and Church leaders spoke up when they sensed error was attempting to penetrate the ranks. These leaders loved the Church too much and believed the Gospel too fully to stay silent when someone twisted God's eternal message of truth. On the contrary — they stepped forward to boldly address it!

In the early centuries of the Church, the apostles and Church leaders spoke up when they sensed error was attempting to penetrate the ranks. These leaders loved the Church too much and believed the Gospel too fully to stay silent when someone twisted God's eternal message of truth.

These early Christian leaders firmly believed it was God's charge to them to guard the Church and to contend for the faith. For this reason, they could not sit idly by and do nothing when error tried to creep into the ranks of the Church. They were compelled to speak up and guard the flock over which the Holy Spirit had made them overseers (*see* Acts 20:28).

Love Says, 'Be Careful of Danger!'

If you witnessed a child running into a busy street with a steady stream of cars driving past at great speeds, would it be loving to allow that child to run out in the middle of that street and to do nothing to stop him, even though you knew his presence in heavy traffic could be fatal? Of course not. You'd scream as loudly as possible to get the attention of that child and keep him from harm. And in that act, you would be demonstrating love.

Bystanders who weren't standing in a position to see the dangerous situation as clearly as you saw it might accuse you of being harsh for screaming so loudly. But the gravity of the situation required your urgent action; otherwise, that child would have found himself in danger, in the middle of oncoming traffic.

Like most people, you probably wish to be known as gracious and polite. But in that kind of real-life situation, politeness could have resulted in a tragic outcome — a life that could have been saved if you had acted more urgently.

This is exactly why Jude decided to speak up about error. If he only penned a faint whisper about the problem, it is likely that his voice wouldn't have been heard and those in danger wouldn't have realized the critical nature of the situation. Therefore, Jude acted as any responsible Christian leader should. He lifted his voice and urgently pleaded with his readers to stand against the error that was trying to gain access to the Church in the early years of its existence.

PAUL'S WARNING TO LEADERS: DANGER AHEAD!

When Paul addressed this issue, he revealed how disturbed he was by what truth-modifiers were attempting to do. In fact, he went so far as to write, "Beware of *dogs*..." (Philippians 3:2)! The word "dogs" is from the Greek word *kuon*, which describes *dangerous dogs that roamed the countryside*. Such dogs were known as a wild, uncontrollable, wandering, nomadic collection of diseased dogs that tried to get into people's houses and gardens in search for food.

Paul realized the very real danger these errant leaders posed if nothing was done to stop them. Like the wandering and diseased dogs Paul alluded to, these leaders would rip the Word of God to pieces — alter it, tear it, dismember it, and then refashion it according to their own design.

This explains why apostles and Early Church leaders raised their voices to alert the Church of the danger in their midst. They were actively protecting God's people from the error that was beginning to gain a foothold among them.

When giving his farewell address to the Ephesian elders in Acts 20:29-31, Paul spoke these words: "For I know this, that after my departing shall grievous wolves enter in among you, not sparing the flock. Also of your own selves shall men arise, speaking perverse things, to draw away disciples from them. Watch and remember, that by the space of three years I have not ceased to warn every one of you night and day with tears."

Paul had warned the Ephesian elders about the impending danger for three full years, but he knew in his spirit that grievous wolves would still find an opening to speak "perverse" things inside the Ephesian church after he left, just as he had warned.

The word "perverse" is translated from a form of the Greek word *diastrepho*, which means *to twist*, *to distort*, or *to bend*. This word clarifies a significant characteristic of error — that it is usually *a new version* of *an established, older message* that has been insidiously *twisted*, *distorted*, or *bent* to correspond with current, deceitful objectives.

Deception's Destructive Aftermath

When Paul wrote to the Galatians, his epistle revealed that errant leaders were advancing into the region of Galatia. In Galatians 1:6, Paul referred to this dangerous situation when he said,

"I marvel that ye are so soon removed from him that called you into the grace of Christ unto another gospel."

Paul said that they had been "removed" unto "another" gospel. The word "removed" is from a form of the Greek word *metatithimi,* a compound of the words *meta* and *tithimi.* The word *meta* denotes a *change*, and the word *tithimi* describes *a position.* But when compounded, the new word denotes some kind of *positional change.* This word was often used in Greek literature to depict *defection.*

From the widespread use of this word, we know that Paul was aware that error was being introduced into the churches of Galatia, resulting in the defection of some from the faith that he had preached to the Galatians. Sweeping doctrinal changes were trying to blow through the Church — and like strong winds often do, these destructive winds of doctrine were creating confusion, disorder, and mayhem among God's precious people.

Sweeping doctrinal changes were trying to blow through the Church — and like strong winds often do, these destructive winds of doctrine were creating confusion, disorder, and mayhem among God's precious people.

AN ESSENTIAL WEAPON AGAINST DECEPTION — YOUR SOUND MIND

From Paul's words in Galatians 3:1, it is clear that seducing spirits were infiltrating the churches in Galatia as well. This is why Paul wrote, "O, foolish Galatians, who hath bewitched you...."

The word "foolish" is the Greek word *anoetos,* which depicts *a person who isn't using his mind.* The problem isn't that the person doesn't *have* a mind; that person just isn't *using* his or her mind.

These individuals were feasting on the spiritual error that was being put on their plates without even thinking about the quality of the spiritual fare they were consuming. And people who don't use their minds to assess and think things through are the easiest to lead astray.

Here again, we find the need to use our minds *in order to keep our heads on straight*.

This is a timely warning for those who live at the end of the age when digital devices provide information so quickly that *thinking* is no longer needed. People's minds are inundated with stimulating visual images and constantly updated information. A great deal of that information is unverified but largely believed, because easy access to information has resulted in *mental laziness.* After all, why should a person *think* when the device he is using can do the thinking and analyzing for him?

In every generation, there is always a category of ardent students who read, study, and write. However, in this day of continual bombardment with fast-paced moving images, a growing majority no longer analyzes information the way previous generations did. We are told by experts that a large percentage of the present generation has difficulty comprehending linear texts that require analytical thinking. For some in that number, they have difficulty reading anything of greater complexity than the text messages that provide their main means of communication.

The most recent statistics reveal that the average young person spends eight minutes a day reading. However, a large part of those eight minutes involve reading text messages on their devices, *not* reading real text, such as in a book or article. The present generation's ability *to think* and *to analyze* is becoming progressively diminished and dulled as we approach the end of this age. There is no doubt that this trend will exacerbate the proliferating mass deception in the days to come.

Although digital advancements have brought positive changes to our modern society, these advancements have also been gradually crippling people's ability to think beyond a surface level. The situation is becoming very serious. In fact, many experts assert that this may be the most gullible and easy-to-deceive generation that has ever lived. How ironic that the most brilliant, innovative engineers in history have created a digital world that is now producing what may be the most non-thinking generation in recent times — or perhaps ever!

Although the brain remains a magnificently complex creation, the continual blitz of easily accessed images and information has had a profound impact. People's desire and ability *to think* — to process, gather, and study information to ensure they arrive at an accurate conclusion — has been greatly diminished. This nonstop bombardment of visual messages on social media has had the net effect of causing people's attention span to be radically decreased.

It is our responsibility as Christians to avoid this modern pitfall by keeping our minds renewed by the Word of God and our spirits well-tuned to the Spirit of God. We are *not* to fall into this "thinking" decline with the rest of society and become gullible with the rest of the crowd. Every moment of every day, we're called to keep our hearts sensitive and our sound minds engaged so we can keep our heads on straight!

There has never been a more important time in history for Christian believers to read, study, and meditate on the *Bible*. The way to circumvent spiritual seduction and deception is by knowing, understanding, and being rooted in the truth of God's Word. He is looking for hearts that yearn to continually know *His* higher thoughts and ways and who therefore embrace and submit to His Word as absolute truth.

If the Christians whom Paul was addressing had been *using their brains* and *thinking* about what was being put on their spiritual plates before consuming it, they probably wouldn't have been bewitched. Instead, Paul had to ask them, "Who hath bewitched you...?" The word "bewitched" is the Greek word *baskaino,* which means *to cast a spell on someone.* Paul's language tells us that their thinking was *clouded*, as if they were under a spell. They were mesmerized by a new proposal — a new way of thinking that was leading them off the path of sound doctrine.

The way to circumvent spiritual seduction and deception is by knowing, understanding, and being rooted in the truth of God's Word. He is looking for hearts that yearn to continually know *His* higher thoughts and ways and who therefore embrace and submit to His Word as absolute truth.

This foolishness had grown so fast that in Galatians 1:6, Paul told them, "I *marvel* that ye are so soon removed...." The word "marvel" means *to be at a loss of words*, *to be shocked*, *to be amazed*, or *to be completely bewildered.* Paul was simply flabbergasted that such preposterous error could find its way into the Galatian church. He was likewise astonished that this seduction could happen so quickly, which is why he wrote, "I marvel that ye are *so soon* removed...unto *another* gospel."

Paul identified the type of teaching that was penetrating the Galatian church when he called it "another" gospel. The word "another" is a translation of the Greek word *heteros,* which means *of a different kind.* The usage of this word means false teachers had invaded Galatia with a gospel of *a different kind.* The word "another" tells us that these error-promoting leaders were presenting some elements of the truth to make it sound recognizable and similar to the message Paul had preached, but they were little by little refashioning and repackaging the message, adapting it to meet the objectives of their personal agenda.

In reality, what these leaders were promoting was a twisted version of truth. It was error packaged with elements of truth and then stealthily posed to believers in the guise of authenticity to make it more appetizing.

What these leaders were promoting was a twisted version of truth. It was error packaged with elements of truth and then stealthily posed to believers in the guise of authenticity to make it more appetizing.

In Galatians 1:7, Paul said, "Which is not another; but there be some that trouble you, and would pervert the gospel of Christ." The word "another" in this verse is very different from the word "another" used in the previous verse. This time it is the word *allos*, which means *of the same kind*.

The various uses of *heteros* and *allos* in these two connecting verses present a strong message: that what these false teachers were preaching was *completely different* from the original Gospel that Paul presented to the Galatians. Although it might have contained some elements of the original message, it had become so twisted that it ultimately was nothing at all like the original Gospel the Galatians had heard and embraced when they came to Christ.

Paul's words in this verse may sound rough to a modern society in which people generally are encouraged to believe whatever they wish. Of course, it's true that people have a right to believe whatever they want. But Paul knew the Gospel was under attack in his own generation and would indeed always face the possibilities of subversion. He therefore lifted up his voice and declared that those leaders were perverting the gospel of Christ (*see* Galatians 1:7).

The word "pervert" is a translation of the Greek word *metastrepho*, which means *to bend*, *to change*, *to corrupt*, or *to turn one thing into another.* This word "pervert" depicts the *modification* of something that already exists — to *bend* it, *change* it, and *remold* it — until the original item is *corrupted.* Then that corrupted version is presented as something improved or enhanced — when, in fact, it is a "perverted" adaptation of what was originally intended.

Of course, it's possible that an errant leader had been genuinely deceived himself along the way and was unaware of the dangerous path he was leading others to embark on. But in those early days of the Church, many false leaders came with the full awareness of their self-serving agenda.

False leaders who fit the latter category knew their listeners would reject them if they blatantly and obviously presented a different Gospel. Therefore, over a period of time, they gradually began to bend it, little by little changing it until it had metamorphosed into a message *they* wanted it to be.

This transformation initially began to occur at a snail's pace. Then over a period of time, these errant teachers began to quicken their pace in seducing God's people away from the pure message of the Gospel and into a modified version of the truth — as seducing spirits with doctrines of demons always do. Some of this we will cover in following chapters.

'Teaching of a Different Kind'

This assault against the Gospel was occurring all over the Church in the First Century. For example, when Paul installed Timothy as pastor of the church in Ephesus, Timothy had to immediately deal with spiritual leaders, well-known and beloved in the church, who were beginning to add their own twist to the Gospel. This is why Paul wrote Timothy, "As I besought thee to abide still at

Ephesus that thou mightest charge some that they teach no other doctrine" (1 Timothy 1:3).

Paul did *not* suggest that *every* leader in Ephesus had fallen prey to this attack of seducing spirits and doctrines of demons; he simply stated that *some* had succumbed to it. However, those counted in that number were visible leaders in the church, which is why Paul insisted that Timothy urgently deal with it.

The same is true regarding these end times. Not everyone will be led astray in these last days. Many leaders will stick with the truth and refuse to budge from it. But it's crucial to understand the devil's tactics in this regard. He aims for vulnerable leaders with influence, because when a notable leader presents a corrupted and modified version of the truth, it has greater impact upon larger numbers of people as the ripple effect of spiritual infection begins to spread through the Church.

It's crucial to understand the devil's tactics. He aims for vulnerable leaders with influence, because when a notable leader presents a corrupted and modified version of the truth, it has greater impact upon larger numbers of people as the ripple effect of spiritual infection begins to spread through the Church.

Paul used the words "other doctrine" in First Timothy 1:3 to let us know what kind of teaching the corrupted spiritual leaders in Ephesus were attempting to bring into that church. The words "other doctrine" are a translation of the Greek word *heterodidaskaleo*, which is a compound of the words *heteros* and *didaskalos*. The word *heteros* points to something *of a different kind*, and the Greek word *didaskalos* means *doctrine* or *teaching*. However, when these words are compounded into one, the new word means *a doctrine of a different kind* or *a teaching of a different kind.*

Paul used this word to tell us unquestionably that notable individuals were disseminating *doctrines* and *teaching of a different kind.* As false teachers always do, they mingled basic truth into the mix. But the original message had become corrupted, and a new version had taken its place.

At the time Timothy assumed his Ephesian leadership role, there was a group of leaders infected with spiritual error who later came to be known as *Gnostics.* Gnosticism was a belief system that encompassed a preoccupation with diverse and strange doctrines that led believers from the solid path of the Word of God into bizarre and weird revelations uncorroborated by Scripture. It was an early attempt of seducing spirits to lead the Early Church into error. Although this was a different type of attack from the one presently occurring in this prophetic end-time season in which we live, there are key aspects from that early attempt to infect the Church that we can learn from.

So what kind of attack was this Gnostic error, and what can we learn from it for this present hour we live in near the end of the age? That will be the discussion of the next chapter.

Think About It

1. Jude was preparing to write a letter to a group of believers on a specific subject when the Holy Spirit redirected his focus to a more urgent assignment. The message of the Gospel and the welfare of God's people were in jeopardy of being infected.

   It was time for a mature Christian leader to stand up for truth and defuse the threat, and God enlisted Jude for the task of articulating His heart in a letter. At stake were the destinies of untold numbers of believers that the enemy wanted to neutralize with that particular brand of demonic lie.

   Did the Holy Spirit ever interrupt your normal routine to give you an assignment with eternal ramifications that didn't come neatly packaged or predictable? When that unexpected divine call to action came, were you ready to obey, or did you flounder to know how to do what He asked for? What can you do in this season to ensure that you are fully equipped and prepared to run with Heaven's next unexpected request all the way to its accomplishment?

2. The corrosive spiritual doctrine that some leaders inside the Church were advocating was *accommodation with the world around them in order to provide relief from persecution and from perpetual pressure to conform.*

   Which relationships in your life are your greatest challenges when it's time to boldly stand for God's absolute truth, even on touchy subjects? Can you think of a specific instance in your life when you compromised with truth to avoid confrontation or rejection, but it proved destructive to the relationship in the long run?

3. Compromise and accommodation with the world produces a weak, contaminated Church possessing very little power. From what you know about the direction the Church has gone over the past few decades, try to pinpoint specific examples and patterns within different denominations and "camps" that prove this premise is true.

Chapter Five

EARLY AND END-TIME ERROR — AND THE CHURCH'S EVER-PRESENT ROLE

We've seen that we are dealing with an onslaught of seducing spirits that are trying to lure society into nonsensical thinking and modifications of truth to match a confused culture. These ludicrous doctrines of demons are being packaged as "progressive thinking" to a world gone mad.

As stated in Chapter One, today we are witnessing a society that has gone morally adrift at the end of the age and is being lured into depths of degeneracy and depravity that have not been seen since the days when paganism ruled the earth. The error being disseminated throughout society is being seductively tailored to a modern generation and its wayward trends. This end-time error has been compared by many to times in ancient history when paganism ruled the land. But in the First Century when seducing spirits were trying to find a way to actually get inside the infant Church, those spirits used a very different approach to cater to the culture and the world of that time.

A spiritual battle between truth and error was already fully engaged against the Early Church when the apostle Paul wrote, "Now the Spirit speaketh expressly, that in the latter times some shall depart from the faith, giving heed to seducing spirits, and doctrines of devils" (1 Timothy 4:1). In the midst of the battle that was raging in Paul's day, the Holy Spirit prophesied that an even more shocking invasion of seducing spirits and proliferating doctrines of demons would emerge on the scene in the last of the last days.

The Greek words used in this verse mean that the Holy Spirit was telling them, *"Let Me tell you unequivocally what is going to happen at the end of the age: There will be an invasion of seducing spirits with doctrines of demons that will attempt to lead the world into widespread, wide-scale deception and delusion. I am telling you up front and in language so clear that you cannot misunderstand — unprecedented delusion will enter the world in that hour."*

As we've already seen, it is just as the Holy Spirit forewarned. A great barrage of various assaults is being waged against the Church today from every direction. Seducing spirits are trying to lead society into depravity, produce modifications of God's truth, water down the Gospel, and bring about a convergence of old pagan ideas and restyled forms of mysticism to present to an ignorant generation as new religious concepts.

The Holy Spirit explicitly said this phenomenon would occur at the very last of the last days — and that it would take place inside the Church as some "depart from the faith." Herein, the Spirit sounded a clear warning: We must be aware that in the very last days, some inside the Church will gradually *depart* from the sound teaching of Scripture.

Since we are living in the age when this departing from the faith is prophesied to occur, you and I must predetermine our immovable stance even if times drastically change and all of society turns in the wrong direction. We must settle within ourselves that the absolute, timeless, and unchanging veracity of Scripture will always remain our standard and our guide. We will plant our feet firmly on the solid rock of God's Word and *refuse* to be moved by spirits of seduction that are luring the rest of the world into deception offered in a myriad of forms.

We've seen that the Early Church was itself under assault by various forms of false doctrines as demon spirits attempted to bend, change, corrupt, and modify the Gospel to become something entirely different than what God intended. First, this assault was being waged by *Jewish legalizers* who wanted to alter the message of grace by attaching Old Testament rules and regulations to it. Paul fought these legalistic Judaizers throughout his entire ministry.

You and I must predetermine our immovable stance even if times drastically change and all of society turns in the wrong direction. We must settle within ourselves that the absolute, timeless, and unchanging veracity of Scripture will always remain our standard and our guide.

This error-ridden group fiercely believed that all converts to Christ had to become "Jewish" in their lifestyles and religious practices. It was a doctrinal error so dangerous and one that carried such spiritually deadly consequences that Paul allocated substantial space in his epistles to refute it.

But in addition to these legalistic Judaizers who tried to corrupt the message of Christ, seducing spirits were also working through other errant leaders. The devil was using this other group to mesmerize newly converted believers with far-fetched revelations and teaching that seem bizarre to us today. However, it was a strategy that would have been especially successful to wage against believers in the First Century who had come out of paganism, where strange ideas and beliefs *abounded*.

How Culture Influences Deception

Let me explain further what I mean regarding the enemy's strategic targeting of doctrinal error during New Testament times. A glimpse into the Greek and Roman world of pagan religion will help you understand my point.

Although it is far from our modern way of thinking today, the Greeks and Romans were deeply devoted to venerating a wide assortment of pagan gods, demigods, and other spirit beings. In our humanistic culture today, we classify the ancient stories about these spirit beings as mythology. However, to the early Greeks and Romans, the stories of their gods were not myths or the byproducts of fantasy or imagination. They indisputably believed that gods, demigods, and the other inhabitants of the spirit world ruled the universe, controlled human fate, and directed the natural world around them. The massive fortunes that the Greeks and Romans spent to build and embellish an incalculable number of temples dedicated to their gods is in itself unquestionable proof of how serious they were in the practice of their pagan religions.

As the Roman Empire expanded and its troops were dispatched to conquer new regions, the Roman soldiers often embraced the worship of new exotic, foreign gods. Upon the troops' return to their homelands, they frequently carried these foreign religions back with them. These new deities were then incorporated in the ever-growing list of gods, demigods, and spirit beings that were worshiped in Rome and throughout the empire. By the time the Early Church began to emerge, that list was enormous. In fact, it had grown so long that today it is simply impossible to compile a certifiably complete list of all the spirit beings worshiped or venerated by First Century Greeks and Romans.

The following list provides a small sample of the spirit entities that pagans believed influenced the world around them. (For more on this, *see* Chapter One in my book *No Room for Compromise.*)

If this list were expanded many times over, it would still fall short of enumerating all the gods and goddesses that were revered and worshiped in ancient Greek and Roman societies. Today society is more humanistic in its approach, and its new "religion" attempts to celebrate man as the center. But in the Greek and Roman world, this endless litany of spirit beings to worship and to appease was the pagan population's daily reality.

Greek and Roman pagans believed that the huge array of gods, goddesses, demigods, and spirit beings to whom they prayed and offered sacrifices controlled every aspect of the natural world. Just to give you a taste of how this list included both the mighty and the minutia of life, the following short list is offered of what the people of these ancient cultures worshiped: the gods and spirit beings of *the sky, earth, underworld, dawn, dark, moon, lightning, night, thunder, storms, honor, reverence, hope, truth, security, baking and ovens, thresholds, hinges, door handles, children's beverages, bees* — and the list went on and on.

As a result of this obsession to venerate spirit beings of every type, idols were erected on every street, at every street crossing, and at every prominent location in the city. In the excavations of ancient ruins, in-home shrines and altars have been a common discovery. These objects of worship were dedicated to a wide variety of gods or ancestral deities, which in many cases had been honored by that family for generations.

Such shrines and altars were usually positioned near the central entrance of a home, in a hallway, or in a central courtyard where residents or visitors could make daily sacrifices. This was common in pagan homes, making it clear that the worship of gods, goddesses, demigods, and a wide array of spirit beings was a customary, integral part of daily life for the great majority of people living in the world of that time.

So at the time the Church was birthed, paganism impacted nearly every facet of life and could be found in every corner of Rome's far-flung territories — including every city and region where the Church was being established outside of Israel. Wherever the flag of the Roman Empire was raised, you could be sure that paganism was widely practiced. Except for the Jewish faith and newly emerging Christianity, there was nothing else in the world at that time but ever-widening variations of paganism.

It was an environment where exotic, mysterious, out-of-the-ordinary, and often very bizarre forms of spirituality and outlandish mysticism dominated society. Thus, it was relatively easy to lure Christians who had come out of that pagan culture back into a fascination with mysticism. These new believers had only recently been saved and delivered from these things. So if the bait set before them was enticing enough, they at times could be seduced to revert to some of the fallacies that had been so ingrained in their pre-Christ consciousness. In this type of spiritually diverse environment, people (including Christians) naturally gravitated to manifestations and tales that today would seem bizarre and outlandish.

In the midst of the complex mix of pagan beliefs that permeated Roman society, a new form of error emerged. False teachers who later came to be known as *Gnostics* began to appear on the scene to appeal to the pagan instincts of people in the Church who had been raised as pagans but had converted to Christ. The term *Gnostics* is derived from the Greek word *gnosis*, which means *knowledge.*

In short, Gnosticism was a mix of Christian belief with pagan philosophies, religions, theosophies, and mysteries — mingling it all together to create a "gospel" considered more compatible with the pagan world at that time. Most new Gentile Christians at that time were of Greek heritage and were therefore more easily influenced by philosophical ideas and concepts of paganism. Consequently, Gnosticism tended to appeal to this category of early Christians on a relatively wide scale.

Gnostics claimed to possess *superior knowledge* and *special insight*. They even asserted that their purported insights and revelations didn't need to be proven by doctrine or examination because it was wisdom derived from an unprovable, mysterious realm. Gnostics even boasted to possess knowledge that surpassed Scripture.

These self-styled prophets and teachers claimed that they had supernaturally perceived and seen into other realms that no other human mind had ever perceived and no other eyes had ever beheld. They boasted that they had explored spiritual dimensions no other man had ever explored.

Certainly we who hold fast to the Word of God believe in having supernatural experiences — including dreams, visions, and revelations that are in agreement with Scripture. To throw out all supernatural activity is a wrong response that would hurl the Church into a ditch on the other side of this problem.

But the Gnostics' revelations in the early years of the Church were outlandish and unsupported by the teachings of Scripture, and many First Century Christians were inclined to be attracted to their diverse and strange doctrines because of their own pagan upbringings.

So with fantastical tales, fabricated doctrines, and teaching of a different kind, Gnostics packaged wild, spectacular revelations to draw enthralled listeners into error and excess. And as we consider the context of this phenomenon — that the majority of First Century believers had only recently been delivered from the exotic and mystical world of paganism — it helps us fathom why Gnosticism was able to flourish inside the Early Church.

Sophists vs. Gnostics

But let's go even a step further into the First Century to see how Gnostic revelators, prophets, and teachers were able to maneuver themselves so dangerously into places of prominence in the Early Church.

In the non-Christian world of that time, there was a notable group of wandering lecturers called *Sophists* who were extremely popular in the pagan world. The word "Sophist" is a derivative of the Greek word *sophos,* which is the Greek word for *wisdom.* The Sophists boasted to possess *special wisdom* and were actually the pagan counterpart to the Gnostics who eventually emerged inside the Church.

Sophists were renowned for their skills at rhetoric, and they were paid exorbitant fees for disclosing their insights on a wide range of subjects. Some Sophists were legitimate educators who educated members of the highest levels of society. Others were more flamboyant and less sincere in their claims of intellectual legitimacy. But the Sophists' style and methods arguably influenced the style and methods of the Gnostics, whose influence lamentably became rife in the Early Church.

Sophists traveled from city to city to give lectures to crowds of all sizes, and people often came from great distances to hear them speak. Some worked the circuit so long that they became celebrities of their time — even household names — using sensationalism and controversy to attract listeners.

The Original 'Ear Ticklers'

Although some Sophists were respectably employed to educate the rich and upper class, there was an opportunistic group who tailored their lectures to the whims of each crowd and who would say nearly anything to please an audience. They were the original "ear ticklers" of the ancient world. The aim of this particular class of Sophists was to provide a sensational message that would ensnare listeners to purchase a ticket to their next lecture. They were known to speak for hours on subjects they knew little about and to style themselves as specialists on a wide array of subjects of which they had little knowledge.

These unprincipled and unscrupulous performers simply wanted to provide spellbinding entertainment and sell tickets for seats at their lectures. An early historian named Dio Chrysostom wrote, "They were like men walking in darkness, led only by the shouts of the crowd and the clapping and applause of the masses."[15]

When Gnostics appeared later in the Church, they seemed to have patterned themselves after the Sophists — for they also were sensationalists who told fantastic tales, only with a spiritual twist. They would regale their listeners with vivid recountings of supernatural experiences and deep, mysterious revelations that had no basis in Scripture or apostolic preaching. These so-called revelators posed a serious threat to the Church as it was being established because they were able to appeal to new believers who were former pagans — those who might be more inclined to be drawn to the bizarre and outlandish.

To simply teach scriptural truths was out of the question for these so-called revelators. In their view, the Scriptures were just a starting point. That is why they delighted to tell tales about

[15]Dio Chrysostom, *Discourse 34*.

conversations with angels, visits with never-before-known celestial beings, and unusual mystical happenings. Although uncorroborated with Scripture, the Gnostics' revelations were mesmerizing to their spellbound audiences.

Again, I want to clearly state that the Church must have divine visitations that are Heaven-sent. However, we cannot — and *must* not — promote experiences or doctrines that are not confirmed or supported by Scripture.

Gnostic Errors (A Short List)

The following is a short list of some Gnostic errors that were prevalent during the time the New Testament was being written. Each of these is refuted in the New Testament epistles. As you will see, each of these is also attempting to reemerge at the end of these last days. We are not called to be Gnostic detectives, but it is healthy to know past error in order to recognize it in the present.

Some primary Gnostic errors included the following:

- **The Gnostics claimed that Old Testament Scriptures were inferior and based on old, outdated, and antiquated ideas; therefore, Christians needed to disconnect themselves from the teachings of the Old Testament.**

  It is hard to fathom, but some Church leaders today are also claiming that the Old Testament has no relevance for New Testament believers. Some leaders state that Christians must "unhitch" from the writings of the Old Testament. But anyone educated in Church history or theology understands this was an early premise of Gnosticism in the Early Church that is trying to reassert itself at the end of the age.

- **According to Gnostics, the God of the New Testament was actually a completely different entity from the God of the Old Testament — and the New Testament God was superior. How God worked and judged, how He acted and what He said under the Old Covenant — all of this was to be viewed as archaic, defective, and inferior to the newly styled messages the Gnostics were presenting.**

  This notion was an expedient way to do away with concepts and texts from the Old Testament that made it difficult for Gnostics to concoct a gospel more accommodating to a pagan world. By removing the authority of the Old Testament (which Christ and all New Testament writers referred to continually), they purposed a new type of gospel that they found more convenient. This premise of Gnosticism that existed in the Early Church is trying to reemerge in the end of these last days.

- **Gnostics furthermore proposed the idea that the wrath of the Old Testament God wasn't to be taken seriously by New Testament believers. They said all forms of present or future judgment were dismissed. The Gnostics claimed that the concept of God's wrath was an imaginary doctrine based on religious thinking that should be discounted as unfitting for a loving God.**

  Even today some skillfully allege that the concept of God's wrath is antiquated and outdated. They declare that God's wrath was poured out on Christ; consequently, they conclude, there is no more divine wrath to release in a future judgment. However, anyone educated in theology understands the outright fallacy of this teaching. It is one of the original premises of Gnosticism raising its head again in these last days.

- **Gnostics also held to a doctrine that flesh — indeed, all physical matter — was evil and fading. Only the spirit held significance; hence, it really didn't matter whether one sinned with the flesh.**

  Ultimately, this Gnostic doctrine led people to believe sin was inconsequential and had no effect on anyone who had already come to faith in Christ. It gave the impression that there was no need for continued repentance for any wrong act conducted in the flesh, because the flesh was inconsequential in the vast scheme of eternity. This was one of the premises of Gnosticism that is once again attempting to establish a foothold in the Church in these last days.

- **The doctrine just described above was held by Antinomian Gnostics. The word "antinomian" means *against law* and depicts these Gnostics' aversion to the moral law of God, which they alleged to be an inferior Old Testament concept that had no relevance for Christians.**

  It is difficult to comprehend how this Gnostic premise could find life again, but this is precisely what some are teaching today when they dismiss the textual authority of the Old Testament and declare that the Ten Commandments have no relevance for a modern-day believer. This premise of ancient Gnosticism is trying to gain dominance again in this end-time hour.

- **Gnostics believed that a new, more syncretic gospel was needed that could meld varying religious beliefs. To that end, they attempted to create a message within an environment that was more open-minded, less text-based, and more "inclusive" of other theological beliefs, philosophical ideas, and alternative lifestyles. Gnostics sought to fashion a faith that even unbelievers**

and pagans would consider unobjectionable and be able to participate in.

Errant teachers of New Testament times were doing precisely what some are doing today as they attempt to remove everything objectionable in Scripture in order to create a newly styled gospel and church environment that makes all accepted regardless of what they embrace or endorse. Instead of confronting the reality and consequences of sin and the power of Christ to overcome it, some take the approach to simply make everyone feel good about themselves without confronting the need for inward transformation. This Gnostic premise and practice is being resurrected in these last days.

- **Gnostics sought to penetrate the spirit world, claiming to explore realms where no other man had ever been. They professed to know names of angels not mentioned in the Bible and even developed entire angelic lineages based on their travels into the spirit realm.**

  Do you know those who dwell on experiences that are unsubstantiated by Scripture? This is a Gnostic premise that has found popularity again in these last days. Although we affirm that there are indeed genuine supernatural encounters with God, we cannot base our beliefs on experiences that are uncorroborated by Scripture.

- **Gnostics believed that God expressed Himself through *eons*, a term used for various manifestations of the divine, and they asserted that Jesus was simply one of them. This appealed to people with pagan backgrounds because they had grown up in a polytheistic setting with many gods. However, this doctrine depreciated Christ, the King of kings and the Lord of lords,**

reducing Him to a position as "one among many" divine manifestations.

Because of a lack of doctrinal teaching today, many people in the Church do not believe Christ is the only way to Heaven. The belief that many roads lead to Heaven is a Gnostic concept that is resurfacing at the end of this age.

Gnostics "departed" from the absolute authority of Scripture and apostolic revelation, refusing to base their beliefs on textual truth. Ultimately, those who held to these errant claims lost their spiritual anchor and thereby kept drifting further off course. By choosing to create a modified, more "inclusive" gospel that fit their syncretic view, Gnostics embarked on an ill-fated course that provided no limits to where error would lead.

Paul, Peter, John, and Jude all addressed the Gnostic departures from the faith in their epistles. But they weren't the only ones. Some prominent Early Church fathers like Irenaeus, Tertullian, and Hippolytus all wrote passionate documents to rebuke and refute this plague of early error.

It may be difficult for us to comprehend how early believers who actually sat under the teaching of the apostles to get established in God's Word could have ever been led astray by errant leaders who were so outlandish and out of line with Scripture. Yet this is precisely what happened in the early centuries of the Church when God's people came under this attack of seducing spirits.

As mentioned earlier, what made these errant influences even more challenging for early Christian leaders who were fighting to keep the Church pure was the pagan culture in the regions throughout the vast Roman Empire where the Church was growing. This meant that believers from a variety of pagan backgrounds sometimes attempted to incorporate the familiarity of their past influences into their new life in the Church. As a result, an influx of pagan beliefs was gradually being integrated into the Church through new converts and even some spiritual leaders.

It perhaps becomes less difficult to comprehend how the bizarre, extra-biblical Gnostic claims were able to lead so many early believers astray when we consider the state of modern society. The nonsensical things that society and even some in the Church are purporting to be true today are not so far from the outlandish doctrines that people were embracing during that spiritual attack in the early centuries of the Church.

Today people generally dismiss the tantalizing tales told by Gnostics in early New Testament times. Yet as we saw in the earlier list of Gnostic errors, many Gnostic-like doctrines and behaviors are reemerging and being perpetuated even by notable leaders in the last-days Church — just as the Holy Spirit forecasted in First Timothy 4:1. A sizable number of Christians are being led toward more pluralistic, inclusive positions that are Gnostic in nature.

In fact, the trend toward such pluralistic thinking is increasing so rapidly, *even among young people who attend church regularly*, that many are wavering on the most basic tenets of the Christian faith. Foundational beliefs — such as the virgin birth, the sinlessness of Christ, the need to repent, moral rights and wrongs, and a literal Heaven and hell — are all on the table with the younger generation.

Recent statistical analysis clearly shows that the belief in absolute truth has already regressed to such a point that the majority of younger Christians see no need to convert acquaintances or friends of a different faith to Christ. Instead of sharing the life-saving message of the Gospel, many young people find ways to rationalize their indecision, such as:

- "If what they believe is working for them, why should I bother them with my beliefs?"

- "Who is to say that Christians are right and those people are wrong?"
- "Isn't it possible that there are alternative ways to God and that Christianity is just our particular way of believing?"

Although there are many God-fearing pastors, preachers, and spiritual leaders in the Christian community today, an ever-growing number of spiritual leaders are replicating the grave errors made by errant leaders in early centuries of the Church. In pulpits and congregations around the world, truth is being altered to reflect the inclusive values of a changing culture. A major shift has occurred in many congregations as pure, sound doctrine has been completely replaced over a period of years by "feel-good" messages. Consequently, many people sitting in church pews today are ignorant of even the most elementary tenets of the faith.

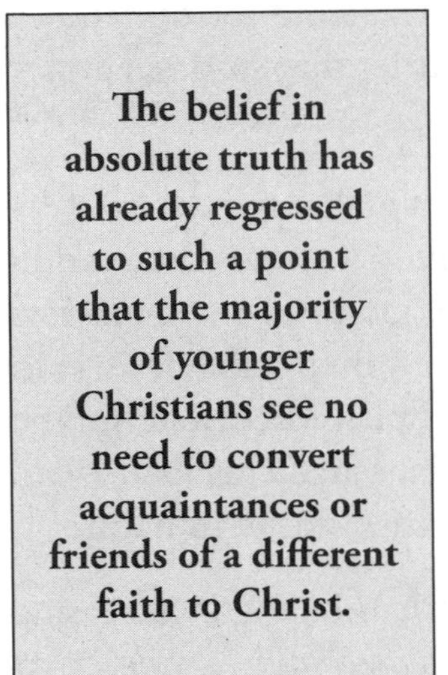
The belief in absolute truth has already regressed to such a point that the majority of younger Christians see no need to convert acquaintances or friends of a different faith to Christ.

Many modern-day church leaders have a strong ability to communicate masterfully. Yet it seems many either lack a basic education in fundamental Bible principles or they have made a deliberate choice to avoid teaching sound doctrine in favor of more popular motivational messages. To those who have taken an unswerving stance on the veracity of God's Word, it appears that many ministers have been duped into taking politically correct positions on many absolute moral issues. These ministers draw back from taking a bold, public stance on any tenet of truth that would put them on a collision course with the society that surrounds them.

As a result, the voice of the Church has fallen silent on many vital matters, choosing to dart around the issues rather than hit them head on. The latter, more courageous stance requires a willingness to potentially fall into disfavor with unbelievers and even so-called Christians who don't hold a solid moral position on many clearly defined, biblically answered questions.

This drift away from the Bible has created a doctrinal vacuum in the Church — a void currently being filled with dynamic business ideas and motivational messages instead of the unadulterated Word of God that the Holy Spirit is bound to honor with signs and wonders. It is certainly true that some of the motivational messages delivered from the pulpit are beneficial in people's lives. However, this type of help is often temporary and can usually be found in books by professionals in the field of psychology who may or may not order their philosophies and thoughts by the standard of Scripture.

It appears that many ministers have been duped into taking politically correct positions on many absolute moral issues. These ministers draw back from taking a bold, public stance on any tenet of truth that would put them on a collision course with the society that surrounds them.

When everything is said and done, only God's Word has the power to permanently transform a life.

It is not too late for the Body of Christ to make a full recovery. In fact, it is never too late as long as there are believers who are willing to hear and hearken to what the Spirit is saying to the Church. However, in order for the Church to receive the divine power it needs for correction, change, and restoration, it must undergo a transformation from the highest to lowest levels. The Holy Spirit is prophetically warning His people that the only way they can thwart a dark spiritual

It is not too late for the Body of Christ to make a full recovery. In fact, it is never too late as long as there are believers who are willing to hear and hearken to what the Spirit is saying to the Church.

season that potentially looms ahead is to heed the Holy Spirit's warning and apply His prescribed solutions found in His Word.

Paul knew the danger of errant teaching and warned the Church to stand against it. The foundational teachings of the apostles were under assault by leaders who claimed to be on the cutting edge of where the Church needed to go. These so-called spiritual charlatans tried to lure early believers into changing theological positions on a wide array of subjects by enticing them with extravagant tales and "comfy" doctrines that would make the Christian faith more interesting and less offensive to the society around them. Those who were lured into this net of deception were ultimately caught in the trap of an apostate belief system.

Another Form of Early Error

Within that early "net of deception" used by the enemy to lure believers away from their strong stance on God's Word was another group of errant leaders called the Nicolaitans. Jesus spoke against this group when He appeared to the apostle John to deliver His messages to the seven churches of Asia (*see* Revelation chapters 1-3).

The Nicolaitans said in effect, "We're living too separately, too strictly. Pagans don't understand us. We don't go to their theaters, their bathhouses, or their temples. Maybe we should compromise just a little to open up dialogue between us so they'll accept us." Jesus referred to this mindset as "the deeds" and "the doctrine" of the Nicolaitans in Revelation chapter 2 (*see* Revelation 2:6 and 15).

In Greek, the word "Nicolaitan" is a compound word comprised of the words *nikao*, meaning *victory* or *to conquer*, and *laos*, meaning *laity* or *people*. When these two words are compounded into one, the new word means *those who conquer the people* or *those who have victory over the people*.

The doctrine of the Nicolaitans was a doctrine of compromise that brought defeat to the people of God. Different parts of the Early Church had fallen prey to this error, and Jesus firmly addressed the matter when addressing the church in Pergamum (*see* Revelation 2:15). After the Pergamene congregation had withstood wave after wave of horrific persecution from the outside, evil was found lurking in their midst — an evil more deadly than the physical persecution they had witnessed and experienced.

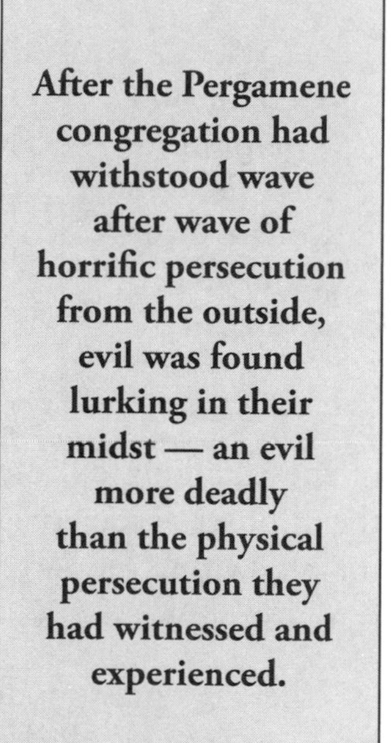

The Nicolaitans were encouraging believers to compromise their faith in order to coexist peacefully with the world. This seduction from within was more dangerous to the effectiveness and the future of the Early Church than any external opposition that would come against God's people.

This mirrors exactly what some are saying today: "Just tone it down. Don't be so strict. Sometimes you have to 'go along to get along' with the unsaved. If you do this, maybe the world won't view you as so obstinate and unyielding."

Whenever God's people compromise their faith, they lose. They lose power. They lose holiness. They lose victory. When God's people compromise their stand for God, it always results in their defeat.

Jesus loved the Nicolaitans, and He died on the Cross for them, but He hated their teachings and doctrines. Like Jesus, we need to take a strong stand against compromise. We must walk in love toward those around us, but we must also walk in holiness. To walk in power, we must walk by a higher standard — and that standard is the Word of God.

When God's people compromise their stand for God, it always results in their defeat.

There is no getting around this spiritual law. Compromise is spiritually fatal to the individual Christian believer and to the life of the local church. God calls on His people to make the decision to have *no compromise* in their lives.

This is the day we live in, when people are tempted to compromise their faith and to modify what they believe because of the changing culture surrounding them. As we've discussed, the mindset of society is changing, and what once was considered morally wrong is now completely acceptable, even when it is contrary to the Word of God.

There is a mass modification taking place in the culture, but as believers, we are called to be different. We are not called to compromise in order to think and act like the world. The Word of God is unchangeable, and so must we be as believers. Underneath the pressure to compromise our faith, we must yield to the Word of God and the Spirit of God for the strength to stand. Like Antipas, we can stand strong against the pressure and hear Jesus say, "Well done. You are one of My faithful ones!" (*see* Revelation 2:13).

No Longer Drifting, but in Full Denial

So this was the situation in the early centuries of the Church. Regarding the Gnostic error, Paul, Peter, John, and Jude all confronted it head on in their epistles.

But when Paul wrote about end-time events in his second epistle to Timothy, he forecasted an astonishing sequence of changes that would come about in society at the very end of the age. Chief among the elements of this seismic shift in society would be an extremely serious spiritual defection that would take place inside the Church.

In Second Timothy 3:5, Paul said there would come a time when people would have "a form of godliness" but would "deny" the power of it. Let's move carefully through these words because they hold great pertinence for our times.

The word "form" is the Greek word *morphosis*, and it means *an outward shape* or *form*. It speaks only of an outward shape and nothing of content.

Let me use the example of a mannequin to make my point. Although mannequins were once primitive in appearance, today they can nearly look human. Some are so developed they would outwardly pass for a real human being to a casual onlooker. In fact, I've personally had the experience of turning to speak to someone, only to discover it was a mannequin in a store! It had such a dimensionally accurate outward form that it passed for a real human being. The form was correct, but, of course, it was nothing but an empty form with no life.

The mannequin example depicts well the meaning of the word "form" in Second Timothy 3:5. It refers to an outward shape or form, but says nothing of content.

But also in this verse, Paul spoke of a "form of *godliness*," so we need to look at the meaning of the word "godliness." It is a translation of the word *eusebeia*, which in this case denotes *piety* or *religiosity*. This would include actions, clerical clothing, religious styles, religious words, religious phrases, religious symbols, and other external religious trappings that people associate with someone or something that is *religious*.

When these words are used together to form the phrase "form of godliness," it portrays something like a mannequin dressed in religious clothes. Imagine a mannequin dressed like an ecclesiastical minister — in clerical clothing with a white collar, a gold chain with a gold cross across its chest, and posed with a Bible in its hands. A good mannequin artist could dress it to appear as a real minister of the Gospel. In fact, a person might even actually mistake it for being a real minister. It would certainly have all the right outward trappings, yet it is nothing more than a shell — a form dressed in religious clothes.

By using this illustration, Paul predicted a time would come at the end of the age when some within the Church would dress themselves in religious paraphernalia — yet like mannequins, they would be inwardly dead.

Paul said that these particular individuals would "deny" the power of authentic godliness. The word "deny" in this context means *to reject* or *to renounce*. By using this word, Paul forewarned of a time when spiritual leaders, confronted with truth and power but no longer embracing it, would reject and rebuff its operation.

This was Paul's declaration — that the end of the age will see apostasy emerge inside the Church. It will dress itself in the guise of the Christian faith, but like a mannequin, it will contain no life or power. When confronted with the true power of the Gospel that can transform lives, this particular category of "defecting" individuals will reject God's truth and embrace a lie. This is a picture of *an apostate Church.*

When I was a young man reading this verse, I wondered, "Who could this possibly refer to?" I knew of no denomination that denied outright the basic doctrines of the Bible, so it seemed like a far-fetched idea to me at that time.

This was Paul's declaration — that the end of the age will see apostasy emerge inside the Church. It will dress itself in the guise of the Christian faith, but like a mannequin, it will contain no life or power.

But in this day we live in, this no longer is an unlikely concept. We are living in a strange age when "spiritual mannequins" are all around us — whether dressed in religious garb or sitting in our pews. They speak in religious terms; they even use Bible language and symbols. But they are not true, living witnesses of the Gospel of Jesus Christ; they are simply hollow shells that imitate the real Church.

We are seeing the departure from the faith that Paul prophesied about, and it is snowballing with the passing of time. At first, this departure was a slow drift. However, the trajectory has become more pronounced in recent years, accelerated over the past several decades by influential portions of the historical Church choosing to abandon the clearly stated, foundational truths of the Bible.

I am thankful for the strong spiritual heritage that many of our traditional denominational churches have forged within the Church at large. Historically, most of them were born in revival and in the power of the Spirit, pioneered by men and women who believed the Bible and gave their lives to the preaching of the Gospel. Some of these traditional denominations still contend for the faith and pour multiplied millions into worldwide evangelism.

The denomination in which I was reared is a strong example of this latter category. I am myself the by-product of this denomination, which not only fervently teaches the Bible, but also tirelessly gives and labors to fulfill the Great Commission around the world.

We are seeing the departure from the faith that Paul prophesied about, and it is snowballing with the passing of time.

However, not all traditional churches have stayed loyal to their original God-given message and mission. Although the historical tenets of some traditional denominational churches remain largely unchanged, the actual practice of their faith represents *a shocking departure* from those foundational truths. Ironically, those same tenets often remain intact within the manuals and creeds of these denominations, all of which were written in part to define the framework and substance of their faith — to *defend and keep the faith*!

However, in order to meet the new cultural norms that exist in modern society, these denominations have gradually moved in the direction of modifying the Gospel wherever needed to avoid controversy or to better "fit in." This trend has gone so far that the apostle Paul would be hard-pressed to recognize the Gospel message at all in what is preached from many of these denominational churches. The pure truths of Paul's epistles have largely been replaced with a gospel of inclusion that emphasizes social justice and social action on wide-ranging subjects.

As a result, a watered-down Gospel has been presented in these last days that marginalizes sin, does not recognize the need to repent, and suggests that the real problem with human beings is psychological or medical and can be treated by acceptance, inclusion, right conditioning, and even medication. The need to be washed in the blood of Jesus and transformed by the power of the Holy Spirit is not even on the radar of these particular denominations. This ominous departure from the truth of Jesus Christ has swung so far that now these denominations are promoting *inclusivity* as if *that* is the message of the Church in this hour — not Jesus' saving, sin-cleansing power.

An example of this ominous departure can be seen in the Washington National Cathedral in Washington DC. The leadership of the National Cathedral proudly states that it is a long-time supporter of the full inclusion of lesbian, gay, bisexual, and transgender people in the life of the Church and considers LGBTQ equality one of the great civil rights issues of the Church in the Twenty-First Century. (Note: LGBTQ is the acronym for "Lesbian, Gay, Bisexual, Transgender, and Queer.")

The Washington National Cathedral website states, "As one of the nation's most iconic faith communities, Washington National Cathedral strives to be a house of prayer where all are welcome. As we live into that expansive, inclusive identity, we at the Cathedral want to be as clear as we can be that all means all. Every person is loved by God. We can preach that from the pulpit, but the most emphatic way we can say it is to live it by uniting same sex couples in marriage at the altar in our Cathedral."[16]

Certainly it's true that every person is loved by God. In fact, mankind was so loved from the beginning that God sent His Son Jesus to die as the ultimate Sacrifice for sin in order to reconcile us to Himself and purchase our eternal freedom (*see* John 3:16). But equally true is Ephesians 5:5, which tells us that fornicators, unclean persons, covetous, and idolaters have no inheritance in the Kingdom of Christ and of God. Ephesians 5:12 stresses that

[16]Gary Hall (Former Dean), "LGBT Advocacy," https://cathedral.org/initiative/lgbt-advocacy/.

it is a "shame" to even speak of such things among God's people, let alone to bring them right into the Church.

Celebrating same-sex wedding ceremonies at our altars is a slap in the face of Scripture. Everyone should be loved and respected, regardless of his or her lifestyle choices. All must be seen as precious souls for whom Jesus died and who can be changed by the power of God. But our responsibility to love and respect a person does not mean we are required to endorse everything that person does. *Friend, it's time to get our heads on straight regarding this issue.*

I wish the example of the National Washington Cathedral was an exceptional case, but it's not. This trend to throw open the doors to every possible lifestyle, no matter how unscriptural, under the banner of God's love and tolerance is creeping into historical denominational churches all across the world. This movement is attempting to infiltrate nearly every major denomination with a demonic pressure to conform to the new social norms. Churches are under increasing pressure to accept and endorse same-sex marriage at the altars of their churches — even though it is a clear violation of Scripture.

Certain denominational churches have *stepped away from* — and in some cases actually *denied* — what their biblical creeds state in order to accommodate a society in sin rather than to confront it as God's prophetic voice.

The creeds of most traditional denominations are similar and remain, for the most part, historically correct. However, in practice, certain denominational churches have *stepped away from* — and in some cases have actually *denied* — what their biblical creeds state in order to accommodate a society in sin rather than to confront it as God's prophetic voice.

This is certainly not true of all traditional denominational churches, but the evidence is clear: Liberal progressive thinkers are negatively affecting the way many of these churches practice their faith. Even more grievous to contemplate is the fact that this departure from basic truths of the Bible is occurring in denominations that were once considered to be holdouts for the Gospel and the power of God.

A departure of this magnitude takes place *slowly* over a period of time and can often go unnoticed until the departure has swung *far* from the foundations of Scripture. Seducing spirits with doctrines of demons have gradually lured believers away from a rock-solid position on Scripture in order to accommodate the moral mess in the world rather than to change it. It's a little here, a little there — a small modification here, a minor alteration there — until finally a church or denomination that started out blazing hot with the fire of God becomes a hollow shadow of its former glory, an outward form with no power.

It's a little here, a little there — a small modification here, a minor alteration there — until finally a church or denomination that started out blazing hot with the fire of God becomes a hollow shadow of its former glory, an outward form with no power.

This drift begins so gradually that those who are in the process of departing will probably not even realize what is happening. But little by little, bit by bit over a period of time, these people are involved in a transition that is moving them *away from* what they once believed and adhered to — and *toward* a very different positioning before God.

Eventually this process of departure reduces a church or denomination to little more than a humanistic goodwill organization that lacks the power of God and endorses only the portions of Scripture that society finds comfortable. As a result, people stream into hell, rarely confronted with the truth they need in order to repent and be transformed by the power of the Holy Spirit.

This modern-day "departing from the faith" that I've just outlined didn't explode on the scene overnight while the Church slept. It began as a slow drift in some religious circles. However, over the past decades, the pace has accelerated until today it often manifests as a blatant rejection of Scripture if a particular issue is at all in conflict with the modern moral mindset.

Those of us who are not part of the traditional denominations can see it clearly as outside observers. Yet it is imperative that we who identify with the Pentecostal / Charismatic part of the Body of Christ check to see if the slow drift of departure is occurring within our ranks as well. That's what the next chapter is about.

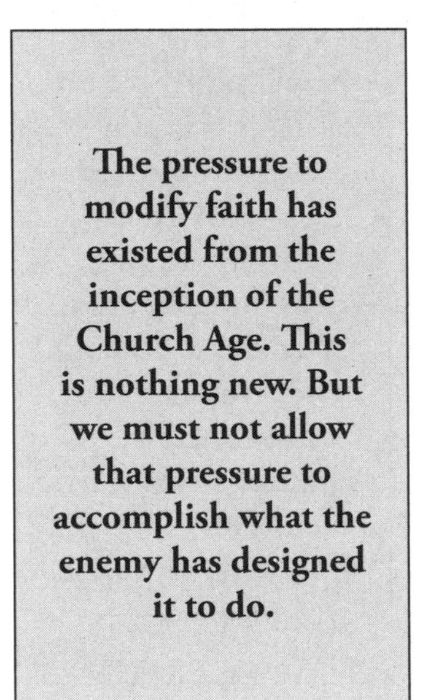

The pressure to modify faith has existed from the very inception of the Church Age. Pressure still exists today to dilute the faith to be more accommodating to the lost world. This is nothing new. *But we must not allow that pressure to accomplish what the enemy has designed it to do.* It is not *our* faith; it is the Lord's. We do not have the right to adapt the faith — only to *keep* it. We must therefore refuse to deny the faith — the eternal truths and time-tested doctrines of the Scriptures. We must protect that faith, guard it, and hold tight to it, even if it requires giving our lives for it.

Think About It

1. In these end times, man's pursuit of the supernatural is displayed everywhere we turn — in best-selling novels, television shows, and movies that glorify the occult. More and more people are being drawn to participate in "contemporary pagan" religious movements, festivals, and rituals.

   Those who hold fast to God's Word in these last days must not remain passive in their own pursuit of God's manifested power, for His plan from the beginning was that signs would follow the preaching of the Word (*see* Mark 16:20). If Christians back off from the true, the seekers of the supernatural will have only the false to satiate their hunger.

   Are you one who yields to the Holy Spirit when He wants to use you in the gifts of the Spirit (*see* 1 Corinthians 12:7-11)? What steps can you take to learn how to yield to Him more fully when He wants to confirm His Word by demonstrating His supernatural power through you?

2. The Gnostic view was that God's wrath was poured out on Christ, leaving no room for a future release of divine wrath in judgment. There's a familiar ring to that claim for some who make up the modern Church. That claim may wear a different set of clothes, but it still walks the earth today.

   Have you personally encountered this "resurrection of Gnosticism" in some parts of the Church? Have you witnessed a church or denomination redefining certain "objectionable" portions of Scripture so that wrong is no longer called wrong and everyone feels "okay" in their sin? How would you describe the fruit that has resulted in people's lives personally who chose to dilute God's truth to accommodate their sin? Have you noticed a difference in the spiritual health and effectiveness of congregations who have made this compromise of the faith?

3. Paul declared that apostasy would arise in the Church at the end of the age. It would dress itself in the guise of the Christian faith, but like a mannequin, it would contain no life or power.

   Have you ever encountered a "spiritual mannequin" in the form of a denomination, a local church, a Christian leader? The Holy Spirit will help you discern what is truly of Him and what is merely dressed in religious garb (*see* 1 John 2:26,27). You will know the "hollow shell" from the real — and you will be responsible for your response to that knowledge.

   So what should your response be when you recognize a "mannequin"? How do you personally remain true to your commitment to God's truth as you "keep the faith"?

Chapter Six

A FRESH STREAM VS. A MIGHTY RIVER

Where does the Pentecostal/Charismatic Movement stand in the midst of modern society's drift away from long-held moral standards based on Scripture?

It's a significant question for us to answer — especially since this movement constitutes the largest single Christian spiritual movement to ever occur since the days of the book of Acts.

Let me begin discussing the Pentecostal/Charismatic Movement with an example. Many years ago, my wife and I and our young sons regularly traveled by car to conduct meetings in churches across North America. On one occasion, we encountered a small river in British Columbia, Canada, with waters that ran sparkling and crystal clear. That lively, bubbling river we so enjoyed was called the Columbia River.

Then later when we arrived in Portland, Oregon, on that same trip, we encountered the Columbia River again — but this time the river's immense size overwhelmed us. We were shocked to see how that small, crystal-clear river had grown into such a gigantic force.

By volume, the Columbia River is the fourth largest river in the United States and has the greatest flow of any river into the Pacific Ocean. It is 1,243 miles in length from its source to the Pacific; it flows south from British Columbia through the state of Washington; its powerful waters cut through volcanic strata that separates the states of Washington and Oregon to form the breathtaking Columbia River Gorge.

While en route to the Pacific, the Columbia River is fed by at least 60 tributaries and sub-tributaries, several of which are major rivers. The main stem has 14 dams, along with 450 smaller dams scattered throughout the watershed area, and the drainage basin is nearly the size of France. Its waters irrigate 670,000 acres of land in central Washington, and its flow is harnessed to produce one-third of the United States' total hydroelectric potential. At its deepest point, it is 170 feet deep, and at its widest point, it is 600 feet wide.

When we saw the immense size of the Columbia River in Portland, it took us off guard. We recalled the crystal-clear stream we had experienced only a few days earlier. *If I wanted to capture in Oregon some of the fresh, sparkling water I'd seen in Canada, would it be possible to separate it from the massive body of water before me?* Of course not. The pure water I'd encountered earlier had been mixed into the huge river that had been fed by 60 different tributaries!

That pure water I experienced in Canada was in there somewhere, but because it had merged with multiple streams, the purity of that original water had become integrally comingled in the broader river. As much as I would have liked to take a drink of that sparkling, clear water that flowed near the river's source, recapturing it was not possible because other streams had entered the mix.

I use this illustration because it frames well what I want to say about the outpouring of the Holy Spirit that has occurred since the beginning of the last century.

The Beginnings of the Modern-Day Outpouring

The first outpouring of the Spirit commenced on the Day of Pentecost and has continued throughout the Church Age whenever hungry hearts have been receptive to it. Some argue that the gifts of the Holy Spirit passed away with the death of the apostles, but a study of Church history reveals that this is not the case. In fact, anyone who alleges this is either ill-informed or intellectually dishonest.

There have always been "seasons" when the gifts of the Holy Spirit were more in operation throughout the Body of Christ than in other seasons. In certain periods, spiritual gifts seemed to ebb because they were not sought, permitted, or understood. But when believers' hearts became hungry and open to seek the gifts of the Spirit once more, those gifts once again began to operate. An examination of Church history will verify this to be correct.

But when we analyze what was happening in the Church at the end of the Nineteenth Century, we see that it was a period when the miraculous work of the Holy Spirit had ebbed and was nearly nonexistent in the traditional Church. Then a certain group within the Body of Christ began to cry out for God to move again — and as always happens when people make room for God's Spirit,

Then a certain group within the Body of Christ began to cry out for God to move again — and as always happens when people make room for God's Spirit, He began to move mightily.

He began to move mightily. A crystal-clear river of God's power flowed from Heaven into meetings that were being conducted in Kansas on January 1, 1906, under the direction of Charles F. Parham.

CBN News reported about the original event that occurred in Topeka, Kansas:

> **In October 1900 in Topeka, Kansas, a small band of believers led by Charles Parham started Bethel Bible School. The school "invited all ministers and Christians who were willing to forsake all, sell what they had, give it away, and enter the school for study and prayer, where all of us together might trust God for food, fuel, rent and clothing." No one paid tuition or board and they all wanted to be equipped to go to the ends of the earth to preach the gospel of the Kingdom as a witness to every nation. The only textbook was the Bible. Their concerted purpose was to learn the Bible not just in their heads but to have each thing in the Scriptures wrought out in their hearts.**
>
> **As they searched the scriptures, they came up with one great problem — what about the second chapter of Acts? In December 1900, Parham sent his students to work to diligently search the scriptures for the Biblical evidence of the baptism in the Holy Spirit. They all came back with the same answer — when the baptism in the Holy Spirit came to the early disciples, the indisputable proof on each occasion was that they spoke with other tongues.**
>
> **Armed with this head knowledge, they now sought to have it worked out in their own hearts. Parham called a watch night service on December 31, 1900. He assembled about 75 people including the 40 students. One of the students, Agnes N. Ozman, asked that hands might be laid upon her to receive the Holy Spirit since she desired to go to foreign**

lands as a missionary. According to Parham, after midnight on January 1, 1901, he laid hands upon her and: "I had scarcely repeated three dozen sentences when a glory fell upon her, a halo seemed to surround her head and face, and she began speaking in the Chinese language and was unable to speak English for three days. When she tried to write in English to tell us of her experience, she wrote the Chinese, copies of which we still have in newspapers printed at that time."

They continued the prayer meeting for two more nights and three days. According to Parham, "We all got past any begging or pleading; we knew the blessing was ours." The rest, as they say, is history.[17]

Six years later when Parham held a public meeting in Topeka, the front page of the *Tonganoxi Mirror* newspaper reported:

Rev. Chas. F. Parham, who claims the distinction of having organized the religious sect known as "The Holy Rollers," is in Topeka arranging for a mass meeting Sunday in the city auditorium. Reverend Parham says he founded it in Topeka, nearly six years ago. The order created quite a sensation when it was in the throes of conception. The following of Parham kept a watch tower of prayer at work night and day, and the petitioner asked that the miracles spoken of in Acts be repeated for their benefit. They declare that their wishes were granted January 1, 1906, and that they were able to speak all languages....[18]

Within ten years, the ripple effects of that tiny prayer meeting in Topeka spread out far and wide. That meeting launched several major healing ministries and ultimately gave birth to the

[17]Gordon Robertson, "The Roots of Azusa: Pentecost in America," http://www1.cbn.com/churchandministry/the-roots-of-azusa-pentecost-in-topeka.

[18]"Charles Parham Meetings," *Tonganoxie Mirror*, August 2, 1906, https://www.newspapers.com/clip/25275435/1906_aug_charles_parham_meetings/.

Assemblies of God, the Church of God, the Church of God in Christ, and the Pentecostal Assemblies of the World — as well as several other denominations and thousands of missionaries who started churches all over the world. All of this was accomplished in ten years with no formal organization and in spite of the limitations on communication and travel that were part of life at the turn of the century.

At the dawn of a new millennium, God answered hungry hearts and poured out a sparkling, clear river of the Holy Spirit's power. Today that river has become so vast that it stands as the largest Christian spiritual movement in 2,000 years of Church history.

At the dawn of a new millennium, God answered hungry hearts and poured out a sparkling, clear river of the Holy Spirit's power. Today that river has become so vast that it stands as the largest Christian spiritual movement in 2,000 years of Church history.

Like the Columbia River I first experienced in Canada, the early outpouring of the Holy Spirit started as a pure, small stream, pouring forth from the throne room of Heaven. However, over the years, many different rivers, streams, and tributaries have flowed into that stream. And although the original, crystal-clear water is still present, it can be nearly unrecognizable at times as a result of its intermingling with so many other streams along the way.

Where I Personally Fit in the Stream

Before you read the following paragraphs, I want you to understand that I am a full-blown, unequivocal Charismatic in every sense of the word.

I was born and raised in Tulsa, Oklahoma, where my parents faithfully attended and served in a Southern Baptist church and taught us that we were to serve Jesus as the highest priority in our lives. At an early age, I was born again at the altar of our church. However, in 1974 at the age of 14, I began to sense a hunger for more, just like many other Christians. It was a journey that would lead to the day when I was gloriously filled with the Holy Spirit and prayed in other tongues.

Being raised in Tulsa, Oklahoma, exposed me to several major ministries that were headquartered in Tulsa. Oral Roberts, T. L. Osborn, and Kenneth E. Hagin were three of these ministers whom I had heard about as I was growing up. Because these ministries were so connected to other prominent Charismatic ministers who visited the city, I was able to frequently attend meetings led by historical Charismatic ministers, some of whom dramatically impacted my life. I shall forever be grateful to Full Gospel Business Men's Fellowship International (FGBMI) for their monthly meetings, where God's power visited us on a regular basis, and for the Kathryn Kuhlman miracle services I attended in Tulsa, where I witnessed miracles beyond my imagination.

Decades later, where do I stand on these matters? I am still a full-fledged Charismatic who prays in tongues, lays hands on the sick, casts out demons, and believes all the gifts of the Holy Spirit are operational in the Church today. The baptism in the Holy Spirit empowered and transformed my life, and I shall forever be thankful for it.

Then in 1991, God sent me and my family to the Soviet Union to participate in another great and historic spiritual movement as the Iron Curtain fell. A people long-starved for truth regarding the Savior of the world came in droves to hear and to respond by surrendering their lives to Jesus Christ. Since that time, I have experienced the book of Acts in all its aspects — miracles, signs, wonders, and mighty deeds as God has moved upon these precious lands. When modern Church history is recorded, I am confident that what has occurred in the lands of the former USSR will be memorialized as one of the greatest advancements of the Gospel to ever occur in such a brief window of time.

My View of the Charismatic Movement Today

The modern Pentecostal/Charismatic Movement started as a Heaven-sent stream of living water to empower the Church to launch into worldwide evangelism at the end of the age. When the outpouring of the Holy Spirit first began at the outset of the Twentieth Century, it occurred primarily outside the traditional Church. It attracted poorer and less educated people — as well as those who, for various reasons, were deeply needful of a touch of God in their lives. As for Christians who considered themselves part of the more established, affluent denominational Church world, this outpouring of the Holy Spirit was largely shunned. Nonetheless, God's power had been unleashed, and it was unstoppable.

By 1914, the Assemblies of God was organized, and other Pentecostal denominations soon followed. These early Pentecostal groups recognized a need to undergird what God was doing by creating a centralized dogma of faith to keep the movement doctrinally on track, form a structure for accountability, and educate people to become mature ministers of the Gospel. Early leaders were energized by the Holy Spirit and burned with fire from Heaven to press on with their message to reach the masses.

Eventually spiritual leaders understood that in order to reach the largest numbers of people possible, they needed to move beyond the walls of church buildings. So by the late 1940s and 1950s, evangelists with enormous tents traveled from city to city to accommodate the multitudes who were being touched and miraculously healed by the power of God.

To reach even a greater number of people, materials were transformed into books and magazines, and ministries launched into radio — all of which resulted in growing crowds. Even people from the traditional churches were beginning to take note of what was happening and to consider the message that these Spirit-filled ministers so victoriously preached and so often demonstrated with signs and wonders following.

In the '50s and '60s, Full Gospel Business Men's Fellowship International established a growing influence with people in the business community as droves of businesspeople from traditional churches began to get filled with the Holy Spirit. These businesspeople then took the message of the baptism in the Holy Spirit back to their traditional churches. As a result, what was once considered a fringe movement began to slowly move into the mainstream.

In the 1960s, certain Pentecostal/Charismatic ministries also launched into television, which began to produce unparalleled growth among believers, even across denominational boundaries. At this same time, universities, colleges, and schools founded on a Pentecostal/Charismatic belief system began to proliferate.

Another significant event occurred in 1967, when a group of Catholic students on retreat at Duquesne University began praying for a fresh outpouring of Pentecost. At that retreat, God answered their prayers, and those present were baptized in the Holy Spirit and spoke in other tongues.

That group of students left the retreat with a yearning to bring the news of their supernatural experience to others in the Catholic Church. Eventually word about this event was sent to the University of Notre Dame, where a similar incident had occurred and had launched a worldwide Charismatic movement among Roman Catholics. The Holy Spirit began to move so profoundly among Catholics that the news of it even reached the Vatican.

The Holy Spirit began to move so profoundly among Catholics that the news of it even reached the Vatican.

In 1992, Pope John Paul II called the Charismatic Movement a "gift of the Holy Spirit to the Church." And on the eve of Pentecost 2004, he stated, "Thanks to the Charismatic Movement, a multitude of Christians, men and women, young people and adults, have rediscovered Pentecost as a living reality in their daily lives. I hope that the spirituality of Pentecost will spread in the Church as a renewed incentive to prayer, holiness, communion, and proclamation."[19]

It is impossible to exaggerate the importance of what happened in 1967 when those Catholic students received the baptism in the Holy Spirit. This was God's power entering the traditional Catholic Church, which meant the movement was finally touching people in every religious circle — men and women of every class, who were both educated and uneducated and who represented every financial sphere.

By the end of the 1970s, the movement stopped widely using the term "Pentecostal" and became known primarily as "the Charismatic Movement."

- Charismatic churches were being established.

[19]Pope John Paul II, "Celebration of First Vespers of Pentecost," *Homily of John Paul II*, May 29, 2004, http://w2.vatican.va/content/john-paul-ii/en/homilies/2004/documents/hf_jp-ii_hom_20040529_vigil-pentecost.html.

- Charismatic denominations and faith associations were springing up.
- Charismatic universities were opening that attracted thousands of students.
- Charismatic publishing houses began to publish a flood of books.
- Charismatic magazines were rolling off the presses.
- Charismatic ministries were advancing in the use of radio and television to broadcast their messages.
- Charismatic missionaries were being dispatched all over the world.

In the midst of all these developments, a strong emphasis on faith, miracles, and the gifts of the Holy Spirit continued with a strong emphasis on the teaching of the Bible.

Then in the 1980s and 1990s, new voices began to flow into the Charismatic Movement, like the tributaries that flow into a river. Although these unknown voices broadened the movement, they also inserted doctrines and practices that were disconnected from the past and represented new streams very different from the original pure flow.

Today the Charismatic Movement is like a massive river, filled with water from tributaries of nearly every conceivable spiritual environment. Just as tributaries can equally bring vital minerals and detrimental contaminations into a river, these spiritual streams brought both good and bad elements into the Charismatic Movement. Most of the original leaders in this movement have died and gone to Heaven, and new voices have often replaced them that have little direct historical or doctrinal connection to the original voices.

Today the Pentecostal/Charismatic community of believers is a conglomeration of voices from different sectors of the church with no unified creed or set of foundational doctrines. And this huge river, filled with the waters of so many Charismatic "tributaries," just keeps getting wider and wider.

Today the Pentecostal/ Charismatic community of believers is a conglomeration of voices from different sectors of the church with no unified creed or set of foundational doctrines. And this huge river, filled with the waters of so many Charismatic "tributaries," just keeps getting wider and wider.

The scope of the community of Pentecostal/Charismatic believers is enormous, encompassing the largest segment of the Body of Christ in Church history outside of the Catholic Church. Worldwide, there are approximately 1.2 billion Catholics, 560 million Protestants, and 260 million Orthodox believers, for a total of 2.5 billion Christians, which is 33 percent of the world's population. But of that total number, nearly 700 million believers purport to be Pentecostal/Charismatic. That's approximately 1 out of every 4 Christians! This is an amazing statistic, considering this movement started in contemporary history not much more than 100 years ago with a tiny Bible study in Topeka, Kansas.

The Dangers Today

There is no question that we have witnessed a manifestation of the Holy Spirit's outpouring prophesied by the prophet Joel (*see* Joel 2:28,29). But the Charismatic Movement is in danger today because it has assimilated so many various theological positions. It is comprised of believers in nearly every denomination, every theological camp, and every eschatological belief. It includes those who could be described as seeker-friendly, traditional Pentecostal, Word of Faith, Third Wave — and every other spiritual "label" you can imagine. The Charismatic Movement has attracted millions of people from a myriad of different faith backgrounds. This is beautiful in one respect because it signals the removal of barriers within the Body of Christ. However, theologically it has muddied the waters.

Believers who identify as Arminian, Calvinistic, Baptist, Presbyterian, Methodist, Lutheran, Catholic, Episcopalian, Church of England, Assemblies of God, Word of Faith, Seventh Day Adventist, and so on, are all rubbing elbows together in worship. But all of these various groups who have received the baptism in the Holy Spirit and speak in other tongues are still on different pages theologically. The wide variety of believers who call themselves Charismatics have no central dogma to hold them together and to help determine what is or isn't sound doctrine. And this isn't even to mention the many "maverick" or fringe groups that have no recognized background or affiliation and have also introduced New Age and spiritism ideas and practices into the Charismatic Movement!

The Charismatic Movement has attracted millions of people from a myriad of different faith backgrounds. This is beautiful in one respect because it signals the removal of barriers within the Body of Christ. However, theologically it has muddied the waters.

Like a mighty river, the Charismatic Movement is massive, with so many different streams flowing into it that it has become a conglomeration of doctrines, beliefs, practices, styles — and a great deal of doctrinal confusion. Some of these practices and beliefs in certain sectors of the Charismatic

Movement are so bizarre that people seek leaders and ministries within the movement who can serve as "safe havens." In other words, many are in search of groups who offer an approach to the Spirit-filled life that anchors believers securely to the Word of God and to the pure stream of the Holy Spirit.

Many are in search of groups who offer an approach to the Spirit-filled life that anchors believers securely to the Word of God and to the pure stream of the Holy Spirit.

Although many recognize and appreciate the multiple flavors of the Charismatic Movement, they nonetheless find it desirable and necessary to navigate to specific groups where they feel safe. I am an example of this, for I have found my place within a spiritual company who hold fast with a rock-solid commitment to the authority of Scripture, to the moving of the Holy Spirit, to biblical morality, and to walking in integrity before God and men — and, in the midst of it all, who demonstrate common sense.

We must never forget that a river with no banks always runs the risk of flooding and contaminating the surrounding areas. The present-day Charismatic Movement that I deeply love lacks such banks.

I would describe these essential "banks" as follows: 1) a set of foundational, agreed-upon elements of dogma and doctrines solidly rooted in Scripture; and 2) spiritual authority that enables leaders within the movement to keep every part that makes up the whole on track. At the very least, ministers within the Charismatic Movement have an obligation to hold unswervingly to the teaching of sound doctrine, to provide themselves with accountability in an association of ministers, and to order their lives as closely as possible to the inerrant teachings of Scripture.

In Summary

I am a staunch believer in the Charismatic Movement. I see it as a supernatural move of the Holy Spirit, and I am grateful to be a part of it. But for this movement to accomplish all that God intends, it needs help to keep within its God-ordained banks. If the mighty river called the Charismatic Movement keeps rushing ahead in its present trajectory without cultivating a strong, broad foundation based in Scripture, it runs the possibility of growing so varied that it veers off course. And the further that river flows off its intended course, the more diluted it will become in its effectiveness to reap the end-time harvest of souls.

But it doesn't have to be that way. God is calling Charismatic Christians to *wake up* and redirect their trajectory once more toward the foundational doctrines of His eternal Word. If the believers who make up the Charismatic Movement today will hold fast to Scripture and form systems of accountability to keep its leadership on track, this movement will continue to grow into the strong, vibrant river of God's truth and manifested power that He has always intended it to be.

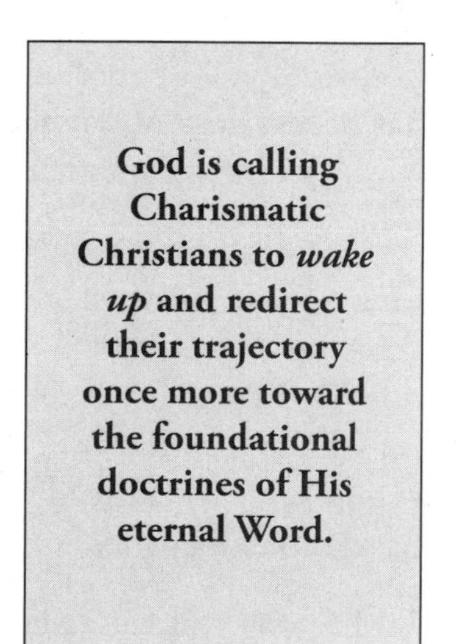

This present-day state of affairs in the Charismatic Church worldwide is *not* what God wants, and it proves the overwhelming need for *sound doctrine* and *solid Bible teaching*. It also emphasizes the urgent need for those of us who are part of the Charismatic Church *to keep our heads on straight* during this last season of the end-time Church.

Sadly, this movement has already drifted so far that some who call themselves Charismatic Christians no longer believe in hell and are inclined toward universalism. Consequently, those who adhere to this set of beliefs no longer focus on missions. Although many say they believe in the absolute authority of the Bible, their actions show they are prone to relinquish part of it if needed in order to fit their preferred belief system.

The Danger of Doctrinal Ignorance

As a whole, Charismatics are skilled at exhorting and using the Bible for illustrative sermons. This is not a bad thing in itself. However, the verse-by-verse teaching of the Bible that would serve as a mighty stabilizing force is becoming a relic of the past. The movement has grown so huge *so relatively quickly* that a solid scriptural foundation hasn't been properly put in place for millions who call themselves Charismatic Christians. In short, there has been a loss of "quality control" in terms of sound doctrine within the Charismatic ranks of the Body of Christ.

The cluttered atmosphere that has developed within these ranks — the spiritual "noise" created by a nonstop stream of new voices and theological ideas that lack a centralized core set of doctrines rooted deeply in Scripture — is an ideal environment for seducing spirits with doctrines of demons to enter and to lead people off track. Already many are largely unfamiliar with certain basic Bible doctrines.

In a very real sense, many Charismatics have been on a restricted spiritual diet for decades. As a result, they are knowledgeable about a certain set of doctrines, such as salvation, faith, healing, and prosperity, but when it comes to other crucial Bible doctrines, they are generally uninformed. This state of ignorance exists even concerning basic doctrines that should be known and embraced by all who claim to be Spirit-filled, such as the doctrines of the gifts of the Spirit, baptisms, and the laying on of hands (*see* 1 Corinthians 12; Hebrews 6:1,2).

This environment of doctrinal ignorance among Charismatic believers is as serious as that of traditional denominational churches that blatantly reject the authority of the Bible in the practice of their faith. The Charismatic dilemma generally is not a deliberate rejection of truth as is occurring in many traditional churches. Rather, the widespread ignorance of the basics within Charismatic circles often leads people to accommodate error without knowing it — often in the guise of inclusivity and the "love and acceptance" of everyone with their variant beliefs and lifestyles.

The spiritual "noise" created by a nonstop stream of new voices and theological ideas that lack a centralized core set of doctrines rooted deeply in Scripture is an ideal environment for seducing spirits with doctrines of demons to enter and to lead people off track.

If we're not careful, this state of doctrinal ignorance among Charismatics could produce a hybrid faith that contains a mix of confused theological ideas. Therefore, we must not abandon reason in the name of inclusivity. We have to realize that *what* we believe is as important as *believing* itself. *This is another reason we need to keep our heads on straight.*

A Comparable Situation to the Early Church

As stated at the first of this chapter, a battle for truth versus error was already raging in the Church when the apostle Paul prophesied that an even more shocking invasion of seducing spirits with doctrines of demons would emerge at the very end of the age. Although the Holy Spirit was alerting the saints to error that would occur as the Church Age was nearing its close, the Early Church was already waging war with spiritual influences that were attempting to modify the faith. In many respects, they were fighting a battle comparable to the battle that is being fought for faith again in these last days.

All New Testament epistles confront error, but even long after the New Testament had been fully written, this assault on truth with the infiltration of error continued for nearly three centuries. Jude wrote that believers were to "earnestly contend" for the faith (Jude 1:3), so Early Church leaders set out to contend for the faith as they were commanded. That precious faith had been given once and for all to the saints, and those early spiritual leaders were aware of their God-given responsibility to protect it at all costs and to teach it to others in its purest form possible.

That precious faith had been given once and for all to the saints, and those early spiritual leaders were aware of their God-given responsibility to protect it at all costs and to teach it to others in its purest form possible.

As a result, Early Church leaders ardently began to write doctrinal statements to precisely define the core tenets of the Christian faith and to spell out those fundamental doctrines that can never be placed on the negotiating table. These doctrinal statements were an early attempt to help keep the Church on the right trajectory during those early years of expansion into new geographical territories. Each time new territory was gained for the Gospel, believers encountered exotic ideas and philosophical beliefs that would try to wriggle their way into the belief system of new believers in order to refashion the message and thereby pollute the Scriptures.

Early Church fathers brilliantly penned those early doctrinal statements, which were based on the apostolic teachings contained in the New Testament. The creeds written in these ancient documents clearly and succinctly articulated the essential core of the inspired teachings of the New Testament. They were so superbly written that they became tenets of faith for the Church — and they still remain the non-negotiable beliefs of the Christian faith today.

As this age nears its close, we will be witnesses of what the Holy Spirit alerted us concerning these last days. More and more, we will see seducing spirits with doctrines of demons actively steering society, including some in the Church, into spiritual lunacy. That means we need to know exactly what these foundational, non-negotiable truths are. Equipped with the immutable, eternal truths of God's Word, we will be better able to recognize truth versus error and to stand strong as His representatives in a world gone mad.

The Charismatic Movement is desperately needed to help advance the cause of Christ to the ends of the earth. It is a God-sent movement to energize the Church with the power of God. In fact, the Church *must* have the supernatural work and equipment of the Holy Spirit to accomplish this Christ-commissioned task of reaching the world with the Gospel before Jesus returns. But it is absolutely imperative that Christian leaders step forward in this last hour of the age to do all they can to protect the Charismatic Movement and to keep it on track and doctrinally anchored to the Scriptures.

In the following chapter, we will look at Second Timothy 4:2-5 to see what Paul further stated about error at the end of the age and what must be done to refute it. When it comes to the matters we're about to discuss, *it is crucial that we keep our heads on straight*!

Think About It

1. Wherever people make room for God's Spirit, He begins to move.

   Is there anything of self — self-interest, self-justification, self-promotion, self-preservation — cluttering your inner "room" reserved only for the Spirit of God? If you will allow Him to help you clear the debris and make room for Him, He will begin to move in ways you haven't yet experienced to prepare you for His purposes. And what He will do for you as His child, He will do for all His people. As they make room for His Spirit, His Spirit will move.

2. Consider the direction that the Pentecostal/Charismatic Movement has gone over the past decades. God desires that barriers to be removed within His Body (*see* Ephesians 4:13-16). However, there must be a unified pursuit among Christian leaders to protect the purity of the faith — established firmly on His foundational, non-negotiable truths — so that the waters of the Word flowing out from His Body are not muddied.

   What are the non-negotiable truths that rise immediately in your heart and cause you to put your "stake in the ground" — i.e., your immovable commitment that these truths must never be compromised or diluted in the name of unity within the Church? Why is it so essential that these foundational truths never vary according to the trend of the times or the preferences of man?

3. Ignorance leads to accommodating error without realizing it. Can you think of a time in your own life when you strongly believed something to be true, only to find out later as you gained more knowledge and wisdom that you had been in error regarding that area of belief? How can you safeguard

yourself and those in your own personal sphere of influence from "allowing an anchor to jostle loose" through ignorance regarding one of those foundational tenets of belief that matters most?

Chapter Seven

COULD YOU PASS A DOCTRINE TEST?

We are living in the middle of an amazing outpouring of the Holy Spirit that the devil would like to derail. Most spiritual leaders are giving of their very best to navigate these tumultuous times and to know how to minister in a world that seems to make less sense every day. However, some are sadly deviating from the solid path of God's eternal truth as they try to become more "relevant" to the world around them. This downward trend is often not intentional, but it doesn't change the fact that it is occurring within the ranks of the modern-day Church.

It's crucial that each of us determines to do our part to protect and uphold the plan of God being fulfilled on the earth in the days ahead. With that in mind, it would benefit us to delve deeper in the Word to see what more the apostle Paul stated about error at the end of the age and the Church's responsibility to combat its infectious spread.

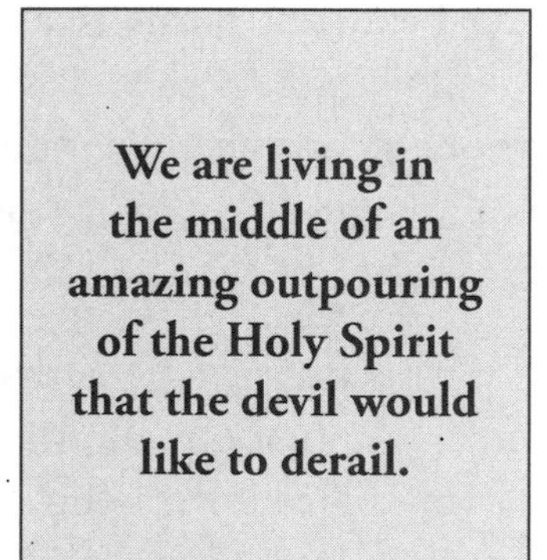

We're about to take a close look at these matters in this chapter. We'll also discuss what Paul wrote in Second Timothy 4:2-5

regarding God's antidote for the end-time rise of deception: *knowing and declaring truth in its purest form possible.* Later we'll explore some of the historical doctrines of the Christian faith that are rooted in Scripture and are therefore immutable and non-negotiable tenets of faith for Christians worldwide. Finally, at the conclusion of this chapter, I want to provide a suggested compilation of the foundational Christian "tenets of faith" that you can study and utilize to fortify your own walk with God.

It's crucial that each of us determines to do our part to protect and uphold the plan of God being fulfilled on the earth in the days ahead.

First, let's consider the significance of what we discussed in the last chapter — that when the New Testament was still being written, poisonous error was being comingled with truth. I thought about this again recently when I read a historical account of a woman who gradually poisoned her entire family by mingling small traces of poison into their daily food and drink over a prolonged period of time. The regular doses of the lethal substance were so small and well-disguised in her beautiful meals that the family didn't know what they were swallowing. As they sat around the table eating food that they thought had been lovingly prepared for them, they were unknowingly ingesting a toxic substance that, over a long period of time, proved to be fatal.

This illustrates the danger of mixing truth with even *traces* of error. At first, small amounts of error can be tolerated without lasting harm if the believer soon returns to a steady diet of healthy spiritual fare. However, if the spiritual food containing even small amounts of error is consistently ingested over a long period of time, that error will begin to sicken believers and can eventually prove to be spiritually "fatal" — leading to the shipwreck of their faith (*see* 1 Timothy 1:19).

As we've seen, the Early Church was being fed hazardous teachings by men who had been lured off course by seducing spirits. Paul therefore urged Timothy *never* to relinquish his God-given assignment to deliver the pure Word of God whenever he stood in any public forum to speak into people's lives.

A Revival of the Bible

You wouldn't have to look any further than Paul's epistles to Timothy and Titus to realize that this pressure to modify the faith had been around since the very inception of the Church (*see* 1 Timothy 1:3-7; 6:3-5; 2 Timothy 2:16-18; 3:1-8; Titus 1:11-14). Satan cannot destroy the truth, so he attempts to minimize it by diluting the message and diminishing it, making it seem as if the Gospel is on equal footing with other ways of thinking. This is why we must take a firm stance on the eternal integrity of Scripture and resolve to receive nothing, believe nothing, and follow nothing that we can't find solidly proven in the Bible.

In this late hour at the end of this age, it is of paramount importance that spiritual leaders accept responsibility to speak truth and to call the Church back to the authoritative voice of the Scriptures. If the Bible is even unintentionally depreciated, both society *and* the Church will drift into destruction. Therefore, it is imperative that we return to the Word of God and experience *a revival of the Bible.*

Making all of this even more significant is the vacuum being left in the absence of numerous key Christian leaders who for years have carried the torch for the authority of the Bible and boldly declared it to society. These stalwart pillars in God's Kingdom are getting older, are retiring, or have died in recent years. The dearth of strong leadership that's been created by their departure is very real, and the vacancies they have left *must* be filled.

The Body of Christ is in great need of quality spiritual leaders who are willing to pick up the torch and boldly declare God's Word to an end-time generation as the absolute, dependable, infallible, reliable, unchanging Word of God. This is truly the responsibility of *every* person called to a leadership position in this hour. Each must be diligent to safeguard biblical truths and provide God's people with spiritual food that will produce long-term, healthy results.

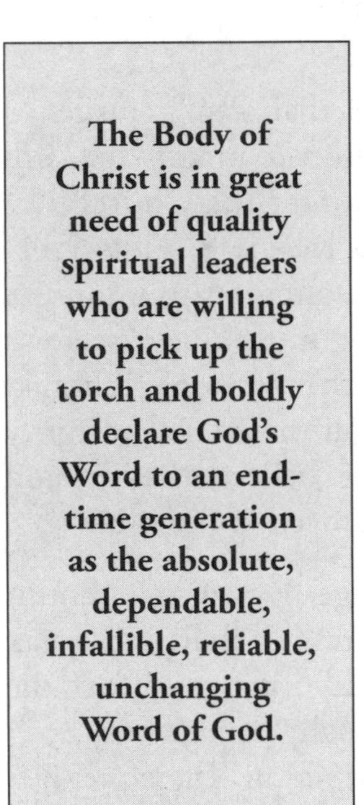
The Body of Christ is in great need of quality spiritual leaders who are willing to pick up the torch and boldly declare God's Word to an end-time generation as the absolute, dependable, infallible, reliable, unchanging Word of God.

Anyone who has children knows that babies tend to put everything in their mouths. As a parent, I've pulled bugs, toys, even trash out of the mouths of our sons when they were very young. As babies, they were prone to put everything in their mouths that their hands could grab.

Likewise, the Church is filled with people who ought to be spiritual adults by now, but they are still spiritual infants because they have not been exercised by the Word of God (*see* Hebrews 5:12-14). For this reason, there are large numbers of believers who, like infants, have put a lot of spiritual poison into their spiritual mouths that is not safe for consumption. Not only will the mixing of truth with false doctrine weaken their foundation and minimize their ability to produce fruit that is eternal, but it could also eventually pull them so far off course that it leads them to a "shipwreck" in various areas of their lives.

In these last days as seducing spirits with doctrines of demons try to infiltrate the Church, it is imperative that spiritual leaders accept the responsibility of guarding God's flock. Their first and primary charge is to provide the people with a strong scriptural foundation to hold them secure. Second, they must stay alert to recognize and remove toxic elements believers have "put in their mouths" before they ingest the error and allow it to lead them off track, away from the sound teaching of Scripture.

Spiritual Cupbearers — Who Are They Today?

All of this makes me think of cupbearers in ancient times, who were either officers of high rank or highly trusted servants whose charge was to taste the drink served at the tables of prominent individuals to whom they were assigned. A food taster had a similar role regarding the food prepared for the individual, and often the cupbearer and the food-taster roles were combined into the same position.

Although the settings for such meals were fabulously designed and beautifully executed, and the food and drink were of the finest quality, the fact remained that those with sinister motives could clandestinely mix the rich fare with concealed poison. Because of this, a highly trusted man who would risk his life to protect such an individual was appointed as "cupbearer." His responsibility was to personally sample the food or drink himself before it was served to see whether it was safe for consumption.

After consuming a portion of the food or drink to be later offered to the person of prominence, these professional tasters were observed to see how they fared. If the food or drink had negative results, it was withdrawn from the menu and tested to determine what ingredients had caused ill effects to the cupbearer — or to determine if poison had been possibly mingled with what was to be served.

If a cupbearer fell ill or died, this news was brought to the attention of those who prepared the food to see what they had mingled into the food or drink to produce such serious or even catastrophic results. Although the cupbearer had been negatively affected, his heroic sampling of the food and drink *before* it was served to people at the table spared the lives of those who would have ignorantly consumed the sickening or deadly ingredients.

Roman history tells us that the Roman Emperor Claudius died in 54 AD — most likely as a result of eating poisonous mushrooms that had been secretly inserted into his meal at the order of his wife, Agrippina, who was the mother of Nero. Because Claudius' cupbearer/taster never fell ill from eating the mushrooms before they were served, it was widely believed he failed to sample the food before serving it. Others speculated that he possibly mingled the poison into the food himself or knew of the conspiracy.

Of course, every person who gets sick or who dies from consuming deadly food or drink isn't always intentionally poisoned. Sometimes poisoning occurs unintentionally because ingredients were not inspected before adding them into the mix to make sure they were not tainted in some way. But food poisoning can typically be prevented. If the kitchen is made sanitary, if spoiled ingredients are removed from the mix, and if the menu is tested before being served, most cases of poisoning can be avoided.

Let's apply this analogy to the Church in this hour. We have seen that the Holy Spirit prophesied in First Timothy 4:1 that seducing spirits with doctrines of demons will attempt to lure believers off track as the age comes to a close. The word translated "doctrines" in this verse is the Greek word *didaskalia*, a word that portrays *information that has been masterfully designed and packaged to make it attractive and appealing to listeners.*

In First Timothy 4:1, Paul used this word to tell us that at the end of the age, seducing spirits — working through people who are themselves deceived — will masterfully package error in such a way that it will be attractive and appealing to many Christians. If Christians living in the last days truly comprehended that they were consuming poisonous spiritual food, they certainly wouldn't consume it. But because the error will be so masterfully presented, many believers will buy into teachings of seducing spirits. That is *clearly* what the Holy Spirit prophesied in First Timothy 4:1.

This brings me back to the example of cupbearers. In these last days when toxic spiritual influences abound, it is imperative that spiritual leaders remember that there is no one more prominent, noteworthy, or beloved in God's eyes than His blood-bought people. Therefore, what His ministers — those He gives charge over the spiritual welfare of His people — offer the saints for their spiritual diet is of paramount importance.

There is no greater violation of duty that a spiritual leader could commit than to serve poisonous spiritual fare that produces a sickening or "fatal" result in Christ's beloved Church. Hence, it is essential that spiritual leaders are willing to first sample the food they're about to offer to know if its effects are going to be healthy or unhealthy.

As end-time leaders, we must be able to provide assurance to those seated around the table that the spiritual food we present is safe and fit for consumption. We must show from the fruit displayed in our own lives that the spiritual fare we offer will produce long-term, healthy results, empowering people to live a life pleasing to God.

I wish to elaborate just a bit more on the role of Christian leaders as spiritual cupbearers in these last days. As mentioned earlier, historical cupbearers not only tested solid food before it was eaten, but they also sampled the wine before it was drunk by those at the table. In the same way, those who stand in spiritual leadership must be willing to test not only the *spiritual meat* being offered to the people, but also the *spiritual wine* that people are being persuaded to drink.

As end-time leaders, we must show from the fruit displayed in our own lives that the spiritual fare we offer will produce long-term, healthy results, empowering people to live a life pleasing to God.

In Scripture, wine is often used as an example of the Holy Spirit's influence in the life of the Church. When the power of the Holy Spirit is poured out on God's people, it often produces a spiritually "intoxicating" influence that changes the way people think and behave. It brings God's people under the control of the Holy Spirit that powerfully produces the life of Christ in them (*see* Romans 8:5,6).

In Ephesians 5:18, Paul encouraged us, "Be not drunk with wine wherein is excess, but be filled with the Spirit." The Greek tense makes it a *command*: We are to be constantly filled with the Spirit's intoxicating, transforming influence. The godly results of such a supernatural Spirit-infilling are enumerated in Ephesians 5:19-21:

> **Speaking to yourselves in psalms and hymns and spiritual songs, singing and making melody in your heart to the Lord; giving thanks always for all things unto God and the Father in the name of our Lord Jesus Christ; submitting yourselves one to another in the fear of God.**

We need a constant infilling of the Holy Spirit that subjugates us to the Holy Spirit's control and changes us into a people saturated with His presence. However, especially in the spiritual climate of these last days, we must be sure that the wine we are drinking is truly the wine of the Holy Spirit. As we discussed in the last chapter, there are many unknown voices emerging in the Charismatic community in these last days. We must be careful not to indulge ourselves in every spiritual manifestation that is presented without exercising discernment. Both spiritual leaders and followers must assume responsibility to ensure that the wine being offered to us to drink is in reality the work of the Holy Spirit.

We need a constant infilling of the Holy Spirit that subjugates us to the Holy Spirit's control and changes us into a people saturated with His presence. However, especially in the spiritual climate of these last days, we must be sure that the wine we are drinking is truly the wine of the Holy Spirit.

When the emphasis of the Bible is diminished on a wide-scale basis, many within the Church have historically lost their ability to discern what is and isn't a true move of the Holy Spirit. In those times, movements have drifted into nonsense that is presented as a move of the Spirit, which has frequently led to incorrect perceptions about the Holy Spirit.

It is true that the Holy Spirit can move in sundry miraculous ways, including unconventional ways. However, you must never forget that He knows the mind of God (*see* 1 Corinthians 2:11), and He never moves in ways that are contrary to the very Scriptures He inspired. All of this is meant to encourage you to use your brain and to know that God expects you to think *before* you deeply consume spiritual meat or wine in these last days, because not all of it is safe for consumption.

Prove All Things — Hold Fast to the Good

In First Thessalonians 5:21, Paul wrote of the need to test doctrines and manifestations before they are embraced. He said, "Prove all things; hold fast to that which is good." Let me tell you a story to demonstrate the point I wish to make about this verse.

I once bought a violin in Moscow that was almost of a certainty an authentic Stradivarius violin. Before I purchased it, I studied how to recognize a real Stradivarius compared to a well-made copy. After convincing myself that I had found a real Stradivarius in an antique shop, I purchased it. But after an examination by a violin expert, that violin proved to be nothing more than a very old, fabulous fake. Only an experienced eye would have been able to discern that it wasn't authentic. Today that fake Stradivarius hangs on the wall in one of my offices as a reminder that everything that looks real *isn't necessarily real.*

I share this example because it is pertinent to the situation the congregation in Thessalonica faced. One or more persons in that church claimed to possess a gift of prophecy, but it wasn't an authentic gift of the Spirit. It was an imitation that resembled the real gift so closely that people in the church had embraced it. The person or persons who were demonstrating this so-called gift of the Spirit must have also been fairly influential, because evidently the congregation as a whole had taken the false demonstrations very seriously.

These bogus prophets were prophesying that Jesus had already returned — and as you can imagine, when these believers realized that the prophecies were false, they were so distressed by the *inaccuracy* of the prophecies, they were tempted to turn a deaf ear to *all* prophetic utterances. But closing their hearts to prophetic utterances would have been a wrong response.

Even though this congregation had been exploited by bogus prophecy, the value of genuine prophecy hadn't changed. It was a true gift from God that the people needed. If they had chosen to keep their hearts closed to that divine gift because of that negative experience, they would have been robbed of fresh words from the Holy Spirit that were a part of their necessary supply from Heaven.

Even though this congregation had been exploited by bogus prophecy, the value of genuine prophecy hadn't changed. It was a true gift from God that the people needed.

Many believers in our own time have been negatively affected by drinking the wine of incorrect spiritual manifestations at one time or another. However, that doesn't mean all unusual spiritual manifestations cannot be trusted.

Never forget that lots of things are used inaccurately in life. For example, a car can be driven in such a reckless manner that it results in a collision — but that doesn't stop us from getting into our cars. It simply makes us more aware of our need to drive carefully and responsibly. If we decided to never drive a car again because someone was fatally wounded in a car accident, that would be an irrational response.

So when Paul wrote to the Thessalonians about this misuse of spiritual gifts, he didn't put a "ban" on all prophecies because of a series of false prophetic experiences. He simply told them to *test* spiritual manifestations before embracing them. Paul told them, "*Prove* all things..." (1 Thessalonians 5:21). In other words, *keep your head on straight when it comes to what you're about to spiritually consume and drink!*

The word "prove" that Paul used is translated from the Greek word *dokimadzo*, which means *to approve after testing.* This word was used in various ways, but it was significantly used to describe the process of testing coins to see if they were real or counterfeit.

Counterfeit coins look very authentic — and there were so many counterfeit coins in circulation in ancient times that it became an accepted practice to test coins to determine if they were real or counterfeit. If tested and proven as fake or counterfeit, they were rejected. Only if the coins were tested and proven authentic were they approved for public circulation and accepted for payment.

That is where the word "prove" comes from that Paul used in First Thessalonians 5:21. Paul didn't tell the Thessalonian believers to reject prophetic utterances; he instructed them *to test* or *to prove* them. God's people are instructed to test both *written* and *spoken* spiritual utterances before fully embracing its substance.

But Paul continued, "Prove all things; hold fast to that which is good." The words "hold fast" are a translation of the Greek word *katecho*, a compound of the words *kata* and *echo*. The word *kata* means *down*, and the word *echo* means *to hold* or *to embrace*. When these two words are compounded to create *katecho*, the new word means *to hold firmly* or *to hold down lest the desired object slip away from you*. It is the picture of figuratively wrapping one's arms around an object and *refusing* to let it go.

Therefore, Paul was urging the Thessalonian believers not to reject all prophecy simply because of a few bad experiences. They needed *to embrace* and *to hold on to* that which was "good."

The word "good" denotes something that is *sound* and *in order*. It has been tested, proven, and shown to be *authentic*. Like a coin that has been tested and proven and is worthy to be put into public circulation, what Paul is commanding us to *hold fast to* has been attested to be dependable, genuine, reliable, and true. Therefore, the Spirit of God is exhorting us *to wrap our arms around* and *hold fast to* those spiritual truths and manifestations that are tested and proven to be *authentic* and *legitimate*, esteeming them as gifts coming directly from *Him* for our good.

Important Questions for Spiritual Leaders To Ask

We saw in First Thessalonians 5:21 how Paul affirmed the wisdom of testing spiritual food and wine before it is consumed. This means there is nothing wrong with asking yourself key questions before you put spiritual food into your mouth to consume it.

As you will see, James 3:1 tells us that those who have spiritual influence will be more strictly judged for what they endorse or present as truth. For this reason, it is wise for spiritual leaders to deeply ponder the content of what they endorse or teach. It is their holy duty to think through a teaching all the way to its logical conclusion before they package and present it to those who listen to them. It is wise for them to ask:

- Is this teaching really biblically based?
- Is this teaching in agreement with the whole counsel of Scripture?
- Is this teaching something I would want my children to consume?
- Is this teaching balanced, or is it possibly a well-packaged diversion?
- Does this teaching comingle someone's opinion with truth in a way that could weaken a believer's character, skew that person's path, or affect the quality of his or her spiritual foundation?

- Is this teaching going to impact people to walk in faith?
- Does it inspire others to bear fruit for God's glory by standing firm on His Word and His promises while drawing nearer to Him?
- Is this teaching aligned with the whole of Scripture, or does it diminish Christ's sacrificial work or mislead in a direction God never intended?
- Is this teaching going to help produce stable, godly Christian character and practices in the lives of those whom I influence?

Those in spiritual leadership must never forget the warning of those Spirit-inspired words in James 3:1: "My brethren, be not many masters, knowing that we shall receive the greater condemnation."

The word "masters" is the Greek word for a *teacher*, and it is the Greek equivalent for the Hebrew word *rabbi*. The word "condemnation" is the Greek word *krima*, and it depicts *a verdict* or *judgment* that results from a formal investigation. In this verse, the Holy Spirit forewarns those with spiritual influence that they will ultimately be scrutinized by God Himself, who will watch to see if what they endorse or teach is in agreement with the entire body of Scripture. That means every word, every phrase, and every nuance that is spoken in a public forum by a spiritual leader is significant to God. We can see just from the witness of this one scripture why it is so important for Christian leaders to always remember that *words have consequences*.

Every word, every phrase, and every nuance that is spoken in a public forum by a spiritual leader is significant to God. It is so important for Christian leaders to always remember that *words have consequences*.

'Death in the Pot!'

In Second Kings 4:38-41, we find a remarkable story concerning a group of men who were studying under Elisha to be prophets. The Bible tells us that Elisha commanded these younger prophetic disciples to go into the field to collect ingredients to make stew, and one of the young prophets inadvertently gathered ingredients from a wild, poisonous vine that looked very similar to a vine that produced good fruit. Because he was unskilled at choosing ingredients, the young prophet unintentionally gathered deadly fruit and mixed it with other healthy vegetables in a pot of stew.

To the untrained eye, the fruit the young prophet collected looked delicious — but if ingested in large quantities, that wild fruit would result in violent vomiting, terrible ulcerations in the bowels, and finally death. An experienced gatherer would have known the difference between the healthy and the deadly fruit. But because of the young prophet's inexperience in selecting ingredients, he accidentally selected the poisonous variety and mixed it into a pot full of otherwise good vegetables. This produced a deadly brew that could have proven fatal to those who consumed it.

When the young prophet returned with large quantities of this poisonous fruit, he shredded it into a large pot; then he mingled it together with meat cut into small pieces and the other vegetables. Finally, he put the pot on the fire to cook, and a stew began simmering that contained hidden death. There is no indication the young prophet intended to hurt anyone. He was simply incapable of selecting correct ingredients due to a lack of experience.

Once the stew was ready, the young prophets poured it into basins and served the others. But Second Kings 4:40 (*NKJV*) says, "Then they served it to the men to eat. Now it happened, as they were eating the stew, that they cried out and said, 'Man of God, there is death in the pot!' And they could not eat it."

Those eating the stew recognized the bitter taste and knew it was deadly, so they cried out, "Death is in the pot!" To remedy the problem, Elisha said, "...Then bring meal. And he cast it into the pot; and he said, Pour out for the people, that they may eat. And there was no harm in the pot" (2 Kings 4:41).

The word "meal" in this verse refers to "wheat." In Scripture, wheat is sometimes used to represent the Word of God. We can therefore see symbolically in this biblical account an example of how dangerous spiritual error can be insidiously mingled into a pot of otherwise good teaching. Those who mingle the poisonous ingredient into the mix may have done so inadvertently, as did the young prophet in this instance.

As a result of spiritual immaturity, a lack of experience, or insufficient Bible knowledge, Christian leaders may mingle poisonous influences into teachings that otherwise would be beneficial to hearers. Some do it unintentionally because they are not mature enough to discern the sometimes-subtle danger of certain spiritual ingredients. That was true of that inexperienced and perhaps very sincere disciple of Elisha, who did not understand that the ingredients he had chosen had long-term, even fatal consequences. Thus, he inadvertently prepared a deadly concoction.

To bring correction to the deadly brew, Elisha knew that they needed to add significant amounts of wheat into the stew to remedy the situation. This is symbolic of what happens when the Word of God is brought into a situation to counteract the effect of poisonous doctrines that are not healthy for consumption. When the "wheat" of the Word is injected in large doses into an otherwise dangerous situation, those life-giving words of truth have the power to nullify the poisonous influence and turn the situation around. The Word of God — scriptural truth injected into situations by the power of the Holy Spirit — can reverse any ill effect of spiritual poison, whether intentionally or unintentionally introduced, that has negatively impacted God's people.

According to James 3:1, those with spiritual influence over others will be held accountable for what they say, what they endorse, and what they serve to saints who are gathered at their table. This is another reason why leaders need to understand doctrinal ingredients and make sure they are bringing forth truths from God's Word that produce life and not death. No true spiritual leader wants the saints to cry out, "Death is in the pot!" when he or she teaches them!

When the "wheat" of the Word is injected in large doses into an otherwise dangerous situation, those life-giving words of truth have the power to nullify the poisonous influence and turn the situation around.

Those in spiritual leadership must see themselves as responsible for what is brought to the table. Like spiritual cupbearers, leaders must know with certainty that no tainted ingredients are being mixed into the pot that might bring eventual harm. Even more, they must be willing to sample the spiritual food and wine themselves to provide assurance to the saints gathered at the table that they can eat with a sense of safety.

That is the way it should be whenever Christians "sit around the table" to listen to the spiritual leaders who teach them. The people should be able to trust that the leaders God places over them will offer *only* safe spiritual food and drink that helps lead them into spiritual health and protects them from potentially deadly harm.

Become a Mindful Consumer

It's true that God's ministers will be held responsible for the doctrines and principles they teach or endorse. However, He also expects His people to use their heads and to actively think through the kind of spiritual food they are ingesting.

Years ago in my travels, I ate in a cafeteria in central Siberia that was visibly unclean, and I *knew* it was risky to eat there. But because I was hungry, I put aside my hesitation and dove into the food. I knew by looking at the cafeteria — *the dirty floors, the dirty interior, the sour smell in the place, and even the dirty plates* — that it was likely the food was not safe to eat. Common sense said, *"Do not eat here!"* If I had listened to my "gut instinct" instead of my appetite, I would have left that cafeteria without eating the food and averted the sickness that I did contract shortly afterward as a result of eating unclean food.

In the same way, if you will listen to your spiritual "gut instinct," you'll know not to consume teachings that are detrimental to your life. If you are listening and staying sensitive to the Holy Spirit in your spirit, He will warn you. And you will help yourself if you'll just pay attention to the spiritual environment! Watch for spiritually dirty floors and plates, and keep alert for a spiritual stench. As you do, you will recognize when you are not in a safe place.

If you find yourself in a dubious spiritual environment and you inwardly sense that it is risky to eat the spiritual food and drink being served there, don't ignore your gut instinct. Just move elsewhere — to a place where you know the spiritual fare that you're being fed is safe.

Your ability to avoid "death in the pot" regarding what you take in spiritually is just a matter of staying sensitive to the Holy Spirit and thinking things through. For instance, consider what you'd do if you found yourself in a dirty restaurant with your family and you sensed your loved ones were on the verge of consuming food that was going to sicken them. Would you stay in there and "eat by faith"? Of course not. So just use the same common sense with your spiritual welfare as you would with your physical well-being in that kind of situation! Don't stick around and consume what could potentially make you spiritually sick!

When questionable spiritual food is being put on your plate, God expects you to respect yourself — and the work He is doing in your life — enough to refrain from eating it and go elsewhere. It's your God-given responsibility to guard your spiritual well-being and to always consider the long-term ramifications of what you are consuming — a responsibility that He expects you to take seriously.

It has always been believers' responsibility to guard their spiritual health and to discern the quality of spiritual food they are consuming. But *especially* in these last days when the Holy Spirit prophesied that strange doctrines will emerge inside the Church, Christians must learn to be "thinking people" who are also spiritually in tune with the Holy Spirit dwelling within.

It's your God-given responsibility to guard your spiritual well-being and to always consider the long-term ramifications of what you are consuming — a responsibility that He expects you to take seriously.

As I said previously, I practice this principle on a daily basis in my personal life. Even though we have an array of Christian TV channels available in our home, I do not allow every program on Christian television to be broadcast into the privacy of our living room. I am very selective about what is allowed entrance into our lives under the label of "Christian." I understand that a little poison ingested over a long period of time, even if it is mixed with good food, can produce ill effects.

I urge you to remove any plate tainted with error from your table and learn to identify and receive only good spiritual food that will make you strong in faith and godly character. Especially in these last days when so many various concoctions of spiritual food are accessible, God expects you to think and not to mindlessly "eat by faith" whatever is placed before you. Use your brain and trust the Holy Spirit within to help you exercise sound judgment, and you'll do well. Because you want to partake of that which is healthy, He will lead you to teaching you can trust.

The Principal Task of Any Preacher or Teacher

This issue of spiritual diet has always been one of great importance for those who are charged to speak the Word of God to others. This is why Paul told Timothy, "Preach the word; be instant in season, out of season; reprove, rebuke, exhort with all longsuffering and doctrine" (2 Timothy 4:2). Before we proceed into the non-negotiable doctrines of the Christian faith that remain true today worldwide, I would first like for us to examine the meaning of Paul's words in this verse.

The word "preach" is a translation of the Greek word *kerusso*, which means *to proclaim, to declare, to announce,* or *to herald a message*. In this context, the word actually described the actions of a *kerux*, who was the official spokesman of a king. It was the job of the *kerux* to announce with clear and unquestionable articulation the desires, dictates, orders, policies, or messages that a king wished to express to the people. Because this spokesman was dispatched to speak for a king, he was required to be accurate, precise, and faithful to the message the king wanted to express.

This means those who act as God's spokesmen are charged to speak His Word accurately, precisely, and faithfully in the way He wants it to be expressed. To make sure we know what public spiritual leaders are supposed to preach, Paul wrote that they are to preach "the word." In Greek, the "word" is a form of the Greek word *logos*, which means *word* and refers to the *written word.*

Making this even stronger is the fact that Paul used a definite article before "word." This unmistakably means that Paul was telling Timothy — and other Christian leaders — that the text he was to preach from was *the* Word of God. This categorically means the principal task of every spiritual leader is to deliver the written Word of God — *the Bible* — when they speak on God's behalf in any public forum.

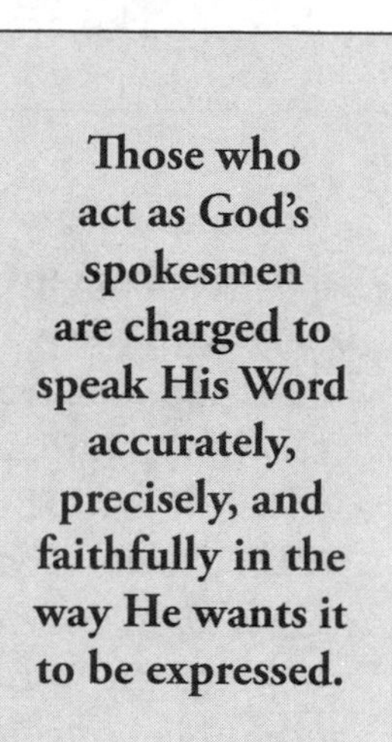
Those who act as God's spokesmen are charged to speak His Word accurately, precisely, and faithfully in the way He wants it to be expressed.

In Ezekiel 3:1-3 (*NKJV*), we see a key guiding scriptural principle that all spiritual leaders should take to heart in light of this core truth that they are entrusted with the task of speaking on behalf of God. Ezekiel wrote, "Moreover He said to me, 'Son of man, eat what you find; eat this scroll [i.e., God's message], and go, speak to the house of Israel.' So I opened my mouth, and He caused me to eat that scroll. And He said to me, 'Son of man, feed your belly, and fill your stomach with this scroll that I give you.' So I ate, and it was in my mouth like honey in sweetness."

This passage was meant to demonstrate that God expects His messengers to fully digest every part of what He desires to say before imparting His message to others. For a messenger to hear God's Word and deliver it without *first* tasting and digesting every part of it himself is strictly forbidden. This includes both the pleasurable parts *and* the bitter parts — for example, both the commendation and the correction. Before God's spokesman can deliver that message in power to others, he must study and seek the Lord to become as intimately aware as possible of the nuances of its intended meaning.

This divine expectation places great responsibility upon spiritual leaders who are called to preach frequently in public settings. Considering the myriad distractions of modern life, it can be a real challenge for them to find time to fully devour and digest the words God gives them to impart before their next meeting. As a result, many sermons are delivered without the power of the Holy Spirit, even though they are delivered in a professional and timely manner. A spiritual leader must fill his inner being with the word he has received from Heaven to impart and allow it to affect him completely. Only then can he step into the pulpit and publicly deliver that message from God with authority and power.

A spiritual leader must fill his inner being with the word he has received from Heaven to impart and allow it to affect him completely. Only then can he step into the pulpit and publicly deliver that message from God with authority and power.

One who preaches a message that he *hasn't* first internalized can be likened to a chef who heartily recommends a dish he has never even tasted. Such a chef may know all about the cuisine he is recommending. He may possess all the right ingredients to produce that dish, and he may even know how to cook and prepare it for others. But if he has never actually tasted that dish himself, everything he knows about it is merely head knowledge. He cannot truly speak about that food with authority because he hasn't had a tangible, firsthand experience with it.

This explains why so much preaching and teaching in the Church today lacks the power of the Holy Spirit. Feeling the pressure to produce spiritual meal after spiritual meal, ministers rush to their Bibles and take out scriptures — like recipes pulled from a cookbook — to cook up something new and different. Trying to keep up with the schedule, they rush from the kitchen to the table to serve meals they have never tasted themselves. And because they rarely take the time to digest these truths on their own, they merely dish out sermons that may be interesting but that are rarely life-transforming.

An individual entrusted to speak on God's behalf must let God's Word go down deep into his belly — his spirit man — that he might be changed, corrected, and nourished by it. Such a leader must swallow the *entire* message given to him with no right to eat of it selectively. As Christ's appointed representative, he must put aside his own feelings and thoughts so the Word can be fully ingested, assimilated, understood, and then delivered in power. There is no doubt that certain parts of these messages will be hard to swallow; nonetheless, one of the requirements of spiritual leaders is to digest *all* that God's Word says.

This principle found in Ezekiel should be taken to heart by anyone who is called to publicly preach or teach the Word of God. It clearly and accurately states that one cannot powerfully bring forth spiritual truths that he hasn't been filled with himself.

Those who preach and teach are required to study, pray, and prepare to teach the Word of God. Once preparation is complete, they then depend on the anointing and inspiration of the Holy Spirit as they speak from their spirits and souls — processing, elaborating, and incorporating human experience to convey what God has shown them in the Scriptures. God's spokesmen are expected to be prophetic voices to the Church. As such, these leaders must stand strong on the side of truth, even if the spiritual atmosphere has changed and the modern Church does not agree with the truth they are commanded to speak.

The example given in Ezekiel 3 plainly means each spiritual leader is to read the message, meditate on it, and deliver it just as Jesus expects. God's message may contain truths that are corrective and therefore possibly unpleasant to hear, difficult to consume, and painful to digest. But there is a supernatural, anesthetizing effect of the Holy Spirit when He speaks difficult truths to His people's hearts. His correction does not discourage, condemn, or leave them in a downtrodden condition. Instead, He speaks truth in a way that protects and soothes as it corrects so that the end result is comfort, encouragement, hope, and strength.

God's spokesmen are expected to be prophetic voices to the Church. As such, these leaders must stand strong on the side of truth, even if the spiritual atmosphere has changed and the modern Church does not agree with the truth they are commanded to speak.

As spiritual leaders, we must speak God's principles — even those difficult to hear — with the anesthetizing effects of the Holy Spirit to help listeners receive the correction without feeling like they are being bludgeoned by truth. He expects us as His spokesmen to deliver His message as He intends and in the power of the Holy Spirit.

I want to interject an important point here before we move on. As we discussed earlier in Chapter Six, many in the Body of Christ have generally become biblically illiterate. In light of this situation, the importance of verse-by-verse teaching of Scripture cannot be overstated, because this approach to the Bible ensures that each truth and subject presented in a passage of Scripture is addressed.

Preaching that centers on scripturally based exhortation has its important place. Although it is not verse-by-verse exposition, it is usually based on broader concepts from the Word that can supernaturally impart strength, courage, and inspiration when done in the power of the Spirit. I greatly respect those who do it well and enjoy hearing them preach. These anointed preachers often stir me to needed action.

But if this type of anointed exhortation is the only spiritual food offered to people — if a deeper, verse-by-verse study of Scripture is not also provided in their spiritual diet — huge gaps will be left in people's knowledge of the Bible. A body of believers fed such a spiritual diet may have a passion to pursue the things of God, but they will lack a depth of scriptural knowledge regarding foundational doctrines that is only gained by a text-based approach to the Scriptures.

There is a supernatural, anesthetizing effect of the Holy Spirit when He speaks difficult truths to His people's hearts. His correction does not discourage, condemn, or leave them in a downtrodden condition. Instead, He speaks truth in a way that cleanses as it provides comfort, encouragement, hope, and strength.

The bottom line is this — the ministry of the Word must include both Bible-based exhortation and verse-by-verse preaching and teaching. Both are vital. When either are emphasized above the other, it leaves significant deficits in the spiritual foundation being built in people's lives.

So this is one vital aspect of faithfully declaring God's Word — that all the truth in all the Scriptures be taken seriously, studied, and taught to the people of God according to the leading of the Holy Spirit. If the giftings and strengths of a pastor lie in other areas besides teaching the Word verse by verse, he must focus on his primary gifting. However, he must also be willing to seek those who can come alongside him to help supply that portion to the people whom God has placed under his charge. The goal should always be to give the people a strong, solid doctrinal foundation on which to base their lives.

The goal should always be to give the people a strong, solid doctrinal foundation on which to base their lives.

We cannot pivot away from the infallible, incorruptible Word of God for even a moment. We must stay dedicated to correct interpretation and to teaching and preaching that is done in the power of the Holy Spirit. This instruction is vital for us to grasp, especially in a day when people are slowly departing from the sound teaching of doctrine. Regardless of what others do, we must determine that *we* will remain clear channels for truth.

Hot Topics and Cultural Issues — *Silence Is Not the Answer!*

A crucial aspect of speaking for God also includes addressing hot social topics and cultural issues on the basis of His Word. This is part of the responsibility of the pulpit. The answers, solutions, or principles to deal with these societal dilemmas are found in the immutable truths of God's Word.

The New Testament writers addressed many hot topics and cultural issues that were relevant to the First Century, such as sexuality, marriage, slavery, addictions, and alcohol abuse, just to name a few. Those who were converting to Christ from paganism came with the baggage of messy relationships, addictions of all kinds, nonsensical thinking, and residual soul damage incurred before they were born again. The spiritual leaders of the Early Church boldly addressed the issues believers of that time faced in their lives, and those timeless answers still speak to us today.

Today the world we live in is also filled with multitudes who have been negatively impacted by society's moral mess. The Holy Spirit prophesied that deluded thinking would pervade much of society at the end of the age — the very point on God's timeline that we are living right now. That means today's spiritual leaders must confront the spreading delusion and speak to the hot cultural issues of this modern era, no matter how uncomfortable they are to address.

Christians impacted by this deception are largely unaware that the influences they are consuming are poisonous and potentially lethal to their destinies and everything good in their lives. They need God's spokesmen to address the subjects that assail them on every side. *Silence is not the answer.*

Today's spiritual leaders must confront the spreading delusion and speak to the hot cultural issues of this modern era, no matter how uncomfortable they are to address. *Silence is not the answer.*

Pastors and spiritual leaders must see themselves in much the same way a father sees his role as the head of his home and family. There are things the children must hear at home from the head of the house — and if they don't, they will be educated by peers, naysayers, and others who are biblically ignorant, willfully or otherwise.

It's simply a fact that if God's leaders will not address these issues, the vacuum will be filled with the voice of the world, which will inevitably lead countless multitudes astray. Leaders who ignore difficult topics have not fully grasped or embraced their God-given responsibility to provide the right response. It is *essential* for God's spokesmen to speak up and communicate what He says on controversial cultural issues in order to help Christians keep their heads on straight in this world that seems to have gone morally crazy.

The Highest Level of Spiritual Warfare

In Second Timothy 4:2, Paul continued, "Preach the word; be *instant*...." The word "instant" is a translation of the Greek word *ephistemi,* which is a military word that means *stay at your post*. It's significant that Paul used a military word when he commanded Timothy — and *all* public spiritual leaders — to preach the Word. The truth is, when a Christian leader declares God's Word in a public forum, it is the highest level of spiritual warfare.

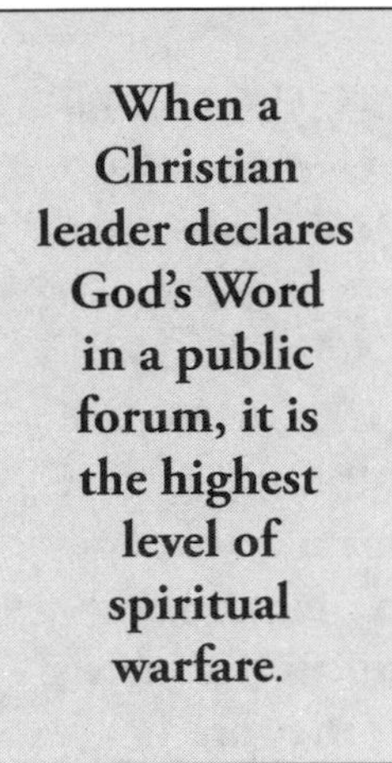

When a Christian leader declares God's Word in a public forum, it is the highest level of spiritual warfare.

The Word of God is sharper than any two-edged sword (*see* Hebrews 4:12). Within the covers of the Bible are all the answers for every problem man could ever face. The Bible can bring new life to hearts, establish order to confused minds, and refresh souls that are being rocked by emotion.

When God's Word is decreed from a person's mouth that is connected to a believing heart, that Word has a life-changing and yoke-destroying effect.

- It penetrates the hearts of people who are in sin.
- It sets people free who are in bondage.
- It shines a light so brilliant that darkness is expelled.
- It heals the body and delivers the mind.

- It brings peace to children and families.
- It breaks strongholds and transforms the mind.
- It changes destinies!

The Bible provides light for the path ahead, freedom for the mind, strength and resolve for the will, healing for the body, and vision for a bright future. There is power in the Word of God that even the devil cannot deny!

The Bible provides light for the path ahead, freedom for the mind, strength and resolve for the will, healing for the body, and vision for a bright future. There is power in the Word of God that even the devil cannot deny!

That's what spiritual leaders are called to preach!

It is therefore no wonder that Satan tries to stop the preaching, teaching, and ministry of the Word. Satan hates God's Word to be declared on the earth because the enemy knows that mental, emotional, and spiritual strongholds are *demolished* when it is proclaimed in power! This is why Paul admonished Timothy and all spiritual leaders in essence, "*Stay at your post, and keep preaching God's message as He intends for it to be preached!*"

A Leader's Position in Good Times and Bad Times

Paul went on to say, "Preach the word; be instant in season, out of season...." Let's look at the words "in season" and "out of season" to see what this means.

The words "in season" and "out of season" are both formed on the basis of the Greek *kairos*, which depicts *a season* or *time*. But the meaning of *kairos* can be altered by adding different prefixes to it. For example, the Greek word *eu* means *good, pleasing, enjoyable* — and when it is affixed to *kairos*, it forms the word *eukairos*, which means *good times*, *pleasing times*, or *enjoyable times*. But if the Greek letter *a* is affixed to *kairos*, it forms the word *akairos*, which means *bad times*, *displeasing times*, or *unenjoyable times*.

By using the Greek words for "in season" and "out of season" — which actually mean *good times* and *bad times* — Paul was telling spiritual leaders to stay at their post and keep preaching God's Word, regardless of what was happening in their environment.

With all this in mind, this verse could read as follows: *"Take a firm stand, and resolve to stay at your post to preach God's Word as God intended it to be preached! Regardless of whether times are good or bad or whether or not you are enjoying the task, that post is your place of responsibility. So dig in and resolve that you are going to be faithful to take a firm stand, no matter what you experience from the atmosphere around you."*

The Pulpit's Complete Task

Paul continued, "Preach the word; be instant in season, out of season; *reprove*, *rebuke*, *exhort* with all longsuffering and doctrine" (2 Timothy 4:2). Paul says it is essential that we have all three aspects of the preaching of the Word in our pulpits — *reproving*, *rebuking*, and *exhorting*. Let me explain the difference between these three facets of the ministry.

- "Reprove" is from the Greek word *elegcho*. In this context, it means *to convict* or *to censure* a listener with the clear preaching and teaching of the Word of God. To "reprove" is to convict with such effectual impact that one is brought to his senses and to the point of conviction for wrong actions and wrong thinking in his life. The listener must choose either to repent or to reject what he now knows to be true.

This is a supernatural work of the Holy Spirit to bring life-altering change to a person's heart, but it requires a personal response from the listener in order to effect that change. This word "reprove" speaks of a crucial part of preaching and teaching that is essential in order for the Holy Spirit to produce purity and spiritual fire in the Church!

- "Rebuke" is from the Greek word *epitimao*. It is the same word that is used in the gospels when Jesus "rebukes" a demon spirit. It is *a correction that expresses disapproval of thoughts, actions, or deeds.* It points out where a person is wrong and provides him with instruction on how to do what is right. It supernaturally represses the prevalence of evil and opposes what is wrong in a person or in society.

  This describes how needful it is for sin and sinful behavior to be corrected and even rebuked by the declaration of God's Word. The absence of a godly rebuke can even lead believers to become calloused to sin and its ravaging consequences.

- "Exhort" is from the Greek word *parakaleo*. It means *to urge, to exhort*, or *to admonish*. It depicts a type of preaching or teaching mentioned earlier that undergirds believers with spiritual strength and admonishes them to press forward toward God's highest will, regardless of the opposition faced along the way. Godly exhortation is strong, anointed, and motivational, and it stirs the listener to cast off defeat and press on toward victory. This kind of preaching and teaching is essential to keep the Church focused on victorious living and the fact that they can overcome the world and achieve every dream God has put in their hearts.

Often in our age when a spiritual leader reproves and rebukes, he is vilified as being narrow-minded, critical, judgmental, or negative, especially in the current climate where political correctness seems to carry more weight in people's lives than does the Bible. Just as I was writing this paragraph, I heard from a pastor who had just experienced a departure of some people from his church. They chose to leave because he dealt with difficult issues from a biblical perspective and was accused of being too narrow-minded.

In some cases, leaders are actually being bullied by people in congregations for fulfilling the divine command of God to reprove and rebuke when it is required. But God's requirements don't change, and He has commanded His spokesmen to speak the Word without compromise, regardless of the consequences.

All three elements of *reproving, rebuking*, and *exhorting* are to be practiced in the Church. Unfortunately, the first two — *reproving* and *rebuking* — have largely been put aside, lest people be offended. As a result, issues that need to be addressed and corrected are often ignored.

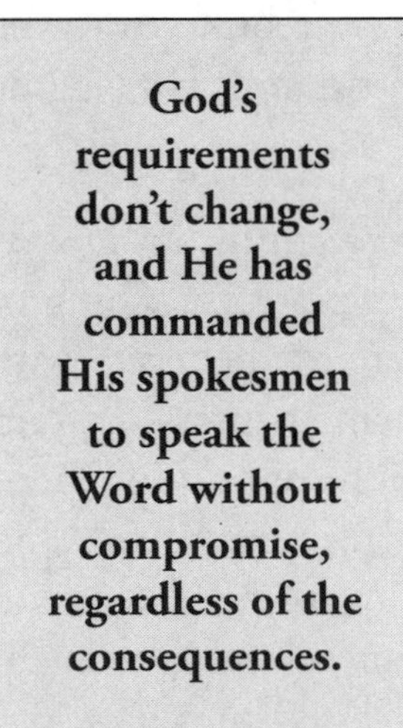

Although this is not always the case, it's true that a good percentage of preaching and teaching consists only of *exhortation* that stirs believers with a positive message. In a world that is filled with negativism, this is vital. Yet although this type of preaching is good, it leaves out the other two vital elements that are so essential for people's hearts to be changed by the power of the Holy Spirit so they can be led to victory.

Sound Doctrine vs. Unhealthy Teaching

In Second Timothy 4:3, Paul wrote, "For the time will come when they will not endure sound doctrine; but after their own lusts shall they heap to themselves teachers, having itching ears."

The Greek text clearly points to the future — *to a last-days season* — when increasing numbers of people in the Christian community "will not endure sound doctrine." The Holy Spirit doesn't indicate how many will be pulled in this wrong direction, but the word "they" in Greek implies *large numbers* of people.

According to Paul, a last-days Christian community will lose their taste for Scripture and will no longer "endure" sound doctrine. The word "endure" is the Greek word *anechomai*, which means they will no longer *put up with* or they will *have no tolerance for* sound doctrine.

The word "sound" is from the Greek word *hugiaino*. It is a word that always portrays something *wholesome and healthy* or that always produces *a healthy state of being*. The word "doctrine" refers to the *long-held teachings and tenets* of the Christian faith.

But in this verse, the Holy Spirit foretold a specific end-time season when a large segment of the Christian community would no longer tolerate such teaching. It actually prophesies that some Christians will begin to gradually lose their appetite for sound doctrine and will actually develop a *distaste* for it. Instead of holding fast to the long-held, wholesome truths of the Bible, they will yearn for messages of a different kind and abhor the sound messages from Scripture that they heard in times past.

Second Timothy 4:3 says, "...After their own lusts shall they heap to themselves teachers, having itching ears." The word "lusts" describes *desires* or *whims*. Paul used this Greek word to inform us that a generation will arise at the end of the age that rejects time-tested truth in favor of teaching that is more in step with the fluctuating whims of the times.

According to the Holy Spirit, new types of "spiritual" teachers will emerge in the last days that will pander to the fleshly preferences of an end-time generation. These so-called leaders will provide a modified version of the Bible that will appeal to a generation that is already adrift. The Holy Spirit forecasts that this category of public speakers will enjoy enormous popularity among their listeners.

Every spiritual leader desires to reach as many people as possible and to speak to a broad audience. However, the leader's aim must never be to gain a following but to speak accurately as God's spokesperson.

Yet the Holy Spirit prophesies that at the end of the age, a host of false teachers will arise, and large numbers of people will be attracted to these leaders who offer modified versions of truth. These *ear ticklers* will proliferate rapidly in these last days as this erring generation "heaps" such teachers unto themselves.

Every spiritual leader desires to reach as many people as possible and to speak to a broad audience. However, the leader's aim must never be to gain a following but to speak accurately as God's spokesperson.

The word "heap" in Second Timothy 4:3 is a translation of the Greek word *episoreuo*, which paints a picture of *piles* of teachers, all intent on appeasing a last-days audience with messages that suit the preferences and even the demands of the majority. Like it or not, this word is the Holy Spirit's warning that large numbers of teachers will go off course at the end of the Church Age — caught up in the spirit of the world and modifying their messages to match the confusion of the end-time culture.

Is it possible that we are currently witnessing this turning away from truth that the Holy Spirit predicted nearly 2,000 years ago? Are we seeing in our own day an accommodating attitude toward the world, which produces a brand of Christianity that blends into the environment around it? Are we witnessing the departure from the faith that the Holy Spirit clearly prophesied?

A Mythical Version of Truth

Paul went on to write, "And they shall turn away their ears from the truth, and shall be turned unto fables" (2 Timothy 4:4).

The apostle Paul foretold that some would discard fixed truth and replace it with "fables." The word "fables" is a translation of the Greek word *muthos*, which is where we get the word *myths* or *fantasies*. By using the word, Paul was *not* talking about myths as we would normally think of myths; rather, he was forecasting that a group of last-days errant teachers will substitute authentic teaching of the Bible with a modified version so far off course that it will actually be a mythical version of truth.

Paul also used the word "fables" in First Timothy 1:4 to describe such false spiritual leaders. He said, "Neither give heed to fables…." The word "fables" is again the Greek word *mythos*, which means *myths* or *fantasies* and is used again to depict newly styled teachings that do not resemble the authentic message of the Bible.

This was Paul's way of describing a popular form of teaching in the First Century. Propagated by distorters of truth, as we saw in the last chapter, this type of teaching was entertaining but incorrect and therefore had no power to transform people's lives.

In First Timothy 1:6, Paul stated those who teach doctrinal nonsense have "swerved" and "turned aside" unto "vain jangling." The word "swerved" is the Greek word *astocheo*, and it means *to miss the mark*. The use of this word means the spiritual leaders in question no longer hit the target of correct doctrine.

The words "turned aside" are a translation of the Greek word *ektrepo*, which is a medical term that describes *a bone out of joint*. By using this medical word *ektrepo*, Paul informed us that when a spiritual leader swerves from truth — *no longer hitting the target of sound doctrine in the message being communicated* — that swerving leader becomes like "a bone out of joint" in the Body of Christ.

If you've ever had a bone out of joint, you know firsthand that the experience is a very *painful* one! Although your overall body may be in good shape, a single bone out of joint creates so much pain that the rest of the body is hugely impacted by it.

Paul used this idea to explain that when a notable spiritual leader gets "out of joint" with biblical truth and begins to swerve away from it, he or she produces inevitable negative consequences that affect many people in the Church. One "out of joint" spiritual leader can create discomfort, pain, and even impairment for the Body of Christ.

One "out of joint" spiritual leader can create discomfort, pain, and even impairment for the Body of Christ.

The Holy Spirit made it clear in Second Timothy 4 that *newly fashioned teachers* with *restyled messages* will produce astonishing mixtures of truth mingled with error, and that many people will be seductively led off track into an inaccurate version of Christianity. *Are we there today?*

Here's How To Keep Your Head on Straight!

As Paul wrapped up his warning to Timothy, he told the younger minister, "But watch thou in all things, endure afflictions, do the work of an evangelist, make full proof of thy ministry" (2 Timothy 4:5).

The phrase "watch thou" is translated from the Greek word *nepho*, which means to *be sober* or *to think straight and not like a silly drunk.* It pictures *clear thinking.* But the Greek grammar is not a suggestion; it is a *command.*

That means this is *a command to think straight* or *to think soberly and clearly.* By using this word, Paul was commanding every spiritual leader to think reasonably concerning what he is communicating to those who listen to him.

The divine requirement is clear: We who are leaders within the Church are to be sober-minded, thinking straight with clear judgment as we fully examine what we are publicly endorsing or teaching. Again, since we will be more strictly judged (*see* James 3:1), it is imperative that we use our minds to think through what we embrace, endorse, and communicate to others.

The phrase "endure afflictions" is important because it tells us that when we keep our heads on straight as so many others are going astray, we may have to put up with some opposition. At the very least, there will be those who accuse us of being relics of the past. We may be told that we are narrow-minded, stuck on old notions while the world is moving ahead, or that we're too "Word-bound" in these changing times.

The phrase "endure afflictions" is a translation of the Greek word *kakopatheo*, a compound of the words *kakos* and *pathos*. The word *kakos* describes something *evil* or *foul,* whereas the word *pathos* depicts *hardship* or *suffering*, or *the putting up with emotional or mental hardness.* Paul here told Timothy — and those who speak for God in the end of the age — that they must prepare and undergird themselves with the understanding that not everyone will appreciate their Bible-based stance.

The word "evangelist" is a translation of the Greek word *euangelistes*, which in a New Testament sense describes a preacher of good news. But there is another, much older meaning that plays a role in this verse. The word "evangelist" — the Greek word *euangelistes* — in its earliest known usage is found on a grave marker from ancient times that commemorated a famous *medium* or *channeler* of that time.

First usages are very important and have an impact on the future use of a word. Because this Greek word *euangelistes* was first used to depict a medium of the spirit world, or one who channeled the voice of the spirit world to the world of the living, this tells us something significant about Paul's intended meaning. He was urging Timothy (and all who speak for God) to do all they can to be the *clearest channels* for God's voice that they can be. The job of God's spokesmen is not to speak for themselves, but to so yield themselves to God's Word that it flows clearly through them to listeners in the purest form possible.

Although Paul was addressing Timothy directly, he was also writing to anyone who speaks for God, which includes not only spiritual leaders, but *every* believer as well. Paul was specifically targeting those who would be alive at the end of the age — which includes *us*. His message was to last-days believers who would witness an epidemic of nonsense in the world around them — a strange season when delusional thinking would try to creep into the Church in unprecedented measures.

But besides those who veer from truth, there will also be a different group of believers who emerge at the end of the age. This latter group will hold fast to the ageless Word of truth, regardless of consequences or opposition, and proclaim its timeless teaching. Let's make sure that *this* is the group *we* belong to. In spite of the difficulties you and I may endure for proclaiming the Bible as utter truth, we must nevertheless stand firm, with our feet solidly planted on the integrity of God's Word.

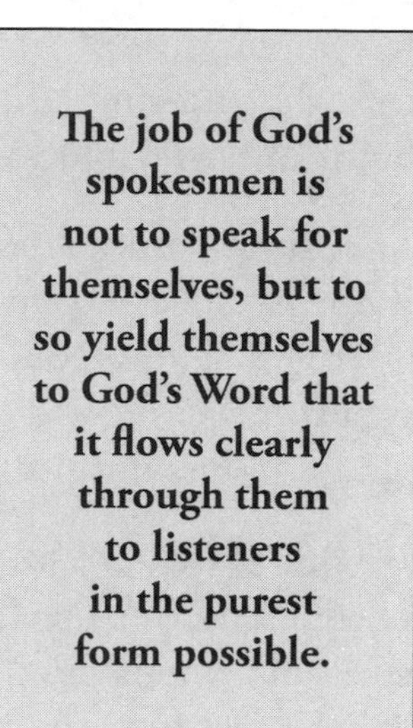

Never forget that when the Bible is taught correctly, it has a sobering effect on people. It helps them keep their thoughts in line with God's truth, bear fruit to His glory in the circumstances of life, and remain stable and secure in times of uncertainty.

We're in the last days that the Holy Spirit prophesied about, warning us that some leaders will go astray in their doctrine. Therefore, it is imperative that we diligently pray for skilled, solid Bible teachers to be raised up who will feed the pure Word of God to those whose hearts are crying out for it.

Are You Sure You Know What the Bible Teaches?

Some in today's Church are ignorant of the most elementary aspects of New Testament doctrine. Some who occupy the pulpits — although they may be masterful communicators and anointed exhorters of the Word — are uneducated in basic Bible principles. Some may not feel capable or qualified to teach verse by verse.

Furthermore, many who know the Bible don't preach it as strongly as they once did because it's not as popular as other types of messages. The temptation is great to shy away from anything, even biblical, that involves correction — "reproving or rebuking" (*see* 2 Timothy 4:2). As a result of these and a myriad of other factors, the end-time drift from Scriptures prophesied by the Holy Spirit in First Timothy 4:1 is indeed taking place.

This underlines the great need to be a real student of the Bible if one is called to stand in a position of spiritual leadership. Just as crucial is the requirement of a spiritual leader to maintain a robust prayer life and an intimate personal walk with God, which always results in spiritual boldness.

But as we have seen, this end-time drift is not an entirely new phenomenon in the Church, because seducing spirits with doctrines of demons also showed up in the early centuries to lead God's people away from the authoritative teaching of Scripture. The Early Church was also combating the infiltration of doctrinal error and spiritual extremes, which led Early Church leaders to come together at certain key times to write a fixed doctrinal statement of non-negotiable New Testament truths.

Such early creeds were established to bring order to the theological madness that was erupting throughout the Christian world. Error-ridden leaders were gradually leading the Church off track doctrinally. Because of this situation, these Early Church leaders set down non-negotiable tenets of the Christian faith and used them to determine right or wrong doctrine.

These fixed doctrines were viewed as the most important tenets of the Christian faith and were never to be modified. Although there was room for dialogue on other points, *these* points were to be embraced and proclaimed as official doctrines of the Christian faith all over the world. And through the centuries, the creeds that these Early Church leaders established have proven to be great aids in keeping the Church on track, at least in these essential, foundational tenets of faith.

Through the centuries, the creeds that these Early Church leaders established have proven to be great aids in keeping the Church on track, at least in these essential, foundational tenets of faith.

Many creeds have been written over the course of the centuries. But in the paragraphs that follow, I want to give you the earliest and most noteworthy creeds of the Early Church that helped form the basis for Christian belief today. These early creeds contain the non-negotiable, immutable New Testament truths that still remain the basis of faith for Christians worldwide.

The Old Roman Creed (circa Second Century AD)

The Old Roman Creed is an early version of what later became known as The Apostles' Creed. Written in the Second Century, it is the earliest known creed of the Christian faith and is widely believed to be the first creed.[20] It was so well known in the Early Church that even Tertullian and Irenaeus cited it in their works.[21]

In the late Fourth Century, an Early Church leader named Tyrannius Rufinus wrote a commentary on this creed in Latin, where he recounted the viewpoint that the apostles originally authored the creed together after Pentecost, before leaving Jerusalem to preach elsewhere.[22] A very early document that has survived from 390 AD described it as "the creed of the Apostles."[23]

[20]John Norman Davidson Kelly, *Early Christian Creeds* (London: Longman, 1972), p. 101.
[21]Kelly, *Creeds*, pp. 100-130.
[22]Rufinus, *Commentarius in Symbolum Apostolorum*, (P.L. xxi. 335B).
[23]Ambrose, from a Council in Milan to Pope Siricius in about AD 390. Ambrose wrote, "Let them give credit to the Creed of the Apostles, which the Roman Church has always kept and preserved undefiled." Ambrose of Milan, Letter 42.5, Tertullian.org.

The text of the Old Roman Creed is as follows:

I believe in God the Father Almighty;
and in Christ Jesus His only Son, our Lord,
Who was born of the Holy Spirit and the Virgin Mary,
Who under Pontius Pilate was crucified and buried,
on the third day rose again from the dead,
ascended to Heaven,
sits at the right hand of the Father,

whence He will come to judge the living and the dead;
and in the Holy Spirit,
the holy Church,
the remission of sins,
the resurrection of the flesh
(the life everlasting).[24]

Nicene Creed (circa 325 AD)

The Nicene Creed was composed in the year 325 AD at the famous convocation of bishops who gathered at Nicaea, a city in Asia Minor, to refute an error about the divinity of Christ that was beginning to be embraced in many churches at that time. Historians state that approximately 300 bishops convened, traveling from throughout the Roman Empire, to develop a doctrinal statement of faith that would refute the doctrinal error that was being propagated at that time. Nearly 1,800 people attended this historical event, if one counted both bishops and other appointed delegates who attended.

The text of the Nicene Creed is as follows:

---

[24]Kelly, *Creeds*, p. 102.

We believe in one God, the Father, the Almighty,
maker of heaven and earth,
of all that is, seen and unseen.
We believe in one Lord,
Jesus Christ, the only Son of God,
eternally begotten of the Father,
God from God, Light from Light,
true God from true God, begotten,
not made, of one Being with the Father.
Through him all things were made.
For us and for our salvation
He came down from heaven:
by the power of the Holy Spirit
He became incarnate from the Virgin Mary,
and was made man.
For our sake He was crucified under Pontius Pilate;
He suffered death and was buried.
On the third day he rose again
in accordance with the Scriptures;
He ascended into Heaven
and is seated at the right hand of the Father.
He will come again in glory to judge the living and the dead,
and His Kingdom will have no end.
We believe in the Holy Spirit, the Lord, the Giver of life,
who proceeds from the Father.
With the Father and the Son
He is worshiped and glorified.
He has spoken through the prophets.
We believe in one holy catholic [universal]
and apostolic Church.
We acknowledge one baptism for the forgiveness of sins.
We look for the resurrection of the dead,
and the life of the world to come. Amen.

The Apostles' Creed (circa 390 AD)

What is called The Apostle's Creed dates back to approximately 140 AD in its oldest form, which is known as The Old Roman Creed (*see* previous discussion). Its present form is believed to date to approximately 390 AD. Early Church fathers referred to it as "the rule of faith." It is considered a condensed compilation of the teachings of the apostles, which is why it was referred to as The Apostles' Creed.

This historical creed covers the unchallengeable core beliefs of the Christian faith. Through the centuries that followed, it was used like a "truth filter" to determine what was and wasn't genuine Christian doctrine. This particular creed is still widely used today in major denominations throughout the Church world.

The text of The Apostles' Creed is as follows:

**I believe in God, the Father Almighty,
the Creator of heaven and earth,
and in Jesus Christ, His only Son, our Lord:
Who was conceived of the Holy Spirit,
born of the Virgin Mary,
suffered under Pontius Pilate,
was crucified, died, and was buried.
He descended into hell.
The third day He arose again from the dead.
He ascended into heaven
and sits at the right hand of God the Father Almighty,
whence He shall come to judge the living and the dead.
I believe in the Holy Spirit,
the holy catholic [universal] church,
the communion of saints,**

the forgiveness of sins,
the resurrection of the body,
and life everlasting. Amen.

Based on New Testament Scriptures and the historical teachings of the Church, these creeds were composed to put forth the non-negotiable doctrines of the Christian faith for every church and every Christian.

After reading these creeds, you'd do well to stop and ponder this question for a moment: *How well do I know these non-negotiable Bible doctrines?*

These creeds don't hold optional or inconsequential doctrines. They are the very center of your faith. Although the creeds are not Scripture in themselves, they contain truths from the Word of God that represent the earliest foundational beliefs of the Christian faith, and they are worthy of your consideration.

As I prepared to write this chapter, I visited a great number of church and ministry websites to read their official tenets of faith posted on their websites. I was struck by the fact that Charismatic churches generally do not have a unified statement of faith that is consistent from church to church and from ministry to ministry.

Some statements of faith are well written; others are minimally stated; and still others are vague, almost giving the impression that they do not want to take a position on major Bible doctrines. Yet it's so important that churches and ministries are able to intelligently communicate what they believe to be the foundational doctrines of the Christian faith on which they are established.

There is no getting around it — *what we believe is very important.*

I understand that people who visit websites aren't going to be interested in reading a theological treatise on doctrine. I also understand that time and space don't permit everything to be included in our tenets of faith that we'd like to include. But based on the teachings of the Bible and these reliable creeds of the Early Church, I want to recommend a set of foundational tenets of faith for your life. The following is provided as a suggested statement of faith to be used by you, your family, your congregation, or even by your church, ministry, or organizational website.

After reading the discussion in this book thus far, if you believe it would be good to update your church or organization's statement of faith, please feel free to use the following as needed.

Suggested Tenets of Faith

THE SCRIPTURES

The Bible, containing the Old and New Testaments, is alone the only infallible, inspired Word of God, and its authority is ultimate, final, and eternal. It cannot be added to, subtracted from, or superseded in any regard. It has God for its Author, salvation for its end, and truth, without any mixture of error, for its matter. The Bible is the source of all doctrine, instruction, correction, and reproof. It contains all that is needed for guidance in godliness and practical Christian conduct. Scripture is inerrant and the authoritative rule of faith and conduct. (*See* 2 Timothy 3:16; 1 Thessalonians 2:13; 2 Peter 1:21.)

GOD

There is One and only One living and true God. The eternal triune God reveals Himself to us as Father, Son, and Holy Spirit — three distinct Persons — with distinct personal attributes, but without division of nature, essence, or being. (*See* Matthew 3:13-17; Matthew 28:18-20; John 1:1; John 14:26; John 17:3; Romans 3:30; James 2:19.)

GOD THE FATHER

God the Father reigns with care over His created universe and over all His creatures, including man, who is created in His image. God orchestrates human history according to the purposes of His grace. God is Father in truth to those who become children of God through faith in Jesus Christ. (*See* Ephesians 1:3-10; 1 John 3:1.)

GOD THE SON

Christ is the eternal Son of God. Jesus Christ was conceived of the Holy Spirit and born of the virgin Mary. He honored the divine law by His personal obedience, and in His substitutionary death on the Cross, He made provision for the redemption of men from sin. He was physically raised from the dead on the third day and ascended into Heaven, where He is seated at the Father's right hand as the Head of the Church. (*See* John 1:1; Hebrews 1:2; Matthew 1:18; Hebrews 5:8; Ephesians 1:7; 1 Corinthians 15:3-8; Acts 1:9; Hebrews 10:12; Ephesians 1:20,21.)

GOD THE HOLY SPIRIT

The Holy Spirit is the Spirit of God and is fully divine. He exalts Christ. He convicts men of sin, of righteousness, and of judgment. He calls men to Christ and effects regeneration. He supernaturally produces Christian character, comforts believers, and bestows spiritual gifts by which believers serve God through His Church. The Holy Spirit seals believers unto the day of final redemption, and He empowers believers in worship, evangelism, and service.

(*See* 2 Corinthians 3:17,18; John 16:8-14; Titus 3:5; Galatians 5:22,23; John 14:16-21; 1 Corinthians 12:7-11; 2 Corinthians 1:21,22; Ephesians 1:13,14; Acts 1:8.)

MAN, HIS FALL, AND HIS REDEMPTION

Man is a created being, made in the likeness and image of God. But through Adam's transgression and fall, sin came into the world. Man thereby incurred not only physical death but also spiritual death and all of its ramifications. Man's willful transgression brought about separation from God and put the entire human race in need of redemption. Jesus Christ, the Son of God, was manifested to undo the works of the devil. He gave His life and shed His blood to redeem and restore man back to God. Because man is created in God's image, every person of every race possesses dignity and is worthy of respect and Christian love. (*See* Genesis 1:26-28; Romans 5:12-15; 1 Corinthians 15:20-22; James 3:9; Romans 3:10,23; Romans 5:14; 1 John 3:8.)

SALVATION

Man's only hope of salvation is through the blood of Jesus Christ. Salvation is the gift of God to man, separate from works and the Law, and is made operative by grace through faith in Jesus Christ, producing works acceptable to God. Salvation is received through repentance by acknowledging Jesus as Lord and placing one's faith in Christ's redemptive work alone. There is salvation in no other name. Salvation is necessary to all men, and when it is experienced, produces eternal life. (*See* John 3:3-5; Ephesians 2:8-10; Acts 4:12; 2 Corinthians 7:10; 1 John 5:12.)

SANCTIFICATION

We believe sanctification is a definite, yet progressive work of grace, commencing at the time of regeneration and continuing until the consummation of salvation at Christ's return. Although sanctification occurs instantly when a person is saved, it is also an ongoing process that occurs as a believer reckons himself dead to sin and alive to God, relies daily upon the power of the Holy Spirit, and submits himself to the control of the Holy Spirit. (*See* Hebrews 12:14; 1 Thessalonians 5:23; 2 Peter 3:18; 2 Corinthians 3:18; Philippians 3:12-14; 1 Corinthians 1:30.)

THE CHURCH

The Church is the habitation of God through the Spirit on the earth. It is visibly experienced in a local congregation of water-baptized believers who are related by faith and fellowship of the Gospel, whose lives and conduct are governed by the Word of God, who exercise the spiritual gifts, rights, and privileges invested in them by grace, and who seek to extend the Gospel to the ends of the earth. The local church is commissioned by Christ to evangelize the lost in the power of the Holy Spirit. It is where believers worship and where saints are perfected and matured. (*See* 1 Corinthians 1:2; Hebrews 10:25; 1 Corinthians 12:12-14; James 5:14.)

WATER BAPTISM

Scripture commands all who repent and who receive Jesus Christ as Lord to be water-baptized. In this act, Christians declare to the world that they have died with Christ and have been raised with Him to walk in the newness of life. Water baptism is not a requirement for salvation, but it *is* a required part of embarking on a life of obedience for every Christian. (*See* Matthew 28:19; Romans 6:4; Colossians 2:12; Acts 8:36-39.)

COMMUNION
(THE LORD'S SUPPER)

The Scriptures established Communion as an ordinance to be celebrated until Jesus comes. The Lord's Supper consists of the elements — bread and the fruit of the vine — which represent the broken body and shed blood of the Lord Jesus Christ and serve as symbols that remind us of our unbroken covenant with Him. In addition, healing and restoration are released as believers receive the Communion elements and by faith appropriate the redemptive work of Christ those elements represent. (*See* Matthew 26:26-28; Luke 22:19,20; John 6:48-51; Acts 2:42-46; 1 Corinthians 11:17-34.)

LAST THINGS

In His own time and in His own way, God will bring this age to its appropriate conclusion. At the end of this age, Jesus Christ will return personally and visibly. The dead will be raised, and Christ will judge all men in righteousness. The unrighteous will be consigned to hell, and the righteous will receive their reward and will dwell forever with the Lord. (*See* Matthew 16:27; 2 Corinthians 5:9-11; 1 Thessalonians 5:1-3; Revelation 1:7; Revelation 22:12.)

RESURRECTION

Jesus Christ was physically resurrected from the dead in a glorified body three days after His death on the Cross. We believe in the return of the resurrected Christ for His saints, both those alive on the earth and those preceding them in death. Both the saved and the lost will ultimately be resurrected — those who are saved to the resurrection of life and those who are lost to eternal damnation and death. (*See* 1 Thessalonians 4:16,17; Revelation 20:6.)

HELL AND ETERNAL RETRIBUTION

The one who physically dies in his sins without accepting Christ is eternally lost in the lake of fire and therefore has no further opportunity of hearing the Gospel or of repenting. The lake of fire is literal. The terms "eternal" and "everlasting," used in describing the duration of the punishment of the damned in the lake of fire, carry the same thought and meaning of endless existence as used in denoting the duration of joy and ecstasy of saints in the presence of God. (*See* Hebrews 9:27; Revelation 19:20.)

THE FINAL JUDGMENT

The Bible teaches that there will be a final judgment in which the wicked dead will be raised and judged according to their works. Whosoever is not found written in the Book of Life, together with the devil and his angels and the beast and the false prophet, will be consigned to everlasting punishment in the lake that burns with fire and brimstone, which is the second death. (*See* Revelation 20:6-15.)

THE GREAT COMMISSION

It is the duty and privilege of every believer and church to actively endeavor to make disciples of all nations. We are charged by Christ to constantly seek to win the lost through our verbal witness, undergirded by a Christian lifestyle and by other methods that are in harmony with the Gospel of

Christ. In accordance with the Great Commission, every church should prayerfully and financially be committed to reach the ends of the earth with the Gospel of Jesus Christ. (*See* Matthew 28:19,20; Acts 1:8.)

Other Foundational Tenets

In addition to the above points, I recommend adding the following to a basic statement of faith. Even though these points are not mentioned directly in ancient creeds of the Church, these are vital to establishing a strong foundation of sound Charismatic doctrine.

THE BAPTISM IN THE HOLY SPIRIT

The baptism in the Holy Spirit is a promise offered to all believers that is distinct from the new birth. With it comes power for life, power for service, and the bestowment of gifts of the Holy Spirit. It is evidenced by the physical sign of speaking with other tongues as the Spirit of God gives utterance. (*See* Matthew 3:11; John 14:16; Acts 1:8; Acts 2:4 ; Acts 2:38,39; Acts 19:1-6.)

THE GIFTS OF THE HOLY SPIRIT

The gifts of the Holy Spirit are supernatural endowments that equip believers, contribute to the edifying and building up of the Church, and demonstrate Christ's power and character to the world. These gifts are operational in the Church today and will continue to operate until the end of the Church Age. (*See* Romans 12:5-8; 1 Corinthians 1:5-9; 1 Corinthians 12-14.)

HEALING

It is God's will to heal the sick through various means — including, but not limited to, the laying on of hands, the prayer of faith, anointing with oil, and the operation of the gifts of the Holy Spirit. Furthermore, healing is provided in the redemptive work of Christ and is available to every believer everywhere. (*See* Mark 16:18; James 5:14,15; 1 Peter 2:24; Matthew 8:17; Isaiah 53:4,5.)

STEWARDSHIP

God is the Source of all blessings. All that we have, we ultimately owe to Him. God commands His people to be good stewards. Christians have a spiritual obligation to the entire world, a holy trusteeship in the Gospel, and a binding stewardship in their possessions. They are therefore under obligation to serve Him with their time, talents, and material possessions as He so directs. (*See* Psalm 24:1; James 1:17; Matthew 25:21; 1 Peter 4:10; 2 Corinthians 9:6,7.)

Finally, the core teaching of Scripture on marriage and family is needed during these last days to provide clear direction for many in today's world who are confused as society continues to veer away from biblical truth and to embrace distorted, unscriptural views about marriage, family, and children.

Believers, churches, ministries, and Christian organizations must be absolutely clear about what the Scriptures state about these subjects, because the lines are being blurred by a society that is going morally mad as we approach the end of the age. I therefore recommend that the following also be added to your official statement of faith.

MARRIAGE AND FAMILY

The Bible teaches that God ordained the family as the foundational institution of human society. The family unit is composed of persons related to one another by marriage, blood, or adoption (or connected through guardianship). Marriage is the uniting of one man and one woman in a lifetime marital covenant. A husband is to love his wife as Christ loves the Church. He has the God-given responsibility to provide for, to protect, and to lead his family. A wife is to submit herself graciously to the servant leadership of her husband and to respect him even as the Church willingly submits to the headship of Christ. She is created in the image of God, as is her husband, and is thus equal to him.

Furthermore, from the moment of conception, children are a blessing and a heritage from the Lord to be treasured and raised up according to the principles of Scripture, and parents are to demonstrate to their children God's pattern for marriage. (*See* Ephesians 5:21-32; Ephesians 6:1-4; 1 Peter 3:1-9; Psalm 127:3,4; Deuteronomy 4:9,10; Deuteronomy 6:7.)

Other wide-ranging points of doctrine are theologically open to intellectual dialogue and even differing views. But regarding these key foundational truths of the Christian faith, there is simply no room for negotiation. These are the immutable doctrines of our faith — and as such, they need to be taught, embraced, and affirmed.

In the preceding chapters, I showed you that even while the New Testament was still being written, poisonous error was being comingled with truth that the apostles stood up to refute. As we have seen, the pressure to modify the faith has been around since the inception of the Church.

In the late hour of this age, it important that spiritual leaders acknowledge what they believe, accept the responsibility to speak accurately and clearly for God as His spokesmen, and call the Church back to the authoritative voice of the Bible. We must dig our heels into Scripture and resolve to *receive* nothing, *believe* nothing, and *follow* nothing that cannot be found in or proved by the Bible.

We must dig our heels into Scripture and resolve to *receive* nothing, *believe* nothing, and *follow* nothing that cannot be found in or proved by the Bible.

In the following chapter, I wish to take you into Peter's words about the paramount importance of God's Word. As Peter made clear in his epistle (*see* 2 Peter 1:17,18), even his unparalleled experience with Christ on the Mount of Transfiguration, as glorious as it was, is outranked by the power of God's written Word!

Think About It

1. The enemy looks for any possible point of access into our personal lives and in the life of the Church. His aim is always to derail and dismantle what God has said will come to pass. The devil's worst nightmare is the fulfillment of God's great plan — the last-days outpouring of His Spirit throughout the earth that precedes Jesus' return. Satan knows the horror that defines his future on the other side of that moment on the divine timeline.

   What have you received from the Lord that is a promise attached to your destiny in Him? Have you made sure that every possible door of access is shut to the enemy so he can't find a way in to derail that promise before you ever reach the moment of its fulfillment?

2. There is a downward trend in progress within the modern-day Church as some spiritual leaders deviate from the solid path of God's eternal truth and try to become more "relevant" to the world around them. Too often this pursuit of relevance has replaced reverence for His holy words.

   Have you ever gotten caught up in trying to blend in with those around you, even if it meant "dumbing down" your firm stance on the Word of God? On the other hand, have you ever chosen to stand out as one of God's spokesmen in a situation and it cost you dearly?

   In this day you will have many opportunities to choose one or the other response. Have you taken time with the Lord to sort out what you're going to do in those challenging moments on the road ahead? *Get it settled* — you're going to stand strong for Him and let Him demonstrate His heart through you the next time truth needs to be enforced to dispel error!

3. Error doesn't always come with a red hat on, announcing its presence. The enemy's ways can be subtle and seductive in their deceptive allure. The Bible says the devil masquerades as an angel of light (*see* 2 Corinthians 11:14).

   Are you solid in your own doctrinal foundation of the basic, non-negotiable truths of the Christian faith? Would you be able to detect "just a pinch of error" being added to a feast of truth so you and those around you could avoid being spiritually sickened? And in such a case, are you ready to stand firm — alone if necessary — as God's "spiritual antidote," ready to speak His truth to help purity be restored?

Chapter Eight

NO HIGHER REVELATION

We've discussed the strong stance against error that the apostle Paul made as he wrote his New Testament epistles inspired by the Holy Spirit. Now let's look at how the apostle Peter addressed the doctrinal errors of his time. I want to take you to *his* words on this matter so you can get a better understanding of the paramount importance of God's Word in our lives. As you will see, everything — including personal opinion and personal experience — must always take a back seat to the authoritative voice of Scripture.

Times may change, and seducing spirits may try to introduce doctrines of demons into the world and even into the Church. But in the midst of it all, there must be those who hold fast to the Word and choose to build their lives on the infallible revelation of God's Word.

Times may change, and seducing spirits may try to introduce doctrines of demons into the world and even into the Church. But in the midst of it all, there must be those who hold fast to the Word and build their lives on the infallible revelation of God's Word — the bedrock of eternal truth that He gave to mankind to live by.

As I've explained in earlier chapters, there were some influential spiritual leaders in the First Century who were attempting to alter the faith. Simultaneously, Gnostic teachers were luring believers into bizarre revelations and teachings that were unsubstantiated by the Word of God. But because their presentations were tantalizing, large numbers of people were being drawn away from the solid teaching of Scripture into off-base teachings and strange spiritual experiences.

Peter addressed these issues strongly in his epistles. And, evidently, when Jude read a copy of Peter's epistle, he was so stirred by it that he wrote to his own readers, telling them to "...earnestly contend for the faith which was once delivered unto the saints" (v. 3). In his epistle, Jude urged those early believers not to give place to the error-filled teaching that was beginning to proliferate in the Church at that time (*see* Chapter Four).

As Peter addressed the problematic leaders who were departing from the time-tested truths of Scripture, he began by describing his own experience on the Mount of Transfiguration. This was quite strategic, for what Peter experienced on that day represented an actual, unparalleled event — far greater than any fanciful tale that was being devised and disseminated in the Church by false revelators at that time. And as Peter chronicled that event, he made it clear that as glorious as that supernatural encounter on the Mount of Transfiguration was, it took a back seat when compared to the authoritative and dependable voice of God's Word.

The Incomparable Weightiness of God's Word

We discussed in Chapter Three that seducing spirits with doctrines of demons were trying to lead the Church astray at that early moment in Church history. False teachers were propagating nonsensical doctrines and outrageous stories of supernatural experiences that had no connection to Scripture.

Certainly God wants to visit His people with amazing supernatural experiences, and He tells us clearly in His Word that this is a vital part of the working of the Holy Spirit in the Church. However, God works only in line with His Word, and the stories with which these false teachers tantalized their gullible listeners were of their own making and could not be supported by Scripture.

These Gnostic teachers were either fabricating stories with the intent to deceive or they were relating actual, demonically inspired supernatural happenings they had experienced by giving access to seducing spirits in their own lives. But whether they intended to deceive or simply deceived themselves, the outcome of their teaching was identical — spiritual infection was being spread through the Church.

It is clear that Peter had encountered some of these delusional teachings that Gnostic teachers were purporting. He was so alarmed by the way these teachers were twisting and distorting the Word of God that he chose to address this disturbing development.

These errant leaders claimed to be part of a superior, elite spiritual group who were on the cutting edge of new ideas. So as Peter addressed them and their twisted doctrines, he began by stating no one had experienced anything that could compare to what had occurred on the Mount of Transfiguration. On that holy mount, Peter, James, and John had been initiated into a small elite group of three who saw, heard, and experienced what no one else had ever seen, heard, or experienced. No Gnostic revelator could ever fabricate a tale to compete with what these three men *actually* experienced that day.

Yet despite the astonishing nature of Peter's divine experience on the holy mount, the apostle made it clear that even this heavenly visitation was eclipsed by the weightiness of God's Word. In fact, Peter declared that there is no higher revelation available to mankind than the Word of God — and that Scripture needs no modifications, alterations, or additions to make it more relevant to a society in a constant state of flux (*see* 1 Peter 1:23-25; 2 Peter 1:19-21).

In Second Peter 1:16, Peter's words actually incriminated notable voices that were twisting truth and fabricating outlandish tales at his time of writing. As we saw in Chapter Five, these leaders were endeavoring to make themselves more popular with large numbers of Christians by altering the Gospel in order to appeal to a wider audience. In addition to twisting truth, they were telling fantastic tales calculated to be attractive to people with pagan backgrounds.

Peter declared that there is no higher revelation available to mankind than the Word of God — and that Scripture needs no modifications, alterations, or additions to make it more relevant to a society in a constant state of flux.

But Peter *absolutely refused* to follow this pattern of modifying Scripture, and he *absolutely refused* to imply that any experience could possibly carry greater weight than God's Word itself. Make no mistake — Peter's words were intended to set the record straight and to establish a plumb line of truth between himself and those who were off base.

Cunningly Devised Fables

As Peter began, he wrote, "For we have not followed cunningly devised fables when we made known unto you the power and coming of our Lord Jesus Christ..." (2 Peter 1:16).

The phrase "cunningly devised" is a translation of the Greek word *sophidzo*, which describes something *cleverly contrived*, *made-up*, *concocted*, *fabricated*, or *invented*. Peter used the word *sophidzo* to assert that these false teachers were concocting tales to appeal to their listeners. Rather than soundly teaching the principles found in Scripture, these usurpers of truth would *use* Scripture in an attempt to substantiate and corroborate their imaginary fables. They'd devise a set of off-the-wall, delusional doctrines and fanciful tales of supernatural experiences and then use a few sparse verses from Scripture in an attempt to validate them. For these imposters, then, the Bible became a tool to build a frame around the error they were promoting to serve their own ends.

All of this was happening in the early days of the Church. Today in this end-time world we live in, errant leaders don't focus on outlandish tales for the most part. Nonetheless, many do allege to have their own upgraded version of truth. In this sense, these modern false teachers are also preaching messages that fit in the "fable" category, because the doctrines they endorse are far afield from the authentic teaching of the Bible. Like the false teachers of the First Century, these last-days errant leaders don't honor the Word of God as a holy treasure of His revelation to man. What some are preaching in various sectors of the Church could actually qualify as fables because their teachings are such a distortion of New Testament truth.

Let me give you an example that occurred not so long ago when one well-known Christian leader asserted that if the Bible is the foundation of a person's faith, that person's faith is "a fragile house of cards" that will eventually come tumbling down. This individual claimed that a Christianity built on the Bible hangs by a thread, and that we must adjust (alter) the message we preach if we're going to reach the next generation, because that generation simply will not believe the Bible as it has been previously believed — as uniquely the infallible, inspired Word of God.

This is simply a heretical statement that should not be tolerated from anyone in a spiritual leadership position, especially a visible one. Not only are the Scriptures the very center and core of *our* faith, but the Scriptures were also the central focus of both Jesus' and the apostles' teaching and preaching.

If members of the next generation are taught the Word accurately and then choose not to believe it, that is their right. But those of us who are older must not abandon or mitigate our belief in the inerrant Word of God just because some in the younger generation don't like it or find it "palatable."

The fact is, those who anchor their faith in the Bible are building their lives on an impenetrable Rock that will hold them up through every season of life (*see* Luke 6:48). Contrary to what the previously mentioned misled leader stated, *the only way to cultivate a well-established foundation is to anchor one's faith in the Word of God.*

Those who anchor their faith in the Bible are building their lives on an impenetrable Rock that will hold them up through every season of life.

Anyone who asserts or even *suggests* that the Bible is out of date is in error. The unfortunate result of errant leaders in the Church taking this unfortunate position is that followers who trust them will be led to believe that the Bible is unreliable and untrustworthy. The people's trust in the Word of God will therefore become diminished, and they will begin to move toward the eventual, "logical" conclusion that the Bible is just another holy book among many other holy books. In other words, many under this type of teaching will come to the dangerous conclusion that the Bible is not really God's Word — that it's just a book of principles, suggestions, and optional, "take it or leave it" spiritual theories. That conclusion is a road that will lead people directly into deception.

Tragically, unless such leaders repent, they and those who believe and follow them will eventually minimize the authority of Scripture and modify it to accommodate the culture. These same leaders will likely even begin to embrace and endorse sexual preferences that are in direct contradiction to certain teachings of the Bible.

You see, once the anchor of Scripture has been cut and cast aside, the ship will begin to veer further and further off course until it is altogether lost in a sea of confusion. This is precisely where the abandonment or modification of Scripture leads *unless* repentance occurs and a return to the Bible as God's authoritative voice takes place.

You are well aware that we live in an amazing age of information — a time when people have more data available to them than ever before. Traditional thinking on many fronts is being challenged, contested, disputed, and questioned. Many are rethinking what they believe. Some of this is positive. For instance, science and better education has opened doors to understanding that didn't exist before.

Once the anchor of Scripture has been cut and cast aside, the ship will begin to veer further and further off course until it is altogether lost in a sea of confusion.

But you and I must remember that what we believe, endorse, or publicly teach can impact people for all eternity. We need to be very careful in this age of questioning not to be so open-minded that we allow our minds to be deactivated, numbed, and closed to truth! When it comes to Scripture, we *must* keep our heads on straight!

This is why I advise all who teach or preach — and everyone who listens to them — to continually ask themselves, *Would the apostles who wrote the New Testament recognize the message I am preaching (or listening to) as truth?* If anyone is teaching information so new, so advanced, and so progressive that the apostles would not recognize it, we can know that this person has swerved far from the Gospel message and has ventured into gray areas.

As ministers of the Gospel, we *must* see Scripture as the central focus of what we are called to communicate. We are never to *use* the Bible simply to build a frame around a point we wish to make. This approach leads to manipulating the Word of God to cause it to say what *we* want it to say.

We must let the Bible speak for itself. Our role as God-called ministers is to study the Bible, to see accurately what it teaches on every subject, and then to present truth as it is presented in God's Word.

You see, the message of the Bible itself *is* the point.

Our role as God-called ministers is to study the Bible, to see accurately what it teaches on every subject, and then to present truth as it is presented in God's Word.

You see, the message of the Bible itself *is* the point.

Defective Doctrine and Its Inevitable Aftermath

Let's go back to what Peter said in Second Peter 1:16: "For we have not followed cunningly devised fables when we made known unto you the power and coming of our Lord Jesus Christ."

The word "fables" is a translation of the Greek word *muthos*. It is the same root from which we derive the word *myths*. By using this word to describe the misleading teachings of errant leaders, both then and now, Peter stated that what they endorse and teach is closer to mythology than to truth.

It is interesting that Paul also used this word "fables" in First Timothy 1:4 where he told Timothy, "Neither give heed to *fables* and endless genealogies...." In addition to that verse, Paul used this word "fables" again in First Timothy 4:7 when he said, "But refuse profane and old wives' *fables*...."

In First Timothy 1:4, Paul connected this fable-like teaching with what he called "*endless* genealogies." The word translated "endless" comes from a Greek word that demonstrates how far off track a teaching can become when it is not anchored in Scripture. It's the word *aperantos*, which depicts something that is *unrestrained*, *far-fetched*, or *off-base*.

Paul used this word *aperantos* in this verse to tell us that lunacy has a way of going *from bad to worse*. If those who embrace, endorse, or teach defective doctrines are not brought back into balance, there is no limit to the excess they can enter into. Why is that? Because they have cut loose the anchor of their belief system from the authoritative voice of Scripture.

If those who embrace, endorse, or teach defective doctrines are not brought back into balance, there is no limit to the excess they can enter into. Why is that? Because they have cut loose the anchor of their belief system from the authoritative voice of Scripture.

Furthermore, Paul also said in First Timothy 4:7 that those who abandon the anchor of God's infallible Word will eventually begin to produce error so disgusting that He considers it "profane." The word "profane" is a translation of the Greek word *bebelos*, which is a word that signifies something so *nasty* that it shouldn't be permitted inside a person's home. In fact, this word *bebelos* was even used to describe *manure*.

By using this Greek word, Paul informed us that defective doctrine — if it is allowed into the Church or into a believer's life — in due course will produce a stinking mess. Deceptive doctrine is nasty — and it has such long-term, detrimental effects that it should be treated like excrement.

Would we tolerate anyone dumping manure in the living room of our homes? *Of course not!* That is precisely why Paul used the word *bebelos* to describe defective doctrines. This was Paul's strong way of saying we must not tolerate error inside the Church or in our personal lives, because if we do, the deception of that error will give rise to a stinking mess in our lives.

But there is another very important meaning to the Greek word *bebelos* that must be taken into account. This was also the very word used among Greeks to describe *one who crossed a threshold without permission* or *an improper entrance into another realm*.

Paul's use of the word *bebelos* therefore may have held an additional meaning — that the errant leaders who were disseminating false doctrines and who told fanciful tales about spiritual experiences may have actually crossed a threshold into another realm that they had no permission from God to enter.

By trespassing into other spiritual dimensions that God never sanctioned them to cross, these leaders made themselves susceptible to deception. As a result, some came back from those other-worldly realms with bizarre tales and weird revelations originating from supernatural experiences that were real but not God-authorized. This may very well be the reason why the errant leaders and their listeners wandered off track.

The Mount of Transfiguration

Let's return now to Peter's words in Second Peter 1:16. The apostle continued, "For we have not followed cunningly devised fables when we made known unto you the *power* and coming of our Lord Jesus Christ." The word "power" in this verse is a translation of the word *dunamis*, which is a well-known and often-used Greek word that describes *explosively powerful strength* and *ability*.

In this verse, as Peter began to relate his experience on the Mount of Transfiguration, he vividly expressed what it actually felt like when the power of Jesus permeated and washed over him on that memorable day. You must remember that this was not Peter's first encounter with divine power. He had seen Jesus heal the sick, cast out demons, walk on water, multiply food, and even raise the dead. Yet despite all that Peter had experienced in his years of following Jesus, he had never observed the magnitude and scope of this kind of power. On that day on the Mount of Transfiguration, along with James and John, Peter experienced Jesus in all of His matchless power, strength, and ability.

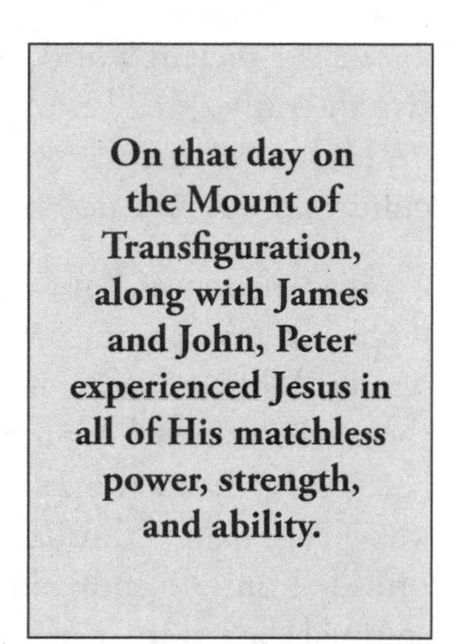

The way Peter chronicled his encounter with the Lord on the Mount of Transfiguration lets us know that this experience made such an impact on him that it was still fresh in his memory many years later. This personal, firsthand encounter was a deeply moving experience for him. On that mountain, Peter had tangibly experienced an unprecedented measure of divine power, seen Jesus in His glory, and heard the audible voice of God.

Eyewitnesses of His Majesty

Peter — still awestruck by this experience — took us by sequential steps through the events that he and the other two disciples experienced when they were with Jesus on the mountain that day. Peter wrote that he and his companions "...were eyewitnesses of his majesty."

The word "eyewitnesses" is a translation of the Greek word *epoptes*, which means *to look on* and was used to describe *a bystander who personally witnessed something with his own eyes.* This word *epoptes* was significantly used by Greeks to describe *individuals who were initiated into the highest levels of mystery religions.*

In the ancient world, pagan mystery religions were very secretive and only a small elite group was allowed into the higher levels. To become a part of the higher echelon in one of these mystery cults, one was required to go through a rite of initiation.

If a person was not willing to become a participant — in other words, *to look on* and *take part in* the initiation — that person was prohibited from going any higher in that mystery cult. But those who *were* willing to actively participate in the initiation process were welcomed into the upper ranks of those religions. Special knowledge gained through access to the secrets of their religion was provided only to individuals who were inducted into the highest spiritual class of their religious community.

Of course, Peter knew all of this when he used the Greek word *epoptes* in Second Peter 1:16, and all these layers of meaning were included when he wrote in this verse that he was an "eyewitness" of Jesus' majesty. The meaning of the word translated "eyewitnesses" makes it clear that Peter was in actuality telling his readers, *"We who were on the Mount of Transfiguration had an encounter that only we have experienced. This staggering encounter with Christ inducted us into the highest level of spiritual experience and initiated us into an elite group of three. Only WE experienced Jesus in this powerful way."*

In the truest sense, by using the word "eyewitnesses" — the Greek word *epoptes* — Peter made a clear statement to his reading audience. He candidly stated that he and the other disciples who were with him on the Mount of Transfiguration saw what no other eye had ever seen, heard what no other ear had ever heard, and experienced a supernatural encounter with Christ that only he and two others — James and John — had ever experienced.

Beholding the Majesty of Jesus Christ

By the time Peter finished describing this supernatural experience, those who were spreading their own false tales must have been captivated — because they would have known his story was real. In just one encounter, Peter had experienced a divine encounter with an extraordinary demonstration of supernatural power and, as a result, had been initiated into an enlightened, exclusive group of three.

Yet even in the recollection of this spectacular experience, notice what stood out foremost in Peter's mind as he recalled this experience. He wrote that he and the other two disciples "...were eyewitnesses of *his majesty*."

The word translated "majesty" comes from the Greek word *megaleiotes*, which was used to illustrate *the splendor and magnificence of a dignitary*. Exalted dignitaries were so splendid in appearance that their presence could cause commoners to fall on their faces in adoration. Peter used this word *megaleiotes* as he recalled his time on that mountain to let us know that *this* was his own response when he saw Jesus transfigured in the manifested display of His full glory. It was such a holy and magnificent divine encounter that it caused Peter to fall prostrate before Christ in humble adoration.

This was Peter's own response when he saw Jesus transfigured in the manifested display of His full glory. It was such a holy and magnificent divine encounter that it caused Peter to fall prostrate before Christ in humble adoration.

Then Peter wrote, "For he [Christ] received from God the Father honour and glory, when there came such a voice to him from the excellent glory, This is my beloved Son in whom I am well pleased. And this voice which came from heaven we heard, when we were with him in the holy mount" (2 Peter 1:17,18).

The revelation of Jesus in all His glory that Peter received that day was still as fresh as ever in the apostle's heart as when he wrote his second epistle. What was revealed to Peter that day on the Mount of Transfiguration changed his life so dramatically that years later, he related this life-transforming account as if it had just occurred.

A More Sure Word of Prophecy

After relating his personal experience of such an unprecedented and unique supernatural encounter, Peter continued by stating that as great as this experience was, something else remained that was more dependable for him and all others to build their lives and their faith upon. He wrote, "We have also a more sure word of prophecy; whereunto ye do well that ye take heed as unto a light that shineth in a dark place, until the day dawn, and the day star arise in your hearts" (2 Peter 1:19).

In this verse, Peter called the Word of God "a more sure word of prophecy." The words "more sure" are a translation of the Greek word *bebaios*, which depicts something that is *authenticated, verified, guaranteed, established, made firm, sure*, or *steadfast*. It speaks of something *proven to be true* and so certain that it *carries legal authority*.

By using this word, Peter was telling us that as wonderful as his experience was on the mountaintop, it was nonetheless a fleeting experience that dimmed in contrast to the Word of God that, as he firmly stated, is "more sure" than anything else. In other words, if Peter had to choose which is most important — experience or the Scriptures — the choice had already been made. He categorically proclaimed that God's Word carries more weight and authority than anything and that *nothing* compares to the absolute and unchanging truths of Scripture.

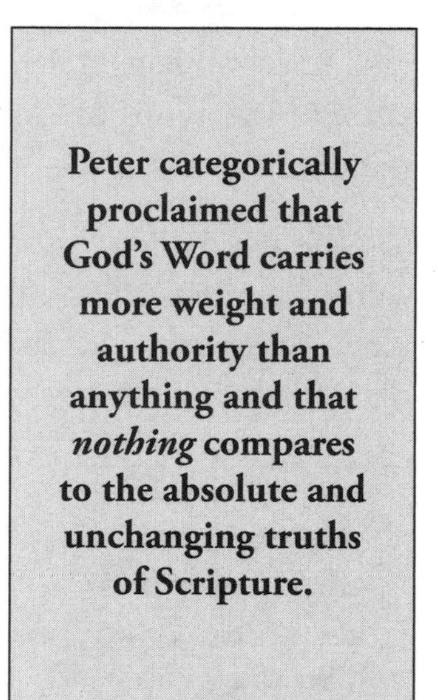

Peter was so convinced that the Word of God is superior to everything else that he went on to stress, "Whereunto ye do well to take heed as unto a light that shineth in a dark place." The phrase "to take heed as unto" is a translation of the Greek word *prosecho*, which means *to give one's full attention to a matter*; *to apply the mind to a thing*; or *to give serious consideration and contemplation to what is being heard, seen, or witnessed*. By using this word in connection with the authority of Scripture, Peter was actually saying, *"If you're going to be preoccupied with something, make sure your preoccupation is with the Scriptures, because they are more dependable than anything else."*

Peter wasn't dismissing the importance of experience with this clear statement, but because Scripture is dependable and without error, Peter wanted his readers — and us — to know that if we are going to have a preoccupation with anything of a spiritual nature, that preoccupation should be upon the absolute truths of God's Word above all else!

Real Spiritual Light

In Second Peter 1:19, as Peter described the paramount importance of the Word of God, he stated that Scripture is "a light that shineth in a dark place."

The word "light" is a translation of the Greek word *luchnos*, a word that refers to an oil-burning lamp that was designed to give long-lasting light to dispel darkness. The word "shineth" describes the action of those lamps. It is a translation of the Greek word *phaino*, which means *to shine* and is used in the present active tense to depict *a light that shines continuously*.

The Scriptures are God's lamp to give continuous light to a people or society that would lie in darkness if the light of God's Word was removed.

If we stopped here, this word already tells us that the Scriptures are God's lamp to give continuous light to a people or society that would lie in darkness if the light of God's Word was removed. Only the light of God's Word drives away spiritual darkness — which is why demonic forces hate the Light *and* the Light-bearers!

But Peter further stated that the Scriptures carry light into each "dark place." The phrase "dark place" is translated from the Greek word *auchmeros*, a word that depicts a place that is *dark*, *dreary*, or *murky*. By using this word,

Peter declared that when the Word of God is heralded, embraced, and believed, it continuously shines its brilliant light into the dark, dreary, and murky places of our lives and the society we live in.

When biblical truth is proclaimed in its purity, it acts in the same way that a lamp provides light for a darkened room in the natural realm. God's truth that is embraced shines light into every sphere of life, bringing understanding and enlightenment and eradicating the ignorance that governs darkened minds.

It is a spiritual law that truth produces light. Whenever a person reads and gives heed to God's Word, allowing its powerful light to shine into his or her life, that light will dispel spiritual darkness. This is true on a personal level, but the effect is greatly magnified when the life-giving light of Scripture shines throughout society at large. Wherever the Bible is widely proclaimed, embraced, and believed, society as a whole is bettered. Widespread agreement based on God's principles serves to drive away many of the ill effects that can accompany spiritual darkness.

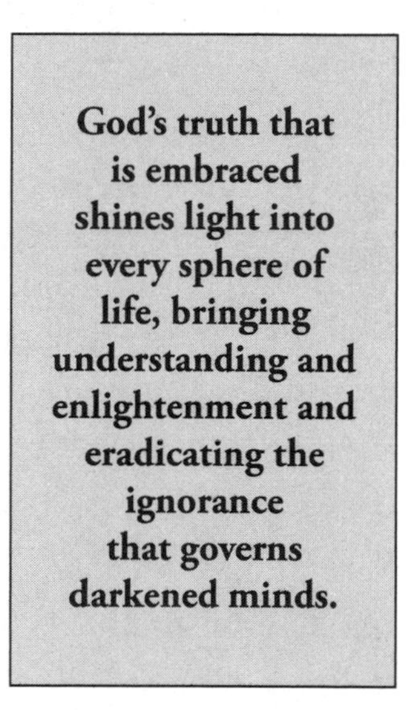
God's truth that is embraced shines light into every sphere of life, bringing understanding and enlightenment and eradicating the ignorance that governs darkened minds.

But in Second Peter 1:19, Peter continued by saying that you must allow the Scriptures to shine their light "...until the day dawn, and the day star arise in your hearts." With this phrase, Peter painted a picture of the morning sunrise that dispels the darkness of night.

When the sun's light first appears over the horizon each morning, its light at first seems dim. But as the sun rises higher in the sky, its light grows brighter until darkness is eliminated altogether. Likewise, when the Gospel first comes to a person or nation, its light begins to shine dimly. But as it is more widely believed and its light becomes more widespread, that person or society is more and more dramatically transformed. In the case of society, every institution begins to be impacted — education, business, government, the entertainment industry, etc. — as darkness of deception is increasingly dispelled.

Scripture simply has to be diligently applied to a person's life or to society as a whole. Every time that occurs, the miracle happens again. Those who once sat in darkness and who lived with its dire effects are transitioned into light and all of its glorious benefits. Just as the sun rises each morning and progressively eradicates the darkness of night, a person or a society that accepts and embraces the truth of God's Word is progressively moved out of the realm of darkness into His light, where transformational change begins to occur.

History has proven this to be true, not only in the past, but even in this present time. Entire nations where darkness once ruled are being changed because of the penetrating light of God's Word. When the Bible is proclaimed, believed, and applied, it eradicates spiritual darkness, ignorance, disease, inequality, poverty, and racism. The Bible is a life-enhancer for all who benefit from its shining light.

In Second Peter 1:19, Peter also likened the brilliant light of Scripture to "the day star." The words "day star" refer to the shining light of the sun and its ability to entirely eliminate darkness. It is a translation of the Greek word *phospheros*, a word that is composed of the Greek words *phos* and *pheros*. The word *phos* is the Greek word for *light* and *pheros* is a word that means *to carry*. When these words are compounded as in this verse, the new word depicts Scripture as the chief instrument God uses to carry light into the dark places of peoples' lives and of society.

This clearly demonstrates why Satan hates biblical truth so much and wants to remove it from society in these end times. As long as the light of God's Word is shining, the effects of darkness are crippled and dismantled. But when His Word is degraded in the hearts of man, spiritual darkness is given license to gather strength. Seducing spirits with their devilish doctrines ensnare people through ignorance and deception as they manipulate those people's ability to see and think clearly.

We see this happening in the world around us today. As the Word of God is losing its once-honored place in the mainstream of society, darkness is filling the vacuum. A society that once had a general knowledge of God and His Word is progressively moving into a critical state of spiritual ignorance. As a result, defective thinking that leads to illogical conclusions with catastrophic results is wreaking havoc in people's lives. The lines between right and wrong are blurred — in fact, they are nearly gone — and people are losing the ability to know the difference even on the most basic level.

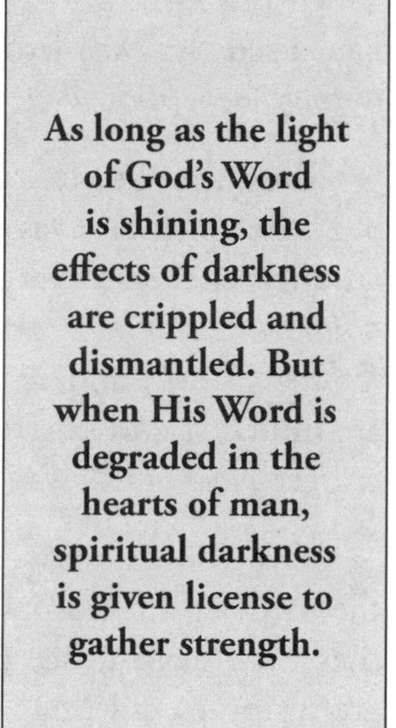
As long as the light of God's Word is shining, the effects of darkness are crippled and dismantled. But when His Word is degraded in the hearts of man, spiritual darkness is given license to gather strength.

Paul referred to the negative effect of spiritual blindness in people's lives and in society when he penned Second Corinthians 4:4. In that verse, he said, "In whom the god of this world hath blinded the minds of them which believe not, lest the light of the glorious gospel of Christ, who is the image of God, should shine unto them."

When Paul wrote that Satan has "blinded" the minds of unbelievers, he used the Greek word *tuphloo* for the word "blinded." This word *tuphloo* doesn't just depict a person who is unable to see; rather, it portrays a person who has been *intentionally and permanently blinded* by someone else who has deliberately removed that individual's eyes. This person hasn't just lost his sight; *he has no eyes to see.*

Paul said Satan has "blinded the *minds* of them which believe not." The word "minds" is a translation of the Greek word *noema*, which is a form of the word *nous*, the Greek word for the *mind.* Paul used this word to denote the *thoughts*, *reasoning*, *opinions*, *feelings*, *beliefs*, or *views* that a person or society holds.

Thus, the apostle was explicitly stating that Satan has "gouged out" the spiritual eyes of skeptics, unbelievers, and members of an unregenerate society to such a degree that *it has affected their ability to see things correctly.* Their *thoughts*, *reasonings*, *opinions*, *feelings*, *beliefs*, and *views* of what they perceive and experience are impeded and obstructed. As a result, they are *blinded* from a correct *view* of the way things really are.

If you have unsaved friends or relatives who seem blind to the truth of the Gospel, this verse may help you understand why they can't seem to see the true state of things or grasp what you are trying to tell them. It isn't that people in this spiritual state are naïve or unintelligent — they are *blind.* Satan has negatively affected their minds and blocked their view by gouging out their spiritual eyes. They have no eyes to see. Spiritual eyes can be created for them to enable them to see the truth, but this will only be possible as the light of God's Word is presented and received.

The fact is, we are living in the last of the last days, and events that were long ago prophesied in Scripture are unfolding before our very eyes. We have crossed the line and entered into the final phase of this last age. Thank God that by studying the Scriptures, we can identify the prophetic timeline and understand the times in which we live.

Armed with this knowledge, we must live soberly and remember that time is rapidly reaching the conclusion of this last-days age. So we must use wisely the time that remains to shine the glorious light of God's Word into the hearts of those whom Satan has blinded. This is why it is so important we don't stop preaching the Bible. And as we preach, we pray that the Holy Spirit gives the people spiritual eyes to truly see the truth presented to them and receive it as the answer to their deliverance.

We must use wisely the time that remains to shine the glorious light of God's Word into the hearts of those whom Satan has blinded.

The Problem Then and Now

The Holy Spirit forecasted that there would be an invasion of delusion into society at the end of the age and that it would even try to find its way into the Church. And we've seen how the danger of deception wasn't a challenge to be faced only by the end-time generation. False prophets and teachers spreading spiritual nonsense through the ranks of the young Church was already a problem that had to be dealt with when the apostles were penning the books of the New Testament.

Yet something was different regarding what the Holy Spirit said about the very end of the last days. He was preparing the Church for an *unprecedented* onslaught of deception in the days leading up to Jesus' return. And as those chosen by God to live in this generation, you and I will witness the events that were long ago prophesied about this time frame.

In First Timothy 4:1, the Holy Spirit clearly prophesied that an emergence of serious deception would arise in the world and even in the Church in this time. We can testify that this is occurring today as innovative and demonic moral agendas are relentlessly advanced, attempting to extend their tentacles into every corner of society and armed with their demand that the world abandon time-tested biblical truth in preference for political correctness that the rest of society approves.

Satan knows that his time is short, so he has released seducing spirits into the earth. These spirits are deceptively leading society and even segments of the Church into inclusionary beliefs and behaviors that are contradictory to the teachings of the New Testament and that would have been considered crazy just a short time ago.

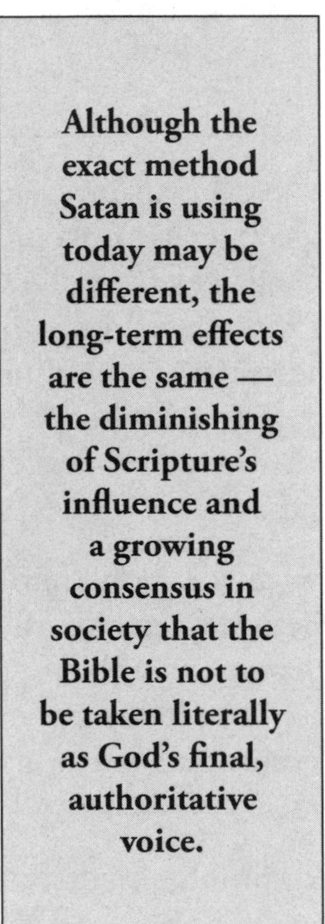

We've seen that in the earliest days of the Church, the apostles were charged with the task of identifying and bringing correction to deluded spiritual leaders. It didn't take long at all after the birth of the Church for these false leaders to "come out of the woodwork" and begin to try to replace truth with defective doctrines concocted to make Christianity more accommodating to society.

Today in this end-time hour, a present-day version of this demonic attempt to deceive is in place and increasing in momentum. Although the exact method Satan is using today may be different, the long-term effects are the same — the diminishing of Scripture's influence and a growing consensus in society that the Bible is not to be taken literally as God's final, authoritative voice.

When Peter wrote his second epistle, he was so concerned about false teachers who were beginning to negatively affect many people that he wrote extensively about the nature and characteristics of these errant leaders. He described vividly how they operate, explaining the process by which they digressed from being spiritually right to being spiritually wrong.

Peter also vividly laid out what the future holds for such false leaders if they don't repent and get back in line with biblical truth. Finally, Peter explained to believers what *they* are to do when they recognize that a spiritual leader has begun to take on characteristics of falsehood.

In the next chapter, we will explore more of Peter's words in Second Peter 2, where he addressed all of these issues. But the takeaway from this chapter that you must never forget is an absolutely essential one: There is *no* revelation higher than God's authoritative voice found in the pages of His matchless, eternal Word!

Think About It

1. God's words, when dispensed from and received into man's spirit, outweigh every other spiritual experience, no matter how glorious or spectacular. There is no higher revelation available, because God's Word holds the articulation of God's heart.

   Do you have a desire to become more intimate with the Lord? Are there areas in your life in which you need His wisdom? Set aside some focused time to get into the Word with a specific purpose in mind: *to know His heart better.*

   God has something specific He wants to say to you, and you'll know by the weight of the words your spiritual ears hear — the way those words quicken your heart and bring a greater understanding of Him and His ways. Every time you make the effort to partake of God's Word with this kind of intentional pursuit, you will tap again into His highest way of revealing truth to you.

2. Spiritual leaders who take the position that the Bible must stay "fluid" and must change with the times start an infectious process of replication among their followers who trust them to speak the truth.

   Have you witnessed that process in action in the lives of people around you? At one time they may have been convinced that the Bible is God's utterly faithful plumb line for absolute truth. Then over a period of time as they sat under this type of toxic teaching, their trust in the Word of God may have become diminished.

   What can you do to help reverse that process in the lives of your loved ones and friends? As you seek God for an answer to that question, stay constant in prayer; keep your spiritual ears tuned to the Holy Spirit's voice; and stay in the Word. Then what you hear, be sure to do. God will honor your hunger for the Word, and your steadfast stance for truth will be a stronger influence on your loved ones than any teacher peddling doubt and unbelief!

3. Only the light of God's Word drives away spiritual darkness, and fervent prayer provides the propulsive power. Can you think of a key situation in your own life when you experienced these truths firsthand? What scriptures did the Lord give you that became a sword in your hand to help turn that situation around?

CHAPTER NINE

A HEALTHY REMINDER TO BELIEVERS AND SPIRITUAL LEADERS

As we have discussed in previous chapters, there were spiritual leaders *inside* the Early Church that were advocating accommodation with the pagan world around them in order to provide a temporary respite from outside pressure. These errant spiritual leaders were beloved and well-known brothers within the Christian community, which therefore made it difficult for fellow believers to see them as evil.

The fact that these individuals occupied leadership positions in certain local churches suggests they had been long-term members of these congregations, since this would have been a requirement for visible leadership (*see* 1 Timothy 3:6). Yet despite these spiritual leaders' high-ranking positions in their local churches and the esteem of their fellow believers, something had caused them to succumb to evil by embracing the philosophy of compromise. The dark path they had chosen offered a temporary reprieve from earthly pressures but carried dangerous eternal ramifications.

When Peter wrote his second epistle, he referred to this insidious attack that was taking place *inside* the Church, saying, "But there were false prophets among the people, even as there shall be false teachers among you, who privily shall bring in damnable heresies, even denying the Lord that bought them, and bring upon themselves swift destruction" (2 Peter 2:1).

In this verse, Peter spoke futuristically when he said, "...There *shall* be false teachers. The words "false teachers" are a translation of the Greek word *pseudodidaskalos,* which is a compound of *pseudo* and *didaskalos.* The word *pseudo* carries the idea of *any type of falsehood.* It pictures *one who projects an image of himself that's false, one who walks in a pretense*, or *one who intentionally misrepresents facts or truths.* The word *didaskalos* is the Greek word for *a masterful teacher.*

When these words *pseudo* and *didaskalos* are compounded, the new word *pseudodidaskalos* depicts teachers who may have begun as authentic, God-called teachers, but over a period of time, they progressively veered off course. Now the message they offer is a *counterfeit* one, which means they have become *counterfeit teachers.* Peter used this word to prophetically forecast that a time "*shall* come" when a particular group of spiritual leaders arises at the end of the age and presents a counterfeit version of truth. They may claim to be on the "cutting edge" of progressive thinking and even of new theological concepts and ideas. In reality, however, this particular category of leaders will be out of sync with authentic apostolic preaching and teaching contained in the pages of the New Testament.

Peter continued by saying, "But there were false prophets among the people, even as there shall be false teachers among you, who *privily shall bring in* damnable heresies, even denying the Lord that bought them, and bring upon themselves swift destruction" (2 Peter 2:1). The phrase "privily shall bring in" is the Greek word *pareisago*. This is a compound of three Greek words: *para*, which means *alongside*; *eis*, which means *into*; and *ago*, which means *I lead.*

The word *para* in this context indicates that the false teachers Peter referenced would walk *alongside* other believers. The word *eis* means they would bring their false doctrine right *into* the church. Finally, the word *ago* suggests that these individuals would hold positions of *leadership* in the church. These false teachers would not be outsiders trying to get inside — *they would be trusted insiders working within the congregation.*

Furthermore, when the Greek words *para*, *eis*, and *ago* are compounded, as they are in Second Peter 2:1, the new word *pareisago* most often denotes *a smuggler attempting to covertly transport illegal contraband across a border while using a disguise or stealth to conceal his activities.*

Deliberately smuggling contraband is not accidental; therefore, Peter's use of this word reveals that these false teachers would be neither ignorant nor innocent concerning their activities; they would know that their words and actions were contrary to the truth. Peter was therefore speaking of leaders who would be willing agents of the enemy, acting seductively to smuggle their false doctrine into the minds of the other church members.

In Peter's time, the process of deception was suggestive and subtle, luring believers into becoming more inclusive and accepting of what pagans believed. The thought was inserted into believers' minds that it would be fine to stop being so adamant about the truth and therefore so separate from the pagan world. What these errant leaders suggested could have sounded like wise counsel, for it promised hope for believers to be spared from many difficulties. In reality, however, it was a demonic stealth operation to compromise the truth. Satan knows that even if compromise does give a temporary reprieve, it always produces a long-term destructive effect on the Church.

Likewise, errant leaders who arise at the end of the age will smuggle their error into the Church so covertly that their misdeeds could be likened to someone who poisons another person slowly over time so that his deadly deeds are very difficult to detect.

There is no doubt that the Greek word depicts *covert activity.* It pictures one who knows he is introducing a new theological concept or doctrine that may raise a flag of concern. Therefore, rather than openly bringing it into the Church, the person looks for a way to sneak it in. This word therefore depicts a conscious effort — at least on the part of the seducing spirits behind the deception — to clandestinely smuggle error into the Church in a veiled way that prevents it from being easily detected.

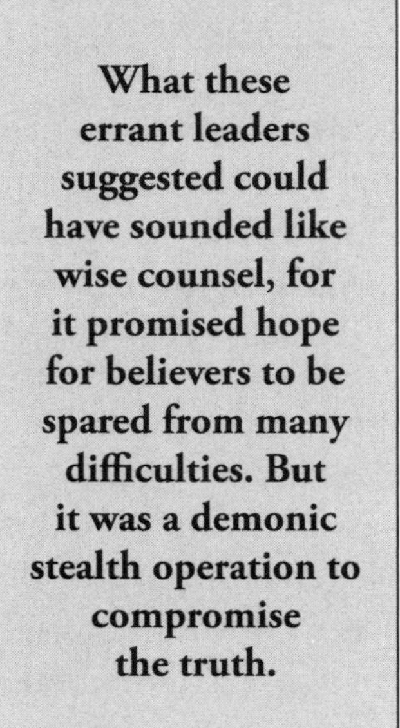

However, besides those in positions of influence who are deliberate distributors of falsehood, there are those who teach error who have actually embraced it as their truth. This means that the perpetrators who are smuggling spiritual error into the Church may be unwitting carriers of deadly spiritual toxins into the midst of God's family. They may not realize the damage they are doing. In fact, these errant teachers may be so deceived by seducing spirits that they have actually convinced themselves that what they're endorsing is unadulterated truth.

Yet the very fact that these false teachers must be careful to covertly insert their new message into the Church is evidence that they at least know something they're purporting is outside of the mainstream of historical faith. This is how seducing spirits are able to work through apostate leaders to stealthily infiltrate the Church. The enemy's strategy is to "breach the walls" and bring in heretical error that will produce a powerless, weakened version of Christianity where sin is tolerated, separation and holiness are ignored, and the need for ongoing repentance is disregarded.

The use of the Greek word *para* from Second Peter 2:1 — in the context of this Greek compound word *pareisago*, translated "privily shall bring in" — is also very significant. As mentioned previously, the word *para* means *alongside*. This alerts us that these spiritual smugglers lay truth and error alongside each other, which often makes the error more palatable to those who listen. This is especially dangerous for the newer, more immature, yet ready-to-learn believers who do not have enough discernment to be able to divide truth from error.

The enemy's strategy is to "breach the walls" and bring in heretical error that will produce a powerless, weakened version of Christianity where sin is tolerated, separation and holiness are ignored, and the need for ongoing repentance is disregarded.

Especially in these last of the last days, it is essential for Church leadership to take their responsibility seriously to guard the flock over which the Holy Ghost has made them overseers (*see* Acts 20:28). As Peter and Jude had to do in their day, leaders must be diligent to watch over the flock Heaven has placed in their charge so that error is not able to take up residency among God's people.

Damnable Heresies

The false doctrine Peter referred to that was being taught at that time was basically a doctrine of compromise. In that time when persecution was at such a high tide, a group of Christian leaders inside the Church arose who decided to mitigate their faith to become more accommodating with the world around them. Does that approach sound familiar to you? Rather than pressing in to the truth and remaining separate from the world, those early leaders advocated a compromise that Peter called "damnable." Even worse, they began to project this dangerous mentality onto other believers who were facing the same intense struggles.

Although this decision to compromise could have provided some temporary relief from external pressures, it was one that would prove to be very costly, leading to a sick, weak, and spiritually defeated Church. Therefore, Peter raised his voice and sounded the alarm to believers everywhere, for all time, that those who embrace a compromising position only contribute to the diminishing of the Church. Sadly, Peter continued to affirm that the individuals he was referring to were real brothers who had chosen the way of deception because they had bartered away truth for a respite from societal pressures.

Peter wrote, "But there were false prophets among the people, even as there shall be false teachers among you, who privily shall bring in *damnable heresies…*" (2 Peter 2:1). Peter warned that individuals would come who would intentionally or unintentionally introduce damnable heresies into the Church, often in a clandestine manner.

Peter raised his voice and sounded the alarm to believers everywhere, for all time, that those who embrace a compromising position only contribute to the diminishing of the Church.

The word "heresies" is translated from the Greek word *hairesis.* Although today the word "heresies" is a strong word that carries the idea of a *false doctrine* or *false teaching*, it actually had a more benign meaning in early Greek literature. The Greek word *hairesis* was simply used to denote *a particular school of thought* or a *choice.*

However, Peter called these heresies "damnable." In Greek, this is the word *apoleia*, which literally means *destroyed*, *decayed*, *rotten*, or *ruined.* This means the phrase "damnable heresies" simply conveys the ideas of *destructive, rotten, or ruinous choices* or a *ruinous school of thought.* By using this phrase, the apostle clearly spelled out what the doctrine of compromise would produce if it wasn't stopped — *destruction* and *devastation.*

In ancient Greek culture, the word translated "heresies" was a technical term used to denote *any sect that embraced intellectual, historical, philosophical, political, religious, or scientific beliefs contrary to the common understanding of society.* Such groups were called heretical because they were divergent from accepted, mainstream beliefs. But over time, the Greek word *hairesis* came to be used differently. In New Testament times, it denoted doctrinal choices — *preferred beliefs* — that were not in agreement or that could not be substantiated by Scripture and were in the long run incompatible with the tenets of the Christian faith.

Thus, a heretical teaching is any belief or doctrine that is divergent from the core beliefs presented in the Scriptures. By contrast, beliefs that are aligned with Scripture — sometimes referred to as *orthodox* doctrines — are referred to as "sound doctrine" in the New Testament because they agree with time-tested truths as presented in Scripture.

In fact, these "heresies" were so incompatible with the Christian faith that Peter called them "damnable heresies." The Greek sentence structure actually reverses these words to say "heresies damnable." In other words, the Greek places the word "heresy" first and the word "damnable" second. With this construction, Peter was emphasizing that if one embraces heretical teaching as part of his regular diet, it will eventually produce a damnable result — that is, it will lead to spiritual *decay, rot,* or *ruin.* This is actually the meaning of "damnable heresies."

So in this verse, Peter vehemently warned believers to beware of errant spiritual leaders who promote "damnable heresies" in the messages they present. In other words, a steady diet of this type of deviant teaching over time will eventually produce decay, rot, and ruin in the life of a believer, in the life of a local body of believers, and, ultimately, in the life of the Church at large.

Denying the Lord That Bought Them

In Second Peter 2:1, Peter elaborated on the nature of this damnable heresy, saying, "But there were false prophets among the people, even as there shall be false teachers among you, who privily shall bring in damnable heresies, *even denying the Lord that bought them....*"

The word "bought" is *agoradzo*, which is the New Testament word for *redemption*. Peter's use of this particular word was not accidental. The errant spiritual leaders he was describing were "bought" — or *redeemed* — individuals. They were not unsaved pretenders trying to get a foothold inside the Church; rather, they were *insiders*, purchased by the blood of Jesus and longtime members of the Christian community. Yet in a crucial moment, they chose to compromise, rationalizing their abandonment of absolute truth as a reasonable, logical option because of the challenging circumstances that surrounded them. This compromise with the world, however, would backfire, ultimately bringing upon them spiritual ruin and decay.

Peter was concerned that their teaching would ultimately spread not only throughout their local body, but throughout the larger Body of Christ, just as a viral or bacterial infection begins to multiply and spread throughout a human body.

Never forget that it takes only a few spiritual leaders getting off track to adversely affect the health of a local church — *if* the matter isn't swiftly dealt with. Physical infections begin at the microscopic level with a relatively small number of contagions and are often very treatable if they are addressed in their early stages. However, if they are left untreated, infections can quickly grow out of control and lead to serious physical complications or even death.

It is similarly true with a spiritual infection. When a spiritual disease is still in its early stages of infecting a local church, it is more easily dealt with. But if left untreated and allowed to fester and spread, a deadly teaching can ultimately undermine the entire local body and then move on to infect a much broader spectrum of believers within the Church.

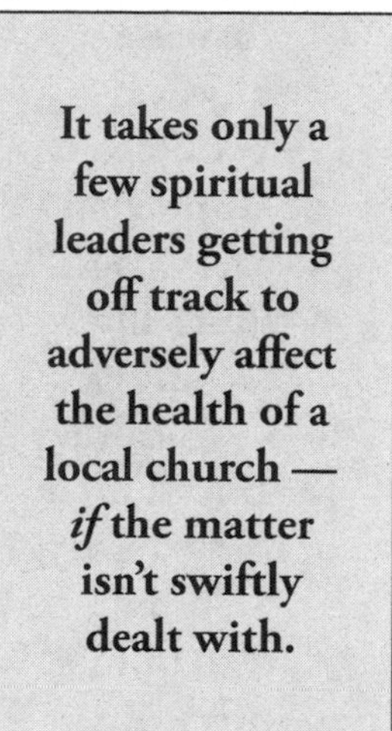

It takes only a few spiritual leaders getting off track to adversely affect the health of a local church — *if* the matter isn't swiftly dealt with.

In the specific case that Peter was addressing, the spiritual infection had entered local bodies through a few church leaders whose influence in their congregations provided a platform from which they could spread their false teaching to fellow believers. Although their numbers were still small at the time, they were already in the process of multiplying inside these churches — *exactly like an infectious disease.*

If the multiplication of this spiritual infection was not stopped by the power of the Spirit, it would have spread from one believer to another to another until it had finally affected not just a few, but entire congregations. Just as a physical infection can be stopped in its early stages from fully developing, God was calling for the Church to immediately *stop* the spread of this infectious teaching.

The most difficult type of spiritual infection to detect and treat is when a trusted spiritual leader has become infected. A spiritual leader is an influential person who touches many lives. False doctrine that finds its way into the heart of one leader, if it is not corrected, will begin to pass to others, just as an infection is passed from one host to the next. If this transmission isn't stopped, it has the potential to eventually infect large sectors of the Church. The point is this: It doesn't take too many erring individuals who are infected with false doctrine to transmit sickness to the Church at large when they hold positions of influence.

We don't know the specific names of the leaders who were the source of false doctrine in the Early Church. At the time of Peter's writing, it seems only a small number had been infected. But Peter knew that if this error wasn't corrected, it would begin to spread like an infectious disease until the entire Church was adversely impacted.

Just as a physical infection can be stopped in its early stages from fully developing, God was calling for the Church to immediately *stop* the spread of this infectious teaching.

Second Peter 2:1 goes on to say that these errant leaders were "denying *the Lord* that bought them." The word "Lord" that is used in this verse is *not* the normal Greek word for "Lord" found throughout the New Testament. In this verse, it is the Greek word *despotes,* which is an administrative term normally referring to a CEO or to one who has authority over others, especially over others in the executive department directly under his control.

The Greek word *despotes* was also used as a technical term to describe the chief steward of large households. This chief steward was over all the other servants in that large household. The others reported directly to him, received instructions from him, were paid by him, and, if the need arose, were dismissed by him. This is the very word that Peter used in Second Peter 2:1 when he wrote "denying the Lord" that bought them.

By using the word *despotes*, Peter let us know that he was describing spiritual leaders who relate to Jesus as their CEO. These are the individuals who have been called by Christ into leadership positions in the Church. They are in the executive department, and they relate to Jesus not only as their Savior, but also as the Chief Executive Officer who called them, who directs them, who corrects them, and to whom they must ultimately answer.

SAYING 'NO' TO THE LORD

Peter said this end-time group of errant leaders would *deny* the Lord who bought them. That word "denying" is a translation of the Greek word *arneomai*, which means *to knowingly deny*, *to knowingly disown*, *to knowingly reject*, *to knowingly refuse*, or *to knowingly renounce*. It refers to *a person who knowingly disavows, forsakes, walks away from, or washes one's hands of another person or group of people.* It depicts something that is done with one's full consent and understanding of what he or she is doing.

But in this verse, the word *arneomai* is used to depict someone who hears what Christ has to say as the One who holds the position of CEO in his or her life, but then rejects His counsel. Those Peter described apparently did not like the instruction or correction the Lord had given. Therefore, rather than accept the Lord's counsel and obey Him, they rejected the counsel of the Lord. The choice before these individuals may have been to disobey the Lord or to obey Him and face the prospect of losing a following. Regardless, they chose to go their own way and to ignore the warning signals of the Holy Spirit.

We have all been guilty of ignoring the promptings of the Holy Spirit at some point in our Christian experience. However, if we are in error — and if we knowingly persist in it — we are opting for an outcome that we will ultimately regret.

Destruction That Rips 'Limb From Limb'

In Second Peter 2:1, Peter also wrote, "But there were false prophets among the people, even as there shall be false teachers among you, who privily shall bring in damnable heresies, even denying the Lord that bought them, *and bring upon themselves swift destruction.*"

The words "bring upon" is a translation of the Greek word *epago*, a word that was used in contemporary writings of New Testament times *to denote the letting loose of wild dogs to tear victims apart, limb from limb*. By using this very graphic word, Peter forewarned that when a spiritual leader denies the Lord's corrective voice and chooses to go his own way, his actions *let loose* his destruction.

This verse does not say God brings destruction upon this person, but that they "bring upon *themselves* swift destruction." This is judgment that they self-release upon themselves. Peter referred to it as "swift destruction." The word "swift" is a translation of the Greek word *tachinos,* which describes something that takes place *suddenly* or *quickly*. The word "destruction" is a translation of the Greek word *apoleia,* and it describes *destruction*, *decay*, *rottenness*, or *ruin*.

By using this word at this juncture, Peter informed us that errant leaders will eventually reap exactly what they have sown. If they sow damnable heresies that are rotten and ruinous into the Church, they will eventually reap a rotten and ruinous situation themselves unless they submit to the Lord's corrective voice and allow Him to bring about a course correction.

An Example of Swift Destruction

How long will an errant leader go on before correction comes from above? I believe an answer to this question is found in the story of Eli and his sons Hophni and Phinehas.

First Samuel 2:12 reveals that Eli's sons were backslidden, even though they were in the ministry. In fact, they had veered off track so seriously that they were even stealing from the offerings given by the people and fornicating with women who worked in the temple (*see* 1 Samuel 2:14,22)! We don't know how long this situation was tolerated, but it seems this situation persisted over a lengthy period of time.

Judgment of this egregious behavior did not come quickly. In fact, God's action against Hophni and Phinehas was not released until they mistreated people so dreadfully that the people began staying away from God's house. First Samuel 2:17 says, "Wherefore, the sin of the young men was very great before the Lord: for men abhorred the offering of the Lord." Because worshipers were tired of the abuse they encountered when they came to the house of God, they eventually began to avoid going to worship there.

When a leader's behavior causes people to turn from His presence, such individuals are teetering on the brink of serious judgment.

For God, that was the final straw. When a leader's behavior causes people to turn from His presence, such individuals are teetering on the brink of serious judgment.

Both Scripture and a careful look at history shows that God is so patient that He even tolerates errant spiritual leaders for a period of time. But First Samuel 2:17 makes it clear that when leaders' actions cause people to steer clear of God's house, those individuals have committed sin that is considered to be "very great" in the eyes of God. That includes the sin of Eli, who refused to deal with his sons and so by negligence participated in their sin. He shut his eyes to their behavior, even though he knew what they were doing.

Eventually Eli and his sons were judged — and when judgment came, it occurred quickly. They experienced a "swift destruction" as Peter described in Second Peter 2:1. God had given Hophni and Phinehas time to repent. It was evident that their behavior was not going to change and that Eli was not going to exercise his authority to stop it. Then came the time when God saw people's obedience to worship Him being negatively affected by these men's actions. At that point, judgment was released, and Eli and his sons were removed *in a single day*.

Not only were Eli and his sons removed, but this event may have also marked the end of Shiloh, the spiritual center at that time and the place where Eli and his sons had been positioned to serve in the house of God. But Shiloh had become infected with Hophni and Phinehas' ungodly behavior, and many Bible scholars believe it was wiped off the face of the earth at this time. So we see that although God gave Eli and his sons time to self-correct, He eventually took action. In doing so, He made it clear that He will not endlessly tolerate errant spiritual leadership.

Although God gave Eli and his sons time to self-correct, He eventually took action. In doing so, He made it clear that He will not endlessly tolerate errant spiritual leadership.

The word "swift" in Second Peter 2:1 is a translation of the Greek word *tachinos,* which describes something that takes place *suddenly* or *quickly*, perfectly depicts what happened to Eli and his sons. Judgment came to this threesome in a "swift" manner because they persisted in their prolonged errant behavior.

Then in Second Peter 2:2, Peter forewarned that *many* will be led astray by errant leaders at the end of the age. He wrote, "And *many* shall follow their pernicious ways...." The word "many" is a translation of the Greek word *polloi*, which refers to *large numbers* of people. In this verse, the Holy Spirit categorically prophesied through Peter that as a result of such false spiritual leaders, large numbers of Christians will be led astray from a scriptural foundation at the very end of the Church Age.

'Feigned Words'

As Peter continued his prophecy about error emerging at the end of the age in verse 3, he warned that "...through covetousness shall they with *feigned* words make merchandise of you...." That word "feigned" in Greek is the word *plastos,* which is a word that denotes *molding* something into a specific form. It is where we get the word "plastic." Peter used this word to regretfully tell us that the errant leaders he was describing and prophesying about would *mold their words* at will to fit their own purposes.

The word *plastos* was also used to describe *forgery* — like one who *forges* a piece of artwork, a type of currency, or someone's signature. Since it is impossible to forge artwork, currency, or a signature by accident, this description is one of deliberate deception. Peter was saying that just as a potter molds clay into any shape that pleases him, these errant individuals mold their words to benefit themselves. The use of the word *plastos* also tells us that they are not committed to absolute biblical truth; rather, they easily modify Scripture to make it say what they want it to say.

Peter's full statement was that "…shall they with feigned words make *merchandise* of you." The word "merchandise" in this verse is a translation of the Greek word *emporeomai.* This word *emporeomai* is where we get the word "emporium," the English word for a commercial center where assorted goods are sold.

But in the time of the New Testament, the word *emporeomai* primarily portrayed *the selling of all types of goods.* It was even used to denote the activity of *marketers* who set up tents in marketplaces to sell all kinds of goods. After the marketers analyzed each new market and determined what would best appeal to each audience, they proceeded to rave with enthusiasm about whatever product they deemed would sell best in each respective community. These ancient marketers were notorious for peddling flawed products that they claimed were fabulous. Their ability to work words to their advantage made them well known in the ancient world. These individuals were masterful manipulators who knew how to fashion their speech in the most effective way to get money out of their listeners' pockets into theirs.

Like the notorious marketers who worked in the natural markets of the ancient world, these end-time errant leaders will seek to reshape, redesign, and remold truth, *almost like plastic,* to meet their own purposes.

It is amazing that these are the words the Holy Spirit chose to speak through Peter to us about a group of deceptive spiritual leaders who will emerge at the end of the age and enter the modern "Church market." And like the notorious marketers who worked in the natural markets of the ancient world, these end-time errant leaders will seek to reshape, redesign, and remold truth, *almost like plastic*, to meet their own purposes. They will willingly modify truth to gain a place in the market — even refashioning truth to fit the whims of an erring generation seeking to have its "ears tickled."

All of this is included in the phrase "with feigned words make merchandise of you." By using the Greek words *plastos* and *emporeomai*, Peter passionately portrayed the type of errant spiritual leaders that will emerge at the wrap-up of the age — leaders who will say anything to establish their voices in the Christian market.

Sleeping Before Judgment

Peter went on to warn us that those who behave so atrociously in the Church are frequently oblivious to the fact that they are playing with fire. That is why Peter added in Second Peter 2:3, "...Whose judgment now of a long time lingereth not, and their damnation slumbereth not."

The word "judgment" in this verse is a translation of the Greek word *krima*, the well-known Greek word for *a judicial verdict of judgment*. The Greek is so strong that it actually conveys the idea of a damning judgment or a condemning sentence. This means the Judge of the earth has been watching all along and has observed that if this category of errant leaders will not heed His voice and change their course, Heaven's court has already issued a final verdict of judgment against them. In fact, Peter went on to clearly state that this impending judgment of them and their actions "lingereth not."

The words "lingereth not" are translated from the Greek words *ouk argei*. The word *ouk* is the strongest way of saying *emphatically not*! The word *argei* is a form of *argos*, a word that means *to linger*, *to delay*, or *to be idle*. When used together, these Greek words mean this judgment is *not sitting idly* and lingering. Errant leaders may not be aware of it, but while they reshape, refashion, and "sell" their new concoctions of truth to the Christian market, judgment has already been released and is en route to their addresses.

In fact, Peter said that their "damnation slumbereth not." The word "damnation" in Greek is once again the word *apoleia*, which describes *destruction*, *decay*, *rottenness*, or *ruin*. Here this word is used to foretell the future harvest these errant leaders will reap because of what they have wrongly sown into God's Church. As noted previously, the individuals Peter described have sown rotten and ruinous heretical teachings; as a result, they are destined for a harvest of spiritual rot and ruin themselves.

The Judge of the earth has been watching all along and has observed that if this category of errant leaders will not heed His voice and change their course, Heaven's court has already issued a final verdict of judgment against them.

The word "slumbereth" in Greek is the word *nustadzo*, a word that is only used one other time in the New Testament. Besides here, the only other time the word *nustadzo* is found in the New Testament is in Matthew 25:5, where Jesus was relating the story of the five wise virgins and the five foolish virgins.

When the five wise virgins realized their bridegroom was coming, they made preparations for his arrival by trimming their lamps and filling them with precious oil. The five foolish virgins also knew the bridegroom was coming, but these latter five mistakenly thought they had time to prepare for his arrival. All the virgins went to bed and "slumbered" — but when the bridegroom arrived, only the five wise virgins who had filled their lamps with oil in anticipation of his arrival were ready. That word "slumbered" is the same word *nustadzo* used in Second Peter 2:3.

Jesus told His listeners that when the bridegroom arrived, the five foolish virgins were awakened out of their slumber to realize that they waited too late to make their preparations; regretfully, they learned it was too late to make amends.

The Holy Spirit uses this same word "slumber" from Matthew 25:5 as He speaks through Peter's epistle. The implication is that just as the foolish virgins did not realize the lateness and seriousness of the hour, many errant leaders who emerge at the end of the age will not realize the imminent nearness of the judgment that is knocking at their door. But Peter stated that while these false leaders spiritually slumber in the face of judgment, the judgment that Heaven's court has issued against them and their actions is *not* slumbering.

Just as the foolish virgins did not realize the lateness and seriousness of the hour, many errant leaders who emerge at the end of the age will not realize the imminent nearness of the judgment that is knocking at their door.

The persistent unrepentant behavior of errant leaders may mean they have convinced themselves that they will evade judgment. It is entirely possible that through continual disobedience and denying of His voice, their hearts have become hardened and their consciences calloused to the tender dealings of the Holy Spirit. They may no longer sense the Holy Spirit's conviction as He tries to bring correction and get them back in line.

Does God Really Judge People Today?

God placed judgment for our sin upon Jesus at the Cross, and we are thankful for it. But the Bible makes it clear that God will judge any spiritual leader or believer who wrongfully handles believers — persistently taking advantage of the flock of God or teaching destructive teachings that lead people away from the time-tested, foundational, and never-changing principles of God's Word.

The apostle Paul sounded the alarm about this divine judgment in First Corinthians 3:16,17. He wrote, "Know ye not that ye are the temple of God, and that the Spirit of God dwelleth in you? If any man defile the temple of God, him shall God destroy; for the temple of God is holy, which temple ye are."

In these verses, Paul depicted the Church as the "temple" of God. The word "temple" is the Greek word *naos*, a word that describes a highly ornamented temple whose interior is highly adorned with ornamentations of gold, silver, and precious stones. To picture what this word means, you must imagine arched and vaulted ceilings; elements of marble, granite, gold, and silver; hand-carved etchings; and continual plumes of incense smoke rising in the air as a part of worship.

When Paul wrote that we are the "temple" of God, he was referring to *a highly decorated shrine* like the kind I just described — only this time he was portraying the Church as that holy temple. Paul's readers had grown up in Greek culture and had seen temples their entire lives. So when Paul used this word *naos*, it would have been natural for images like the one I described to flash through their minds. They knew that the word *naos* always depicted *a highly decorated shrine*. The temples of their times were beautiful buildings with tall, vaulted ceilings, marble columns, granite floors, hand-carved woodwork overlaid with gold and silver, and burning incense billowing into the air around the front of the altar.

The Church is the actual temple of the Holy Spirit in the earth today. We are specially fashioned by God for the habitation of the Spirit — paid for by the blood of Jesus, sanctified by and endowed magnificently with the riches of the Holy Spirit and the Word of God.

The Church is so precious to God that in Revelation 1:20, it is symbolically presented as "golden." Gold was the most valuable commodity of early New Testament times, so this was God's way of declaring that absolutely nothing is more valuable or precious to Him than the Church.

We are specially fashioned by God for the habitation of the Spirit — paid for by the blood of Jesus, sanctified by and endowed magnificently with the riches of the Holy Spirit and the Word of God.

The Church is so precious to God that Paul stated, "If any man defile this temple of God, him shall God *destroy*." The words "defile" and "destroy" are both translations of the Greek word *phtheiro*, which means *to spoil*, *plunder*, *destroy*, *empty*, or *wipe out*. There is no doubt about Paul's intention in using this Greek word in this context. It plainly means that if anyone wrongfully handles the Church — spoiling it, plundering it, destroying it, or emptying the Church of its truth and its power — the law of sowing and reaping will kick into action and that individual will himself be spoiled, plundered, destroyed, emptied, and wiped out.

The bottom line is this: If someone wrongly handles the house of God, the law of sowing and reaping will be activated and that person will reap exactly what he or she has sown. This may not be popular exegesis in today's current spiritual atmosphere, but it is the clear teaching of Scripture. Wherever this principle is taught and understood, a sense of grave seriousness and sobriety is imparted to those who are leading God's people.

The stakes are not only high — they are eternal. Therefore, it's crucial that leaders understand that their choice to teach doctrines unsupported by Scripture to God's people truly does result in serious consequences.

A Chronicle of God's Judgment

In Second Peter 2:4-6, Peter went on to elucidate the consequences of rebellion against God: "For if God spared not the angels that sinned, but cast them down to hell; and delivered them into chains of darkness, to be reserved unto judgment; and spared not the old world, but saved Noah, the eighth person, a preacher of righteousness, bringing in the flood upon the world of the ungodly; and turning the cities of Sodom and Gomorrah into ashes condemned them with an overthrow, making them an example unto those that after should live ungodly."

With these verses, Peter was declaring that it is *certain* God will hold errant leaders accountable for gross error they bring into the Church. Chronicling God's consistent behavior concerning rebellion in past history, Peter showed how:

- God judged angels that rebelled against His authority.
- God judged the entire ancient civilization of Noah's day that rebelled against His authority.
- God judged Sodom and Gomorrah and reduced them to ashes because of their rebellion against His authority.

Peter's point was this: Scripture shows that God is consistent in how He deals with rebellion. So how could anyone assume that God will shut His eyes to errant leaders who have modified biblical truth and led others astray?

Judgment Passed on Sinning Angels

To make this point, Peter referred to Old Testament examples of judgment, and his first illustration was the judgment that befell angels who sinned. In Second Peter 2:4, Peter wrote, "For if God spared not the angels that sinned, but cast them down to hell; and delivered them into chains of darkness, to be reserved unto judgment."

The word "spared" is translated from the Greek word *pheidomai*, which indeed means *to spare*, but also means *to treat something leniently*. This word emphatically means that God was not *lenient* even with the angels who rebelled against His authority. He held nothing back when He judged those sinning angels. In this passage, then, is the solemn warning that God will not make allowances for anyone who belligerently defies His voice.

Peter wrote that God "...cast them down to *hell*; and delivered them into chains of darkness, to be reserved unto judgment." The word "hell" in this verse is the Greek word *tartaros*, which describes *an underground cavern where rebellious spirits were assigned to reside until the time of judgment*. By using this horrible word, Peter informed us that the angels who sinned certainly did not escape divine retribution. Perhaps a better translation would be that God cast them down into *a place of detention*.

Peter continued, "For if God spared not angels that sinned, but cast them down into hell; and *delivered* them into chains of darkness." The word "delivered" is taken from the Greek word *paradidomi*, which refers to the act of *handing something over*. The idea depicted here is graphic and dramatic. It is the picture of God Himself holding these rebellious angels by the scruff of their necks and personally handing them over to a place of detention until a later time when they will be permanently judged. The implication here is that the sin of these angels was so great that God would not ask other angelic beings to execute this judgment for Him — He carried out this judgment *personally*.

Verse 4 also says God delivered them into "chains," which is a translation of the Greek word *seira*, which indeed describes chains. In Jude 6, he used the Greek word *desmos* to describe this "chaining" of rebellious angels. The word that Jude used here depicts *unbreakable bonds* or *unbreakable chains*, which means this particular category of angels would be *permanently bound* forever.

However, the word *seira* that Peter used is also closely connected to the Greek word *siros*, a word that denotes *underground pits* that served as *granaries* for crops. It is from this ancient word that we derive the concept for the huge granaries that hold crops today. An even earlier meaning of the word was *a dungeon*, *pit*, or *cavern*. This idea coincides perfectly with the theological concept of *tartaros* — a fallen-angel detention center or subterranean abyss where errant spirits were sent.

Peter even revealed what this subterranean detention center was like when he wrote that God delivered them into chains of "darkness." The word "darkness" is from the Greek word *zophnos* and describes *dense blackness*; *unceasing, neverending darkness*; or *a place mute of all light*.

Wouldn't this be the ultimate judgment to be pronounced upon an angelic creature who had been created to live in the light of God's glory? To bind them in unbreakable chains and place them in dungeons that are forever black would be the most terrible judgment of all for a former creature of light.

The Flood of Noah

Once Peter finished establishing that God was not lenient with errant angels, he moved to his second illustration of God's steadfast judgment. In Second Peter 2:5, he wrote, "And [God] spared not the old world, but saved Noah the eighth person, a preacher of righteousness, bringing in the flood upon the world of the ungodly."

Peter again stated, "And [God] spared not the old world...." The word "spared" is again the Greek word *pheidomai*, which means *to spare*, but also means to treat something *leniently*. This word emphatically conveys that just as God was not lenient with angels who sinned, He was also not lenient with the world that existed at the time of the Flood. God held nothing back when He judged the world at that early moment in history. Peter was once again giving the solemn message that God is just and will not make allowances for anyone who consciously defies His voice.

The phrase "old world" is very significant. The word "old" is a translation of the word *archaios*, which in this case means *ancient* or *archaic*. The word "world" is a translation of the word *kosmos*, which in this case means *the ordered world*. In other words, the word *kosmos* in this verse refers to *civilization*, *culture*, and *society*.

Peter once again showed that God is no respecter of persons, nor is He a respecter of civilizations. God's justice is so steadfast that when the world of Noah's day persisted in their egregious sinful behavior and refused to repent, God judged that entire ancient civilization. In fact, He judged it so entirely that He wiped it out — leaving only a handful of Noah's family surviving.

Just consider what happened to the ungodly world of that time while Noah and his family were resting safely in the protective care of God in the ark. Peter described the deluge by saying, "...Bringing in the flood upon the world of the ungodly" (2 Peter 2:5). The words "bringing in" is a translation of that word *epago*, the Greek word that denotes *the letting loose of wild and vicious dogs to literally rip a victim to pieces, limb from limb.*

God's justice is so steadfast that when the world of Noah's day persisted in their egregious sinful behavior and refused to repent, God judged that entire ancient civilization.

This is the same word we saw earlier in Second Peter 2:1 where Peter depicted judgment that errant leaders "bring upon" themselves. Using this same word, he illustrated in verse 5 what the flood did to the ancient civilization that existed before the flood. In other words, the flood was like ferocious wild dogs that literally tore the old world to pieces until nothing remained of that ancient civilization.

The Great Flood was indeed a cataclysmic event. The unrepentant and belligerent behavior of that ancient civilization required the steadfast justice of God.

This devastation was so complete that Peter used the Greek word *kataklusmos* to picture it. The word *kataklusmos* is the Greek word that means *to inundate, flood, overwhelm, to submerge with water*, or *to completely deluge.* The Greek word *kataklusmos* is where we get the word *cataclysmic.*

The Great Flood was indeed a cataclysmic event. It did not matter that it would wipe out all historical records of that early civilization or that it would destroy all of man's progress until that time. The unrepentant and belligerent behavior of that ancient civilization required the steadfast justice of God.

Sodom and Gomorrah

Finally Peter came to his most dramatic illustration of God's judgment. In Second Peter 2:6, he wrote, "And turning the cities of Sodom and Gomorrah into ashes condemned them with an overthrow, making them an ensample unto those that after should live ungodly."

Notice Peter said, "And turning the cities of Sodom and Gomorrah into ashes...." The words "turning into ashes" is translated from the Greek word *tephroo*, which means *to completely reduce to ashes* or *to incinerate*. It is the same word that the Roman historian Dio Cassius used to describe the volcanic activity that occurred at Mount Vesuvius. According to Cassius, the inner rim of Mount Vesuvius was constantly growing brittle.[25] From time to time, this brittle ridge would collapse and crash down into the deep throat of the huge volcano. Eventually the entire top of the mountain collapsed, settled into the throat of the volcano, and disappeared under the ash of the volcano.

The historical usage of this word in connection with Sodom and Gomorrah seems to mean that the territory where these wicked cities were located were burned so catastrophically by the fire and brimstone that fell upon it that the ground in that area became extremely brittle. Not only was the territory completely covered with ash, but eventually this brittle geographic area collapsed. And when it did, the entire region where these evil cities had been located sank into the earth so that there wasn't even a hint left of it. I find this very interesting since the Dead Sea, where biblical history says Sodom and Gomorrah once existed, is geologically the lowest point on earth!

Peter continued by telling us that God "*condemned* them with an overthrow." The word "condemned" is translated from the Greek word *katakrino*, which is a compound of the word *kata* and *krino*. The word *kata* means *down*, and *krino* means *a judgment* or *a sentence*. This word pictures *the damning judgment or condemning sentence of a court*. Peter's use of this word tells us that Sodom and Gomorrah's unrepentant ways brought down a severe judgment upon them by the court of Heaven. The reprobate people of those two wicked cities may have rebuffed the idea that God was watching and would deal with them, but Heaven's court was in session and the verdict of God's court was that they did not deserve to exist.

[25]Dio Cassius, *Roman History*, LXVI.21.

In fact, Peter stated, "And turning the cities of Sodom and Gomorrah into ashes condemned them with an *overthrow*, making them an ensample unto those that after should live ungodly." The word "overthrow" is translated from the Greek word *katastrophe*. You may have guessed that this is where we get the word "catastrophe." What happened to Sodom and Gomorrah was *a catastrophic event*. In fact, it was so catastrophic that when the event was finished, there was absolutely nothing left of these areas but smoke.

We know this because Genesis 19:28 says that when Abraham got up the morning after fire and brimstone fell on Sodom and Gomorrah, he looked toward the region where the cities had been the night before and all he could see was smoke: "And he [Abraham] looked toward Sodom and Gomorrah, and toward all the land of the plain, and beheld, and lo, the smoke of the country went up as the smoke of a furnace."

A Sculptor's Small-Scale Model

Peter went on in Second Peter 2:6 to say that God made "them an *ensample* unto them that after should live ungodly." The word "ensample,"or "example," is translated from the Greek word *hupodeigma*, a word that was first used to describe *a sculptor's small-scale model*. Before a sculptor makes a larger, finished product, first he makes *a small-scale model* or *a prototype* of the final sculpture he wishes to create. Before that large-scale model is created, the sculptor first meticulously works on his prototype to make certain each detail of measurement or dimension is perfected. When this small-scale model is proportionally exact and has met his stiff artistic requirements, the sculptor then uses this preliminary model to guide the process as he enlarges and amplifies it into the true-to-size, final work of art.

With the use of this word *hupodeigma*, Peter was clearly warning that the fate of Sodom and Gomorrah is a prototype of a coming future judgment that will be released at the end of all ages upon a society that is "ungodly." The word "ungodly" in this case is a form of the word *asebes*, a Greek word that denotes those who are *impious*, *irreverent*, or *dishonorable* toward the things of God.

As I pointed out in Chapter Two, the apostle Paul prophesied that society at the end of the age would become lawless (*see* 2 Timothy 3:1-5) — that is, living with no deference or respect for the established, time-tested law of God. Here Peter described that same last-days generation by using the word *asebes*, a general term to describe *a people who have generally lived disregarding all things sacred and scriptural.* And when Peter wrote that the fate of Sodom and Gomorrah was an "example," he was categorically foretelling that the destruction of these two cities would be like a sculptor's small-scale model or a prototype of a final judgment that is still to come upon this category of the ungodly.

The fate of Sodom and Gomorrah is a prototype of a coming future judgment that will be released at the end of all ages upon a society that is "ungodly."

We therefore see in these verses that God's just treatment of rebellion has always been consistent — with rebellious angels, with the ancient world at the time of Noah, with the ungodly cities of Sodom and Gomorrah — and at a future time, with a godless society at the end of this age.

Remember, Peter began this chapter by describing a time in the future when errant spiritual leaders would smuggle error into the Church. Then in verses 4-6, he painstakingly chronicled God's dealings with those who err from the truth and who refuse to listen to His corrective voice.

- Since God judged angels that rebelled against His authority…
- Since God judged the entire ancient civilization of Noah's day that rebelled against His authority…
- Since God judged Sodom and Gomorrah and reduced them to ashes because of their rebellion against His authority…
- Then we need to understand that God *will* deal especially with those in spiritual leadership who persistently rebel against His authoritative voice.

In these verses, Peter portrayed a scenario that I would not wish on anyone. However, because he was describing a potential reality for those who err from the truth and who package error for the consumption of other people, this passage of Scripture is actually a demonstration of God's mercy. The Lord dedicated all these verses as a warning to every believer — especially to leaders within the Church.

This passage of Scripture is actually a demonstration of God's mercy. The Lord dedicated all these verses as a warning to every believer — especially to leaders within the Church.

In light of all these documented cases found in Second Peter 2, it's imperative to ask:

- What are we to do to help those who are off track so that they do not reap destruction?
- What role does God expect us to play in helping deceived individuals get set free from the deception that blinds them so they can circumvent judgment?

- What can we do to bring about deliverance in the lives of spiritual leaders or believers who have fallen prey to seducing spirits and doctrines of demons in these last days?

In the final two chapters, we will continue to explore what Peter told us about our role in bringing about deliverance for believers or spiritual leaders who have been led off track. I believe you will clearly see that you have a major role to play in God's supernatural intervention to bring those in error back into alignment with biblical truth.

Think About It

1. In the natural, it is a smuggler's goal to transport contraband items undetected by authorities to a desired destination, camouflaged by legitimate cargo. The spiritual smuggler has the same aim and similar tactics. Laying truth and error alongside each other to camouflage the lie, the spiritual smuggler seeks to make his contraband doctrine palatable so listeners will grant it "safe passage" to their hearts. He is banking on the probability that those who hear won't have enough discernment to distinguish truth from error.

   How well have you prepared yourself in the study of God's Word to ensure that your spiritual eye will immediately spot the "contraband," no matter how cleverly it is camouflaged? What can you do to shore up any gaps in that preparation process?

2. The law of seedtime and harvest has been active and operational since the beginning of creation. It's a spiritual law no man can avoid, no matter how clever he thinks he is. Wayward leaders who lead God's people astray will eventually reap exactly what they have sown.

   Can you think of examples of prominent ministers over the past century who may have started out right, but who then through an array of wrong choices began to sow destructive error in the Church? For every errant minister you think of who followed a path of deception, how many eventually repented and corrected their course? What happened to those who did not repent?

3. In these end times, the marketing of manipulation to achieve the enemy's ends is rampant in every arena of life. Words deliberately molded to fit selfish agendas is the order of the

day. The only way for us to stay clear and free from every deceptive and manipulative pull is to keep our hearts pure and sensitive to the Holy Spirit's leading and keep our sound minds centered in the truth of God's Word.

Just between you and the Lord, assess your own tendency to manipulate or mold words in a given situation to help direct a situation to fit your preference or desired outcome. How well do you fare in that private, honest assessment?

Chapter Ten

THE LORD KNOWS HOW TO DELIVER THE GODLY OUT OF TEMPTATION

For a moment, let's imagine…

Glowing lights in the distance warmed the night sky with color, inviting the quiet attention of a stranger in the land. Sheltered in a tabernacle of rich fabric woven with goats' hair from Mesopotamia, Lot peered curiously through the tent door at the "golden" city on the horizon. Exotic sounds of drums and tambourines played furiously, and westward winds on the plain teasingly delivered the aroma of roasted game seasoned just the way he'd remembered it in Ur.

Resignation settled over Lot like a heavy blanket in winter. Since leaving his uncle's company of seeking travelers, Lot had determined, perhaps for the first time, that his future was his own to command. As he sat in the place of authority at the door of his tent, the great expanse of the plain, as far as the eye could see, beckoned him as the broad boundaries of his future possibilities.

Lot was starved in his senses from walking for the past five years by the faith of his uncle, Abraham. The new sights and sounds of Sodom had already begun to spark and entice Lot's unattended soul. Voices of reason conveyed gently across his mind like a pleasant stream until they mustered the strength of a river that would not be denied.

Everyone knew the goings-on in Sodom — that this wicked city was no place for a man joined in covenant to God. But Lot reasoned with himself more and more convincingly that he could honor his godly upbringing amidst the trending culture and perhaps, as "one of them," even win some over to the faith. After all, Lot was a blessed man, having amassed great wealth in the family trade. He could settle in Sodom, taking some time for himself to enjoy the fruit of his labor while shining as a witness of the goodness of God.

To every beat of the distant drums, Lot's reasonings struck against his conscience with determined rhythmic force. He was oblivious to the creeping temptation besetting him, taking root unnoticed. *But it was coming for his very life...*

So let's talk about Lot, because his story is very pertinent to our discussion in Chapter Nine on errant leaders. Biblically, the scenario just described isn't so far off from what actually happened to this man of covenant and his family, and it serves as a grave warning to us as covenant believers in Christ today.

In Second Peter 2:7-9, Peter presented Lot as a textbook example of an individual who veered off track morally and scripturally. As you will see, by Lot's choice to gradually lay aside his convictions and to convince himself over time that it was all right to go in a wrong direction, a great deal of personal tragedy ensued.

We're going to explore the biblical account of Lot to see why Peter chose to use him as an example of a *believer* or a *leader* who has gone astray.

As we begin, keep in mind that Peter was addressing the issue of false spiritual leaders that will emerge at the very end of the age

(vv. 1-3). He meticulously showed us in three significant examples, as we saw in Chapter Nine, that God is consistent in the manner in which He deals with those who know His voice but refuse to submit to His authority. The purpose of the chapter was to sound a warning to errant leaders, and to *anyone* who is in error, and to tell others what role they are to play when they see a believer or a leader who has gone astray.

But why would Peter use Lot as an example of a spiritual leader gone astray? As you will see, Lot veered off course from the walk of faith he knew. He accommodated the world around him and compromised his experience of faith to adjust to his culture — just as the Holy Spirit warned that some leaders in the Church will do toward the end of the Church Age.

In Genesis 11:26-28, we learn that Abram (later called Abraham) had a brother named Haran, who had a son named Lot. Haran died before Abram departed from his homeland, Ur of the Chaldees, to embark on his journey of faith. When Haran died, Abram and Sarai (later called Sarah) assumed a parental role in Lot's life, as was the custom in many ancient eastern cultures. This meant Abram held a position of authority in Lot's life. And because Abram and Sarai were unable to produce children of their own, Lot in a sense became like their own son and was included as part of their family.

With all this in mind, we can deduce with a measure of certainty that Lot was somewhere in the vicinity on the day Abram announced that God had spoken to him in an audible voice (*see* Acts 7:2,3). This event marked a dramatic shift in Abram's life. Before he heard God speak to him, Abram was pagan by ancient tradition — raised to worship the moon god in the religion that was widespread among the people who lived in Ur of the Chaldees. For Abram to declare that he was departing from his ancient pagan roots to follow the voice of a God no one knew would have been a scandalous situation that created waves in the community and among Abram's family members. It is indisputable that Lot would have been personally impacted by this development.

Because Abram held an assumed parental role in the life of Lot, we know that Lot lived very close to him — close enough for him to observe Abram taking his first radical steps of faith. And when his wealthy uncle and aunt left their comfortable home in Ur of the Chaldees to pursue what the voice from Heaven had spoken to Abram, the Bible tells us that Lot left Ur of the Chaldees with them (*see* Genesis 11:31).

In Chapter Five of my book *The Will of God — The Key to Your Success*, I go into great detail about God's call to Abram and the mistakes he made in the earlier years as he started out on his walk of faith. In that chapter, I cover the fact that God's original instructions to Abram were to go alone, with just Sarai: "Now the Lord had said unto Abram, Get thee out of thy country, from thy kindred, from thy father's house, unto a land that I will shew thee" (Genesis 12:1).

Nevertheless, Abram allowed Lot to accompany him as he set out from his homeland to find this unknown location God had promised him. There is much to learn from this early misstep of Abram, and I urge you to read Chapter Five in my *Will of God* book to glean from that part of this biblical account. But for this discussion, the fact remains that Lot was right there at Abram's side as servants packed up their belongings and mounted on traveling beasts to begin the journey. Along the way, Abram and Sarai settled into one city for several years. Lot was with them during those years as well.

Finally, Abram and Sarai's traveling entourage resumed the journey, eventually entering the land of promise and observing the giants who dwelt in that land. Lot was at the side of Abram and Sarai and would have seen firsthand Abram's response as his uncle observed the giants and realized the formidable challenges facing them in this new and unfamiliar land.

Abram built an altar to call out to God for help, rededicating himself and his family to God's purpose for their lives (*see* Genesis 12:6,7). This was a decisive moment in Abram's faith journey — and we can be reasonably certain that Lot was right there at Abram's side during this event. Lot probably helped gather the stones for the building of that altar, and clearly understood that a recommitment to God's plan and purposes was being made on that momentous day. Lot was even with Abram and Sarai when they sojourned for a brief time in the land of Egypt, and he personally experienced the protective hand of God that was upon them while they were there (*see* Genesis 12:10-20).

The point is that Lot could not have lived and traveled so closely with Abram and over such a long, sustained period of time, and stayed ignorant about his uncle's walk of faith. Lot understood conversion, repentance, and the importance of obedience to the voice of God. He knew that living a life at an altar of surrender and consecration was what God required. In many respects, Lot was a joint participant in Abram's adventures of faith that today we read about and teach to others. Lot didn't just witness it — he participated in it and walked it out alongside Abram and Sarai. Their faith became his faith to embrace as well.

Yet even though this was Lot's history with Abram, the nephew lamentably left his uncle's side when Abram gave him first choice of land to settle in. Lot's choice was to make his home in Sodom — one of the world's most perverse cities at that time (*see* Genesis 13:10-13).

Lot had accompanied his uncle in the walk of faith. Through Abram's example, Lot had learned the importance of following the voice of God and living at the altar of surrender. Nevertheless, when the time came to make a crucial choice that would affect the outcome of his and his family's lives, Lot somehow convinced himself that he could live in compromise without being affected by it.

Although Lot had physically left Ur of the Chaldees, the pagan culture of his homeland had never left him. So at a crossroads moment when he had to make a choice, he was drawn to an environment similar to one he knew as he was growing up. In due course, not only did Lot live in Sodom, but his decision also meant his wife, daughters, and sons-in-law — the entire family — would be affected by that corrupt environment. And as time passed, it seems they all became part of the mess in that notorious city and were negatively affected by its perverse influences.

When the time came to make a crucial choice that would affect the outcome of his and his family's lives, Lot somehow convinced himself that he could live in compromise without being affected by it.

The story of Lot, then, is the story of a man who had a great beginning, but who later departed from the faith that had been imparted to him. Possibly Lot was led astray by seducing spirits who coaxed him to live in the midst of immoral lifestyles and perverse situations that were profane in the sight of God.

In actuality, when Lot chose to relocate to Sodom, he was returning to the same vomitous situation that he and his family had left when they journeyed out of Ur of the Chaldees (*see* Proverbs 26:11). The obscene sexual lifestyles in Sodom were akin in many respects to what Lot had been familiar with when he was young before his uncle had heard and responded to the voice of the true God.

In Sodom, Lot — this man who had known and experienced so much of God's grace — found himself living comfortably in the midst of wickedness, far removed from what he had known, believed, and experienced in his relationship with God. All of Lot's past was put aside as he sought to comingle with the people of Sodom in order to experience a more "comfortable" life.

Lot was not forced to live in Sodom. When he first entered that city and observed its pervasive wickedness, he was afforded the opportunity to turn from it and leave. But Lot chose to put aside his convictions and to enter in to make his home there, knowing that it was not a place for a righteous man to be living or to raise his family.

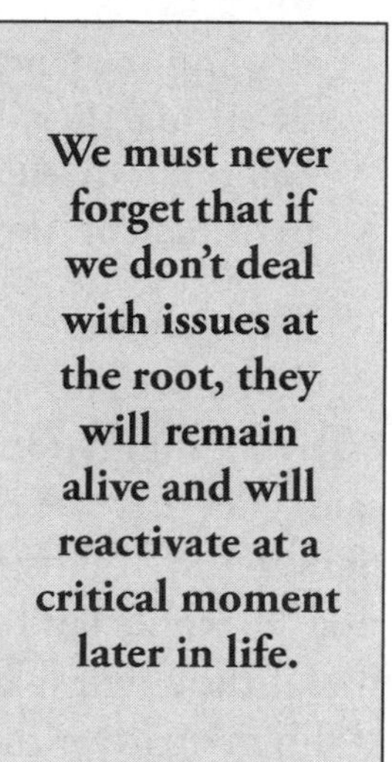

Judging from Lot's decision-making process at this point in his life, it seems that Ur of the Chaldees remained alive in his soul, even though he had walked in faith with Abraham for years. We can learn a lesson from Lot here. We must never forget that if we don't deal with issues at the root, they will remain alive and will reactivate at a critical moment later in life. That is probably what happened when Lot finally entered Sodom. Most likely, the city was a comfort and a draw to his flesh because it was a familiar setting to what he had experienced before he started out on his faith journey with Abram.

Lot's wandering began very gradually. This is usually true with any Christian who backslides or with any spiritual leader who drifts away from what he previously knew, believed, and experienced in his relationship with God and His Word. Lot's story is perhaps the clearest example in Scripture of how a departure from God and His Word progressively takes place in the life of a Christian — or in the life of a spiritual leader, which is the actual topic Peter was writing about as he gave us this example of Lot.

How Does Wandering Begin?

Genesis 13:6,7 tells us that Abraham and Lot were rich with livestock, servants, and material possessions. Eventually, however, the land became so crowded that the herdsmen of both companies became embroiled in continual arguments over territory. It became simply impossible for them to keep living together.

> **And the land was not able to bear them, that they might dwell together: for their substance was great, so that they could not dwell together. And there was a strife between the herdsmen of Abram's cattle and the herdsmen of Lot's cattle.**

The Scriptures reveal that Abram loved Lot like a son and wanted no strife between him and his beloved nephew. So he offered a suggestion that we read about in Genesis 13:8,9. Abram said, "Let there be no strife, I pray thee, between me and thee, and between my herdsmen and thy herdsmen; for we be brethren. Is not the whole land before thee? Separate thyself, I pray thee, from me: if thou wilt take the left hand, then I will go to the right; for if thou depart to the right hand, then I will go to the left."

Genesis 13:10 tells us, "And Lot lifted up his eyes and beheld all the plain of the Jordan, that it was well watered every where, before the Lord destroyed Sodom and Gomorrah, even as in the garden of the Lord, like the land of Egypt, as thou comest into Zoar."

Even in ancient times, Sodom and Gomorrah were known as luxurious cities that were rich and full of financial opportunities. The lights, sounds, and smells of the cities were all in close proximity to the place where Lot was living — and it is entirely possible that the temptation of these cities had been calling to Lot for some time even *before* Abram suggested they each go a different direction. Lot had been a partner in the walk of faith with his wealthy uncle and aunt, but walking by faith had not been an easy journey for any of them.

Traveling in a caravan for years had no doubt been difficult, and Lot might have been thinking that the faith journey hadn't worked out too well for his family. We can't know for sure, but perhaps this is why he quickly lifted up his eyes toward Sodom when Abram made the suggestion that they separate.

Perhaps you personally know of people who reasoned themselves out of God-given callings and assignments because they became weary of the faith journey. Can you recall those who convinced themselves that a life with more creature comforts is what they needed? How many people throughout history have followed the will of God for a season but then, for various reasons, gradually over a period of time coaxed themselves into believing that an "easier" route was better for them and their families?

I ask you to consider that this *may* have been what happened to Lot. But whatever the reason, the fact is that Lot promptly lifted his eyes toward Sodom and Gomorrah when Abram made the suggestion that they part. This strongly suggests that the thought of separating from Abram and going elsewhere was one that Lot had been entertaining even *before* Abram made the suggestion.

Lot didn't barge right into Sodom to make his residence there. He had walked with God long enough to know that Sodom and Gomorrah were not the type of cities where he and his family should live. But Genesis 13:11-13 chronicles Lot's deterioration into compromise when it says, "Then Lot chose him all the plain of the Jordan; and Lot journeyed east: and they separated themselves one from the other. Abraham dwelled in the land of Canaan, and Lot dwelled in the cities of the plain, and pitched his tent toward Sodom. But the men of Sodom were wicked and sinners before the Lord exceedingly."

Evidently Lot eventually coaxed himself into believing it was all right to move into an environment that he knew was wrong. To make his home in that godless environment, he would have had to violate much of what he knew to be true. A move toward Sodom may have been appealing to Lot's flesh and to his natural eyes, but it was nonetheless *not* a place for a man with so much knowledge of and experience with God.

You must remember that Peter used this illustration of Lot as an example of spiritual leaders who deviate from the faith. Like Lot, many times spiritual leaders begin strong in faith and in personal sacrifice to obediently follow God's call. In the beginning, they surrender all to Jesus and perhaps even experience God's miraculous power at various points in their experience.

But along the way — for different reasons — these leaders capitulate to weariness or discouragement and begin to yield to the temptation of believing that life would be easier if they would relax their standards a little. They may start pondering whether becoming more inclusive of those with different views would make life less complicated. They may conclude that it would be acceptable to bend a little here and there and to lessen their strong scriptural stance on hot topics that put them at odds with society.

The fact is, no one who loves Jesus wakes up one day and says, "Today I'm going to depart from a strong stance on the Bible." This type of insidiously gradual departure happens over a period of time — one little step at a time — inching a person closer and closer to tolerating what he formerly believed to be sinful and an abomination before God.

Isn't this exactly what we see in the case of Lot? The Bible tells us that Lot "pitched his tent toward Sodom." So when he pitched his tent in the plain, Lot set it up with the open flap of the tent facing Sodom. In the evenings when he sat under the flap to enjoy the cooler night breeze in that hot climate, he could see the lights of Sodom in the distance. More than likely, Lot could even hear the sounds and catch a scent of the city's different aromas carried on the wind.

As the days passed, Lot may have slowly inched his tent nearer and nearer toward Sodom — until one day he was so close to the wicked city that it was easy for him to decide to simply move right into Sodom itself. In the end, this man — who had learned from his uncle what it meant to walk by faith — chose to make his home right in the center of depravity, convincing himself that this was the best decision for him and his family.

As I mentioned previously, Sodom and Gomorrah were very similar to Ur of the Chaldees — a place that reeked of idolatry and perversion. It was the dark spiritual environment from which God had delivered Lot when Lot ventured out on the walk of faith with Abraham. Having grown up in such an environment may have made it easier for Lot to be drawn to a dark spiritual environment similar to the one he had grown up with in Mesopotamia.

But I want you to see that Lot "pitched his tent toward Sodom." He did not immediately rush into Sodom to participate in its dark spiritual surroundings. But by pitching his tent toward the city, Lot slowly allowed his thoughts to be drawn toward its activities — until finally he was no longer entertaining the idea of Sodom; he actually *moved into it.*

By pitching his tent toward the city, Lot slowly allowed his thoughts to be drawn toward its activities — until finally he was no longer entertaining the idea of Sodom; he actually *moved into it.*

This is a vivid picture of mentally playing with sin. Although at first Lot didn't go to that center of depravity and sin in person; he went there mentally.

If any believer plays with sin long enough in his mind, eventually those thoughts will control him, drag him down, and entice him into actual participation.

Likewise, if any believer plays with sin long enough in his mind, eventually those thoughts will control him, drag him down, and entice him into actual participation. As metal is naturally drawn to a magnet, something in that city pulled on the soul strings of Lot. Eventually he found himself no longer living in the plains near the city, but rather living in the city itself.

A Righteous Man Living Below What He Knew To Be True

Lot had chosen a city destined for judgment as his habitation. But before God rained fire and brimstone upon Sodom and Gomorrah, Lot would reap the benefits of God's covenant with his uncle Abraham. Peter related that God "...*delivered* just Lot, vexed with the filthy conversation of the wicked" (2 Peter 2:7).

The word "delivered" is translated from the Greek word *ruomai,* the very word in Greek that speaks of *a last-ditch effort to save someone who is on the brink of destruction*. Because Peter used this word, we know that God reached into the sewage of Sodom and "snatched" Lot and his family out before judgment fell on the wicked cities of the plain. In other words, Lot's soul was so seared — so spiritually calloused by the many violations he had permitted to invade his heart and soul — that an intervention was necessary to save him and his family. God literally reached into the pit of Sodom and dragged Lot out. Otherwise, he would have lingered there, ending up as ashes in the fiery holocaust that was to imminently consume the whole region.

Yet despite the fact that Lot was living in one of the world's most wicked cities, Peter referred to him as "just Lot."

The word "just" is a translation of the Greek word *dikaios*, which is the New Testament Greek word used most often for *righteous* or *righteousness*. That Peter would call this man "righteous" assuredly tells us that through the muck and mire of a deteriorated believer's life, God is able to see the commitment the person made to Him years before. If God could observe Lot's wayward condition and still call *him* righteous, we can be assured that God sees beyond the sin and deception that binds any hardhearted believer or errant spiritual leader we know.

Remember, Peter was discussing wayward spiritual leaders in his epistle. Therefore, the fact that Peter called Lot righteous tells us that although such spiritual leaders may be deceived and causing harm to themselves, to their families, or even to the Body of Christ, Jesus sees beyond their erroneous shift in direction that violates the commitment they first made to Him. Although they have veered off the path of the true faith, they are nonetheless the Lord's.

But although Peter called Lot "just," he continued by saying that Lot was "vexed with the filthy conversation of the wicked." The word "vexed" is extremely important, for it is a translation of the Greek word *kataponeo,* which is a compound of the words *kata* and *poneo.* The word *kata* carries the idea of *domination*, and *poneo* means *to work to the point of exhaustion.* But when these two words are compounded, the new word denotes *total exhaustion.* Thus, the word "vexed" — the Greek word *kataponeo* — can be translated *to wear out*, *to tire out*, *to break down*, or *to bring to a place of total and complete exhaustion.*

The progression of Lot's moral and spiritual deterioration can be ascertained by the use of this word "vexed." First, he pitched his tent toward Sodom; then later he moved into the city, thinking

He had tried to convince himself that he could live near sin without participating in it, but Lot soon discovered the power that sin possesses. The activities of the city eventually began to wear him out, break him down, and exhaust his strength to resist.

that he could live near sin without being affected by it or participating in it. But the pervasive wickedness that surrounded Lot eventually "vexed" his heart. This tells us the moral and spiritual perversity around Lot began to eat away at his resistance. He had tried to convince himself that he could live near sin without participating in it, but Lot soon discovered the power that sin possesses. The activities of the city eventually began to wear him out, break him down, and exhaust his strength to resist. And at some point after his resistance was lowered, Lot *succumbed* to the environment around him.

The Tragedy of Becoming 'One of the Crowd'

To what degree Lot succumbed to his environment is not known; however, when the angels came to destroy the city and entered it for the first time, they found that "Lot sat in the gate of Sodom" (Genesis 19:1). To "sit in the gate of the city" was an ancient expression that denoted those who were *counted among a city's leadership*. This indicates the level to which Lot had sunk morally and spiritually.

We know for certain that Lot wrongly assumed he could live in the midst of iniquity without becoming affected by it. Then over the passing of time, the pressures of the city caused this man who had previously walked in faith to become so blended into Sodom that he was actually given a position to *sit in the city gates*.

For Lot to even be counted as one of their city leaders makes one wonder. Did he close his eyes to the people's perverse sexual behaviors and silence his voice about their sinful lifestyle in order to get along in his new environment? We can only speculate about this point, but the fact that Lot sat in the gate of the city makes one thing clear — the people of the city saw him as one of their own.

Notice what primarily "vexed" Lot. Peter says he was "vexed with the filthy conversation of the wicked." The phrase "filthy conversation" gives insight to the environment that surrounded Lot every day in his new life in Sodom. The word "filthy" is a translation of the Greek word *aselaeia*, which denotes *unbridled living* with an emphasis on *sensuality*. The word "conversation" is translated from the Greek word *anastrophe*, which describes *lifestyle* or *behavior*. When the two words are combined as one phrase, the phrase emphatically means that Lot was surrounded by *unbridled, outrageous, sensuous lifestyles and behaviors.*

Even the strongest believer can be worn down by the constant onslaught of sinful surroundings. This is the reason Paul instructed New Testament believers to "flee also youthful lusts" (2 Timothy 2:22). Unfortunately, Lot did *not* choose to willingly extract himself from the wicked city he had chosen as his home. Rather, he stayed in that depraved environment so long — living in the midst of it, hearing and seeing its evil effects day by day — that he finally succumbed to it and in some fashion became an accepted part of it with his own seat at the city gates.

When Sin Comes Calling

This reminds me of the Old Testament account when Balaam tried to curse the people of God but could not do it. When his sorcery against them failed, Balaam seduced them into unbridled, sensual living by dangling the prostitutes of Moab before the men of Israel.

Numbers 25:1-3 relates the account: "And Israel abode at Shittim, and the people began to commit whoredom with the daughters of Moab. And they (the daughters of Moab) called the people (the men of Israel) unto the sacrifices of their gods: and the people did eat, and bowed down to their gods. And Israel joined himself unto Baal-peor."

The men of Israel did exactly what Lot had done to himself — they played with danger until danger began to play with *them*. Notice the progression in these that reveal how sensuality and sin lured the Hebrew men into *blatant* sin.

First, the daughters of Moab called unto the men. These prostitutes who served at the altar of Baal were literally flaunting their nearly naked bodies in front of these men, inviting them to come take advantage of their flesh.

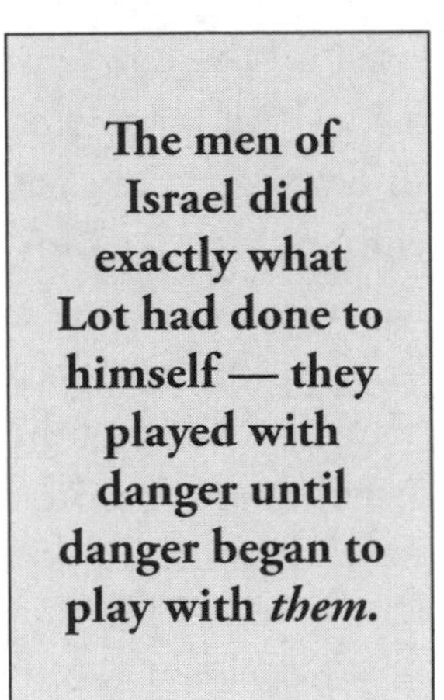

Second, the daughters of Moab called the men into the place of sin. After flaunting their bodies in front of their eyes as if to offer themselves freely to them, the women lured the men to follow them out of their tents to a place where they should have never been. Although God had shown Himself faithful to these Hebrew men, they allowed themselves to mentally entertain lustful thoughts about those women until they yielded to the temptation to draw nearer and take a closer look.

Third, the Moabite women lured the men to a place where sin abounded. We finally come to the third step in the progression of sin. Once drawn to the ungodly location where these women lured them — a place where sensual activity abounded — the Bible says, "the men did eat" (Numbers 25:2).

It just so happened that the food eaten in these pagan temples was near the idolatrous altar where sexual acts occurred. The fact that the men sat down to eat actually implies that they sat down not only to eat, but also *to watch*.

The temptation eventually overpowered the men, and Numbers 25:2 says that the men of Israel "bowed down to their gods." In other words, after inching closer and closer to sin, these Hebrew men sacrificed their godly morals and convictions on a demonic altar. Numbers 25:3 goes on to say, "Israel joined himself unto Baal-peor." This means the men of Israel actually consummated the sexual sin that they had been mentally entertaining as they allowed the Moabite women to seductively dangle themselves before them in the first place.

What we see in the case of the men of Israel is the progression of sin that nearly always occurs in the life of a believer when he or she succumbs to sin. It is the very pattern that gripped Lot.

1. **Sin called unto him** — so he moved his tent into the plains closer to Sodom.

2. **Sin kept calling him to the place of sin** — so he left the plains and unthinkably moved right into the city of Sodom itself.

3. **Sin tempted and seduced him** — to such a wretched degree that he ended up sitting at the gates of Sodom as one of its city leaders (which explains why all the men of Sodom knew where he lived, as is recorded in Genesis 19:4).

4. **Sin vexed him** — which means Lot was conquered by the daily intermingling with and observance of sin, and in some

way, he surrendered to it. No one knows the extent to which Lot succumbed to Sodom, but Peter's words express that in choosing comfort, Lot lost so much as a result.

Dwelling With the Wrong Crowd

I must remind you that Peter called Lot a "just man." In fact, the apostle repeated this fact twice as he wrote about Lot. Peter was making it explicitly clear that although Lot was deceived and had been lured astray by seducing spirits and doctrines of demons, he had not lost his righteous standing with God. Lot was the perfect example of a righteous man or spiritual leader today who has also erred from the faith that he previously experienced as a way of life.

Of course, believers who follow an errant path of deception still lose plenty. They will experience a great loss of covenant blessings in this life, including one of the most precious — the loss of peace. They may even suffer the loss of their families, vocations, and fortunes. We should always remember — and pass on a warning to the next generation — that devastation inevitably follows when a person veers from the path of obedience to the faith.

We should always remember — and pass on a warning to the next generation — that devastation inevitably follows when a person veers from the path of obedience to the faith.

By using the words "just" and "righteous" to describe Lot in this context, Peter was assuring us that deceived believers who follow errant leaders are still saved. However, like Lot, they have been lured astray by seducing spirits that work to modify and contaminate the true faith.

Consequently, these believers have become more accommodating of lifestyles and behaviors condemned by Scripture.

In Second Peter 2:8, Peter wrote, "For that righteous man dwelling among them, in seeing and hearing, vexed his righteous soul from day to day with their unlawful deeds." The word "dwelling" is a translation of the Greek word *egkatoikeo*, and it depicts one who *settles into a home and feels comfortable there.*

Here we find Lot's first two mistakes: He chose the wrong place to live, and he chose the wrong friends. Not only did he choose the wrong friends, but he apparently pushed through the vexation of his soul and came to the point of accommodating their values and their lifestyles. It seems that Lot gradually became comfortable with those he associated with and chose to lay down his convictions in order to experience a piece of the worldly success that could be found in Sodom.

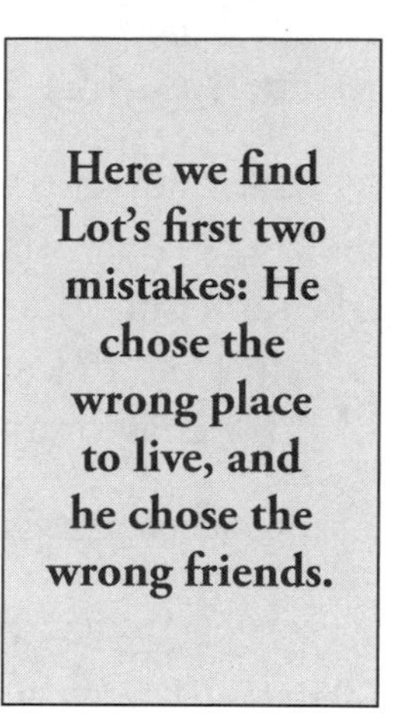

Likewise, most believers and spiritual leaders who falter spiritually do so because they choose wrong spiritual friends, associates, and advisors. Many good men and women of God have been tainted because they listened to the wrong people. They violated their convictions and listened to advice that they knew was questionable in order to be accepted by others or for the sake of promotion. Many started out as good men and women of God but lost their forward progress in His plan by laying aside their integrity through a series of poor decisions.

The decision to dwell among the wrong spiritual friends is always a dangerous step that leads down the road of deception. This is why every believer — *especially* spiritual leaders — must choose his or her spiritual company very carefully!

Numbing the Conscience

Peter continued to tell us more about Lot's spiritual and moral deterioration when he described Lot's position in Sodom. The verse says that Lot was "dwelling among them, in *seeing and hearing*" (2 Peter 2:8).

The words "seeing and hearing" represents Lot's next drastic mistake. Peter's illustration shows us the power of evil influences in a person's life.

Even current statistics prove that if a person watches enough violence on television, his sensitivity to violence will become numbed. The same statistics reveal that if a person watches enough pornography, in time that person will lose his sensitivity to the wrongness of this behavior and become *numb to* it.

What we watch and hear determines what we eventually become.

Lot watched and heard so much wickedness in the activities that transpired around him on a regular basis that he became numb and hardened to the evil of it. In fact, he became so calloused in his heart to the wrong he continually witnessed that he was able to live in the midst of it for an extended period of time.

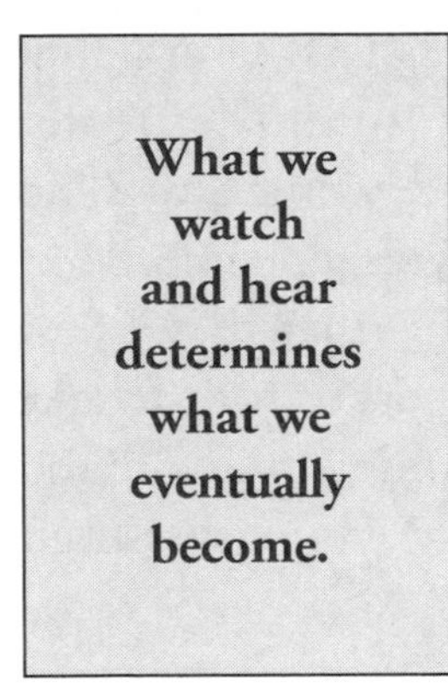

What happened to Lot will occur in any spiritual leader's life who chooses the wrong spiritual friends. If a leader continually subjects himself to watching and listening to people who have veered off the path of Scripture, he may be initially distressed by their unscriptural behavior. However, if he doesn't separate himself from those relationships and *stop* watching and listening to them, eventually he will become *numb* to the wrong. His conscience will become more and more calloused to the seriousness of their questionable behavior, and it is likely that this leader will be more prone to pick up some of his close associates' errant attitudes, beliefs, and behaviors himself.

Lot made the drastic mistake of regularly "seeing and hearing" things that were detrimental to his soul. This was part of the process that led to his becoming vexed in life.

God is plainly telling us that we must guard our eyes and our ears lest we make the same mistake. He has called us to be people of integrity who are not given to compromise.

God has called us to be people of integrity who are not given to compromise.

Spiritual Torture

As Peter continued in his description of how the pervasive sin of Sodom impacted Lot, he wrote, "...Dwelling among them, in seeing and hearing, *vexed* his righteous soul."

This particular word for "vexed" is a different Greek word than the word used before. This time, Peter used the Greek word *basanidzo*, which is the Greek word for *torture*. This word *basanidzo* tells us that at least at first — before Lot became numbed to his environment — seeing and hearing those sinful activities internally tore him to pieces. By willfully living in that dark and sinful environment where he should not have lived, and accommodating what he knew to be wrong, Lot subjected his mind and soul to unrelenting torment, which eventually reached the point of inner *torture*.

Lot mentally played with sin. He dwelt among the wrong crowd. He regularly subjected his eyes and ears to perverse and immoral activities that defiled his soul. All of this caused his life to become a protracted episode of inner torment that eventually led to callousness and deception. In fact, Lot's state of deception and insensitivity to sin became so rank that God had to literally *snatch* him from the fires of judgment.

The Lord Knows How To Deliver the Godly

Since Lot put himself in this position by his own free will, why did God dramatically intervene to rescue him from his own wrong choices? Furthermore, if a wayward believer or an errant spiritual leader does the same, what would cause God to act to snatch him or her out of destruction? Peter continued to use Lot as his example to answer these vital questions.

In Second Peter 2:9, Peter wrote, "The Lord knoweth how to deliver the godly out of temptation."

Because Lot is the example that Peter used in this text, we must turn to the Old Testament to see how God delivered Lot from his deceived way of living. In Genesis 18:1, we read that the Lord appeared to Abraham in the plains of Mamre with two angels. Genesis 18:16,17 says, "And the men rose up from thence, and looked toward Sodom: and Abraham went with them to bring them on the way. And the Lord said, Shall I hide from Abraham that thing which I do?"

Abraham and the three divine visitors walked toward the edge of the mountain that overlooked the valley where Sodom and Gomorrah was located. The Lord told Abraham, "Because the cry of Sodom and Gomorrah is great, and because their sin is very grievous; I will go down now, and see whether or not they have done altogether according to the cry of it, which is come unto me; and if not, I will know" (Genesis 18:20,21).

In the following verses, we discover that the Lord sent these two angels into the cities of Sodom and Gomorrah to make an investigation of the sin that was there. But Genesis 18:22 says, "And the men turned their faces from thence, and went toward Sodom; but Abraham stood yet before the Lord."

Especially notice that last phrase that says, "Abraham stood yet before the Lord." Abraham *knew* what the angels would find in Sodom and Gomorrah because he was well aware of the dark spiritual condition of these cities. But what deeply disturbed Abraham, and rightly so, was that Lot and his family were living in the midst of those perverse cities. Abraham knew that if God's judgment fell on those cities, Lot and his family would be destroyed along with the wicked population.

Abraham's Intercession

This is why "...Abraham stood yet before the Lord" (Genesis 18:22). Abraham understood that if he did not make intercession on Lot's behalf, his nephew and his family would be consumed as judgment fell upon Sodom and Gomorrah. It was for this reason that Abraham stepped forward to intercede for Lot. Abraham's first words of negotiation for Lot's life are found in Genesis 18:23, where it says, "And Abraham drew near, and said, Wilt thou destroy the righteous with the wicked?"

The words "Abraham drew near" reveal Abraham's seriousness to intercede for Lot's safety. This response of an intercessor is essential when we see a wayward believer or an errant spiritual leader who has been gripped with deception that has negatively affected himself and others. Whenever believers or leaders embrace error that will eventually bring destruction to their own lives or to the lives of others, we must step forward as Abraham did to intercede for their deliverance so they can escape the consequences of their disastrous choices. Surely we would want others to do the same for us if we ever fell into a trap of deception that could bring negative consequences to our lives and the lives of those around us!

So we see that even though Lot was living a misguided life in Sodom, Abraham drew near to the Lord and began his life-saving act of intercession. The scenario in Genesis reads like something one would see at a negotiation table as Abraham negotiated a deal to save Lot from the judgment that would soon fall upon Sodom and Gomorrah and the other wicked cities of that ill-fated plain. In Genesis 18:24, Abraham pleaded, "Peradventure there be fifty righteous within the city: wilt thou also destroy and spare not the place for the fifty righteous that are therein?"

Even though Lot was living a misguided life in Sodom, Abraham drew near to the Lord and began his life-saving act of intercession.

Abraham continued to negotiate deliverance for the remnant of the righteous in Sodom and Gomorrah. What if there were 45 righteous (*see* v. 28)? What if there were just 40 (*see* v. 29)? And what if there were only 30 righteous (*see* v. 30)? Or only 20 (*see* v. 31)? Ultimately Abraham aimed for the number 10 as he interceded. At last, Abraham heard the Lord say, "…I will not destroy it for ten's sake" (*see* v. 32).

Once Abraham heard this, he was assured that God would honor His promise and that he had sealed the safety of Lot and his family. Some Jewish scholars say that there were ten members of Lot's larger family living in the city. If this was the case and Abraham understood that fact from the first moment he began to intercede, why did he start his negotiation with the number 50 as he commenced to intercede for the righteous in that city? Even if this is not correct, is there a possible reason why he began with 50 and ended with 10?

You must remember that Abraham was the first to walk by faith as we know the walk of faith today, so it is entirely possible that he may not have known how bold he could be as he interceded for the deliverance of his beloved family. It appears that he cautiously proceeded before he boldly made request to God. But today we do not need to cautiously proceed as we pray for others who need someone to boldly intercede for their deliverance. Hebrews 4:16 states emphatically, "Let us therefore come *boldly* unto the throne of grace, that we may obtain mercy, and find grace to help in time of need."

The word "boldly" comes from the word *parresia,* a common Greek word that was normally used in ancient times to depict a person who *speaks his mind* and does it *straightforwardly* and with *great confidence.*

Because the Holy Spirit uses the word *parresia* in Hebrews 4:16, we know that whenever we approach the Lord in prayer, we need never fear that we are *too frank*, *too bold*, *too forthright*, *too honest*, *too outspoken*, or even *too blunt* as we bear our hearts to Him or request His help. We should never be irreverent, but neither do we need to be ashamed to speak exactly what is on our hearts.

When we go to the Lord, He *wants* to hear exactly what we have to say! The use of the word *parresia* also tells us that God is not bothered when we're honest with Him. He may correct us or take us to the Word to help fix our wrong thinking and believing, but He is always glad when we come to Him and speak freely from our hearts.

But the Holy Spirit continues to exhort us to "...come boldly unto the throne of grace, that we may *obtain* mercy, and find grace to help in time of need." The word "obtain" is a translation of the Greek word *lambano*, which means *to seize or to lay hold of something in order to make it your very own*, almost like a person who reaches out *to grab*, *to capture*, or *to take possession* of something. In some cases, it means *to violently lay hold of something in order to seize and take it as one's very own.*

This means it is right for you to reach out by faith *to forcibly lay hold of* God's delivering power when you intercede for those who are in trouble. And the verse continues to say that if you do this, you will "*find* grace to help in time of need." The word "find" is a translation of the frequently used Greek word *heurisko.* The word *heurisko* simply means *to find.* It expresses the idea of a discovery that is made by *searching.* It's where we get the word "eureka!"

Whenever we approach the Lord in prayer, we need never fear that we are *too frank, too bold, too forthright, too honest, too outspoken, or even too blunt* as we bear our hearts to Him or request His help.

Usually the word *heurisko* points to a discovery made due to an intense investigation, scientific study, or scholarly research. There's nothing left to chance in this kind of investigation. After working long hours and searching for a long time, a researcher's time and effort finally pay off as he finds what he has been seeking. In that ecstatic moment of euphoria, he shrieks, *"Eureka!"* — which means, *"I found it!"*

This means that as you seek God for His delivering power, you will capture exactly what you need from Him. So don't stop seeking it until you have finally laid hold of it and have made it your very own!

But there is something else very important about the word *heurisko* that I must point out. This word doesn't just describe a discovery made for yourself — it can also mean *to acquire something for someone else.* For example, if you know someone in need of deliverance as we have been discussing in this chapter, you can reach out by faith and acquire it for them. Because the word *heurisko* also means *to acquire something for someone else*, it means you can go to our Great High Priest and seek Him for help on behalf of others. You can obtain help for those who are in any type of need — which includes any wayward believers and errant leaders you are concerned about.

The phrase "help in time of need" is a translation of the Greek word *boetheia*, a word with a military connotation. The word *boetheia* can be translated *to help*, as *to help a person with his or her needs*, but the military connotation of this word adds much more meaning and makes its significance even more powerful.

In early New Testament times, the word *boetheia* was first and foremost a military word that depicted the moment when a soldier heard that a fellow fighter was entrenched or struggling in battle or was captured or wounded. Once alerted to this situation, the soldier quickly went to fight for the safety and well-being of his fellow fighter. Just hearing of a comrade in need was all that was necessary to beckon the soldier into battle, and he spared no effort as he went into action to rescue that comrade in arms and to bring him back to a place of safety, security, and protection.

As you seek God for His delivering power, you will capture exactly what you need from Him. So don't stop seeking it until you have finally laid hold of it and have made it your very own!

The Holy Spirit uses this same word to tell us what to do when we ourselves get into trouble, or if we are concerned about others who have slipped into trouble. We are to boldly and frankly come before the Father's throne to ask for help or to intercede for others. Jesus will then go into battle like a mighty Warrior to secure our deliverance or the deliverance of others!

This is "help" that Jesus wants to provide if we will boldly make intercession for those who have slipped and fallen in battle or who have been seduced into a wrong way of thinking, believing, and living. If we are willing to seek the Lord's assistance — and we refuse to stop standing in the gap for them until that divine help is manifested — Jesus will fight for them! He is waiting for us to come boldly before the Father's throne to ask for His delivering power in time of need.

Realizing this, we must draw near to God, as Abraham did on Lot's behalf, and boldly make intercession for erring believers or spiritual leaders who are headed in the wrong direction. And I feel compelled to say — how dare we talk about them and yet fail to pray for them!

We must draw near to God, as Abraham did on Lot's behalf, and boldly make intercession for erring believers or spiritual leaders who are headed in the wrong direction. And I feel compelled to say — how dare we talk about them and yet fail to pray for them!

Abraham absolutely knew what would happen once the angels arrived in the evil cities of Sodom and Gomorrah and completed their investigation of the perverseness they would find. He was deeply concerned because he loved Lot — and that love drove him to intercede. He knew Lot and his family would be devoured in the raging fires that would soon fall upon the cities if he did not intercede for them.

Likewise, if we see a brother or sister who is straying off course or a spiritual leader who has veered into some type of falsehood, we must act as Abraham did and make serious intercession before God on that person's behalf to rescue him from continuing on a course that could adversely impact many more lives than his alone.

Finally, Genesis 18:33 says, "And the Lord went his way, as soon as he had left *communing* with Abraham: and Abraham returned to his place." The fact that this kind of prayer is called "communing" with the Lord tells us that He enjoys it when His children come to Him to make straightforward prayer on behalf of others. God was delighted with Abraham's boldness in prayer, and He will be delighted with you as well when you pray confidently for those who have gone astray.

Furthermore, Genesis 18:33 says that when Abraham's work of intercession was done, he "returned to his place." This powerful statement informs us that because Abraham had ensured the safety of his family through prayer, he could go back home and sleep in peace because he knew that God would honor His Word.

What peace it brings to the soul when we can rest assured that someone has been delivered from destruction because of our prayerful intercession! For this reason, Abraham returned home, went to bed, and slept sweetly that night — knowing that God would honor his request and that Lot and his family would be preserved even if judgment fell on Sodom and Gomorrah.

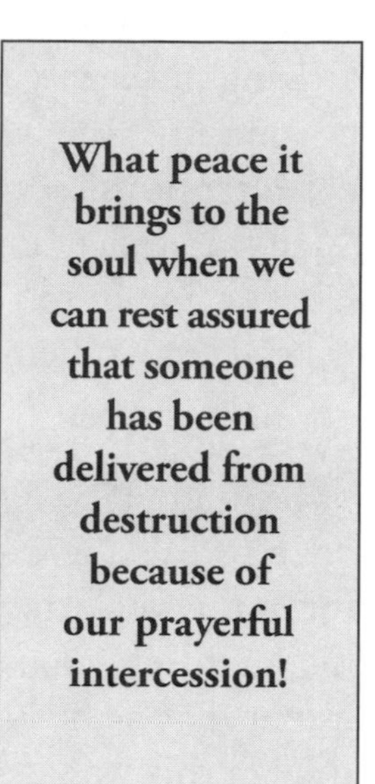

God Remembered Abraham

As the biblical account continues, we read that the angels arrived in Sodom that same night to investigate the sin of the city. When they arrived and met Lot, he beseeched them to come to his house and to not stay in the streets at night. It is probable that Lot knew what the angels would see if they stayed in the streets at night. It is likely that Lot didn't want these angels roaming the city during the nighttime lest they should see the rampant sin.

Lot may have even wanted to shield them from possible sexual advances made by the men of Sodom.

But the Sodomite men were so morally twisted that when they learned two new men were in town and were staying at Lot's house, they "…compassed the house round, both old and young, all the people from every quarter" (Genesis 19:4). These two angels looked like strong, good-looking men and had been in the city for only a brief time. However, the news of two new men arriving in the city had spread like wildfire throughout the entire community. The Sodomites burned with such lust and had such evil intentions for these two new men that verse 5 goes on to say, "And they called unto Lot, and said unto him, Where are the men which came in to thee this night? Bring them out unto us, that we may know them."

Genesis 19:7 states Lot's response when he came to the door of his house: "…I pray you, brethren, do not so wickedly." This verse reveals the extent to which Lot had compromised his life, for in this verse, he does the unthinkable and calls the Sodomites his "brethren." You see, Lot had violated his conscience to such an extent that he had blended his life with the men of the city, even though this was against the righteous standard that Lot inwardly knew to be true.

The full extent of how reprobate Lot had become is evident in Genesis 19:8, where he inconceivably said to the men of the city, "Behold now, I have two daughters which have not known man; let me, I pray you, bring them out unto you, and do ye to them as is good in your eyes: only unto these men do nothing; for therefore came they under the shadow of my roof."

In Lot's errant way of thinking, he believed it was all right for the men of Sodom to sexually take advantage of his daughters in order to spare the angels. But the men of Sodom did not want his daughters — they wanted the men who had come into his house that night. Genesis 19:9 tells us, "And they said, Stand back. And they said again, This one fellow came in to sojourn, and he will needs be a judge: now will we deal worse with thee, than with them. And they pressed sore upon the man, even Lot, and came near to break the door."

In other words, they responded by saying, "Who are you to be a judge of us?" This implies that Lot was not respected as a voice for morality in the midst of Sodom. Something had caused him to lose that moral voice. In fact, the sinners of Sodom found his stance that night to be hypocritical, which indicates that his lifestyle was possibly not too vastly different from their own. The men of Sodom were so outraged that Lot would attempt to tell them how to live that they even threatened to rape him if he did not immediately surrender the male visitors (the angels) to them (*see* v. 9).

Genesis 19:10,11 tells us the angels immediately intervened to deliver Lot from being raped by the men of Sodom that night. It says, "But the men [the two angels] put forth their hand, and pulled Lot into the house to them, and shut to the door. And they smote the men that were at the door of the house with blindness, both small and great: so that they wearied themselves to find the door."

Because the men of Sodom wanted to sexually exploit the new men in the city and were threatening to do even worse to Lot, the angels pulled Lot into the house and shut the door to keep the men away. Then the two angels struck those ungodly men with blindness to stop them.

It is revealing that the men of Sodom were so driven by demonic darkness that even in their blindness, they continued to try to find a way into the house to lay hold of the new arrivals to sexually exploit them. It is also important to note that the blindness that struck the men of Sodom would ensure that the Sodomites would not find their way out of the city when the fires began to fall.

Genesis 19:12,13 records that the angels had asked Lot, "Hast thou here any besides? son in law, and thy sons, and thy daughters, and whatsoever thou hast in the city, bring them out of this place: For we will destroy this place, because the cry of them is waxen great before the face of the Lord; and the Lord hath sent us to destroy it."

Imminent judgment was coming to the city, so Genesis 19:14 says, "And Lot went out, and spake unto his sons in law, which married his daughters, and said, Up, get you out of this place; for the Lord will destroy this city. But he seemed as one that mocked unto his sons in law."

It is interesting that Lot's daughters were married because he earlier stated that his daughters had never sexually known a man. This may give insight to how much Lot's own family had become affected by life in Sodom. Some scholars suggest that Lot's daughters had never had sex with their husbands because their husbands were part of the homosexual community in Sodom; in other words, even though legally married, the couples had never sexually consummated their marriage. If this is the case, it would certainly demonstrate the severity of Sodom's influence on Lot's own family.

Notice the Bible says that Lot "...seemed as one that mocked unto his sons in law." This tells us that the husbands of Lot's daughters had never seen Lot try to lead spiritually. In fact, when Lot suddenly began to speak about the judgment of God, the two men didn't take him seriously. They must have wondered, *So you're a preacher all of a sudden? You've got to be kidding! Who are you to raise a voice about what is right and wrong?* Even though Lot had previously known a life of faith before residing in Sodom, he hadn't led his family spiritually. Therefore, his sons-in-law didn't take him seriously at a crucial moment when it was imperative that he speak as a credible spiritual leader in his own home.

In Genesis 19:15 and 16, the narrative continues: "And when the morning arose, then the angels hastened Lot, saying, Arise, take thy wife, and thy two daughters, which are here; lest thou be consumed in the iniquity of the city. And while he lingered, the men laid hold upon his hand, and upon the hand of his wife, and upon the hand of his two daughters; the Lord being merciful unto him: and they brought him forth, and set him without the city."

Even though Lot had previously known a life of faith before residing in Sodom, he hadn't led his family spiritually. Therefore, his sons-in-law didn't take him seriously at a crucial moment when it was imperative that he speak as a credible spiritual leader in his own home.

The angelic visitors protected Lot and his family the entire night from the twisted men of Sodom who wearied themselves the whole night long to get into the house to sexually exploit the visitors and even Lot. After living in their protection the whole night, the next morning the angels urged Lot to quickly get his family together to leave the city before judgment fell. The Bible says they had to "hasten" Lot, which tells us that Lot was dragging his feet and was not wishing to leave the city he had come to call home.

The angels then warned him again that the city was about to be consumed. How did Lot respond? Genesis 19:16 tells us that he once again "lingered" — not wanting to give up his position, his comfort, or his surroundings, even though they were on the brink of damnation.

> **And while he** [Lot] **lingered, the men** [the angels] **laid hold upon his hand, and upon the hand of his wife, and upon the hand of his two daughters; the Lord — being merciful unto him: and they brought him forth, and set him without the city."**

In other words, the angels *forcibly dragged* him and his family out of the city against their wishes.

It is baffling that Lot — even though the angelic visitors were about to release God's judgment — did not want to leave Sodom. Lot had been warned that the city was about to go up in flames, but he didn't want to believe it would really happen. In the end, the angels had to actually *lay hold* of Lot and his family by the hands and *forcibly remove* them from the city against their wills before it was consumed!

Even with all the warnings they had received, Lot and his family didn't want to depart from Sodom. They held on to hope that God would overlook the sin of Sodom and decide not to pour out His judgment upon the Sodomites whom Lot had come to call his "brethren."

Genesis 19:24,25 tells us what happened when Lot and his family finally evacuated the city.

> **Then the Lord rained upon Sodom and upon Gomorrah brimstone and fire from the Lord out of heaven; and he overthrew those cities, and all the plain, and all the inhabitants of the cities, and that which grew upon the ground.**

In that terrible, cataclysmic moment as those cities were being destroyed, Lot's wife revealed her own inner surrender to the spiritual infection of Sodom's wicked surroundings. Despite the angel's warnings to refrain from looking back, Lot's wife turned to do just that as the destruction of the cities was taking place. In that wayward moment, she was turned into a pillar of salt. In her backward glance, Lot's wife had chosen to step away from deliverance and step back into judgment.

When God was finished dealing with Sodom and Gomorrah and the wicked sister cities of that plain, they were wiped out forever, never to be rebuilt. It was a permanent and lasting destruction of a region filled with man's rampantly perverse and unrepentant sinful activities.

While all these momentous activities were taking place, Abraham was at home sleeping peacefully because he had sealed Lot and his family's deliverance when he drew near to the Lord in intercession. Genesis 19:27,28 tells us what happened when Abraham woke up the next morning. He returned to the spot on the mountain's edge where he had made intercession and looked into the valley below to see what had occurred during his sleep that night. It says, "And Abraham got up early in the morning to the place where he stood before the Lord: and he looked toward Sodom and Gomorrah, and toward all the land of the plain, and beheld, and, lo, the smoke of the country went up as the smoke of a furnace."

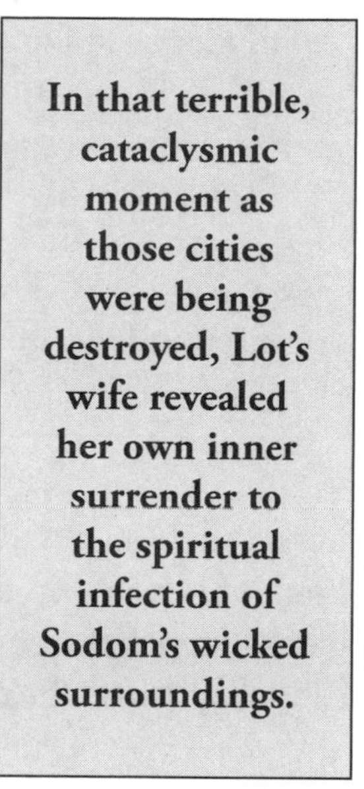
In that terrible, cataclysmic moment as those cities were being destroyed, Lot's wife revealed her own inner surrender to the spiritual infection of Sodom's wicked surroundings.

The entire floor of the valley had sunk, for the earth had swallowed the entire region. Smoke still rose in the air from the fire and brimstone that had fallen upon the cities.

Historians and archeologists generally agree that the ashen remains of the cities of Sodom and Gomorrah are located somewhere near the southern end of the Dead Sea or possibly even at the bottom of the Dead Sea. The Dead Sea remains the lowest geological location on the face of the planet even to this day. God completely destroyed the wicked cities of this plain — and to this very day, that region exists as a testimony to God's judgment upon sin.

Genesis 19:29 concludes by telling us, "And it came to pass, when God destroyed the cities of the plain, that God remembered Abraham, and sent Lot out of the midst of the overthrow, when he overthrew the cities in the which Lot dwelt."

Lot's was an ever-increasing fade and fall from a walk of faith by association until he had become fully acclimated to the sinful environment that surrounded him.

Lot's was an ever-increasing fade and fall from a walk of faith by association until he had become fully acclimated to the sinful environment that surrounded him. This is precisely the gradual process we as believers are to avoid regarding the toxic, unscriptural mindset of modern society: Tolerance leads to acceptance, and acceptance leads to changed ideals, values, and morals. Then a covenant child of God fully embraces the wrong.

God didn't save Lot for Lot's sake; he saved Lot and his family because of Abraham's intercession. Had it been left up to Lot, he would have remained in the city and would have been consumed along with everyone else. Lot was too calloused in his heart to understand the severity of his situation and to know he needed to be delivered. But God remembered Abraham's intercession, and He delivered Lot and his family because Abraham had drawn near to intercede on their behalf.

So Here's What You Must Do

This means that even if wayward believers or errant spiritual leaders do not realize the seriousness of their error, God will listen to us when we pray for them. This is why we must pray for those who are caught in deception. Like Lot, these individuals may be too deceived to comprehend how critical their situation really is. If it was left up to them, they may continue in their course of action, but we can make the difference on their behalf by stepping up to pray for them.

In Second Peter 2:9, Peter concluded his own commentary on Lot by saying, "The Lord knoweth how to deliver the godly out of temptations." How does God execute that deliverance? He responds to the intercession of those who are willing to stand in the gap on behalf of others who do not know to pray for themselves.

You see, when believers have stood in the gap and made intercession for those captured by deception, many have been spared from destruction. So rather than simply criticize those who are in error or bemoan the fact that people are veering from the truth in these last days, believers must once again become engaged as those who pray for their errant brethren's deliverance.

God expects you and me as part of His end-time Church to intercede for errant believers and spiritual leaders who have gone astray in this last season of the Church Age. Make no mistake — the Holy Spirit prophesied that a large contingent of people would depart from the faith in the very end of the age.

This is clearly stated in First Timothy 4:1, as we've discussed earlier in this book. But because we are the ones who live in this last prophetic time frame, part of our responsibility as end-time believers is to get on our knees and earnestly intercede for those who have departed from the faith so they can be rescued and set back on a right path. As people of God who have been entrusted by God to live in this exciting last-days season, we must accept this as part of our divine assignment.

God will likely urge other godly spiritual leaders to intervene according to Scripture and do whatever is possible to help restore those who are in error. However, the general assignment of believers is to intercede — as Abraham did — for their deliverance!

Rather than simply criticize those who are in error or bemoan the fact that people are veering from the truth in these last days, believers must once again become engaged as those who pray for their errant brethren's deliverance.

As you have read the pages of this book thus far, I'm certain you have thought of believers or spiritual leaders who seem to have veered from the clear teaching of Scripture. This indeed is heartbreaking. But rather than simply bemoan this development, you are commissioned by the Lord to use Abraham's example as a model and go before the Lord to intercede for these individuals.

The fact is, if these individuals are deceived, they will not understand the reality of their need to repent. But as you step forward to stand in the gap and pray for them, God may enact a plan to deliver them — because you, like Abraham, drew near to the Lord and interceded for them.

If you were caught in deception, wouldn't you want someone to do this for you?

Think About It

1. Just like Lot, we all arrive at crucial crossroad moments in life in which we have to make a decision that will impact the direction and outcome of our lives from that point forward. There will be a variety of voices trying to influence our decision — including our own soulish thoughts, preferences, and desires — yet only one Voice deserves to be heard. In that moment, it will matter which voice we've allowed to be the loudest in our lives in the years that came before.

   What was your last "crossroads moment"? Looking back on that time in your life and the many voices that vied for your attention — the Holy Spirit, loved ones, the devil, the world, your own flesh, your natural reasoning, your emotions — whose voice became the loudest and the one you ultimately followed? What have you learned from that decision that will help you make a precisely accurate God decision at the next intersection of your destiny?

2. We must never forget that if we don't deal with issues at the root, they will remain alive to possibly reactivate at a critical moment later in life.

   Perhaps the issue looks like a bad habit that used to hinder a person and he may have changed his behavior. But if the root of that issue is rebellion and that person never lays the axe to that root, he might find the former bad habit cropping up again down the road because he never fully repented for saying no to God.

   Can you think of a past sin or hindrance in your life that you've worked on eradicating? Are you assured that you have dealt a death blow to any lingering root system through deep repentance and the power of the Holy Spirit's "axe"? If not, set aside time with the Lord to receive His wisdom on what must be done to ensure that this issue never comes back to derail your progress.

3. You may personally know of people who outwardly seemed to be doing well, but then reasoned themselves out of God-given callings and assignments because they became weary of the faith journey. People's lives may appear one way on the surface while they carry a deeper struggle behind the scenes that no one sees. How would you describe the actual outcome of someone's decision to draw back from his or her divine call? What could that person have done differently in those moments of faltering faith to avoid such an outcome?

Chapter Eleven

HOW SHOULD WE RESPOND?

As we come to the close of this book, we must ask, "What is our responsibility if we see a believer or a spiritual leader take on the characteristics of falsehood, either through doctrinal error or sinful behavior?"

Because we are living in the very last season of the last days, it is likely we will be confronted with some of these difficult issues, whether we want to be confronted with them or not. Most of us know or are familiar with believers or spiritual leaders who have been led astray by seducing spirits and, as a result, have fallen into sin and unbiblical lifestyles or have embraced strange, unscriptural beliefs.

There is nothing more heartrending than to watch a person begin to abandon his scriptural foundations and take on the characteristics of falsehood and deception. It is especially grievous to see leaders with influence deviating from truth, knowing that it will ultimately cause them to lay aside sound doctrine and godly morals as they embrace beliefs and practices that will produce negative results — both in them and in those who follow their example and teachings.

But even though some have gone astray (*see* 2 Peter 2:15), it is critical to remember that the gifts and callings of God are

God is always redemptive, and His intention is to make a way for such individuals to be restored into their vital roles and to function once again in His marvelous plan for this hour.

without repentance (*see* Romans 11:29). These individuals may have been seduced to go in a wrong direction or pursue a wrong course. But if they will repent and get back on track, the call of God is still on them, and they can be used by Him once again.

One of my purposes in writing this book has been to help the reader understand how to respond to those who have gone astray in this end-time season of the Church Age. God is always redemptive, and His intention is to make a way for such individuals to be restored into their vital roles and to function once again in His marvelous plan for this hour.

Compassion for the Spiritually Sick

I want us to turn our attention one more time to the book of Jude, where we find another important passage of Scripture. In Chapter Four, we discussed the writer's words in Jude 3, where he urged believers to "earnestly contend for the faith." Yet with the same sense of urgency, Jude also instructed believers to be compassionate toward those who have fallen into any form of deception. He wrote, "And of some have compassion, making a difference: and others save with fear, pulling them out of the fire; hating even the garment spotted by the flesh" (Jude 22,23).

Often when someone we know and love — perhaps even someone we have trusted in the past —- falls into error or sin, we may be tempted to feel betrayed and angry toward that person. We may wonder how that person could have ever veered off track into such deep moral or spiritual foolishness. However, holding a hostile attitude against those who are walking in doctrinal error or living in blatant sin will not set them free — and it won't help our heart condition either.

It is impossible to understand the spiritual condition of a deceived believer or an errant spiritual leader if your feelings about that person are affected by bitterness or anger. I understand that it can be very difficult to line up your emotional response with the Word of God if the person is a long-time trusted friend or family member, or if he or she is a spiritual leader you have looked to and trusted in the past. However, it is only when your thoughts are cleared of anger and hostility that the love of God in you can be unleashed through earnest, heartfelt prayer to help set that person free from the deception that has led him or her into error.

In verse 22, Jude wrote about sinning believers and errant leaders, saying, "And of some have *compassion*...." The word "compassion" is a translation of the Greek word *eleao*, which in this case refers to *the deep-seated and unsettling emotions a person feels when he has seen or heard something that is terribly sad or upsetting*. These are emotions that may arise, for example, when you see a starving child whose stomach is bloated from malnutrition. You may also feel such emotions if you see an emaciated person dying of terminal cancer or if you encounter a family who is living in such destitute conditions that they are forced to live on the streets with little money or food and with bare necessities.

It is only when your thoughts are cleared of anger and hostility that the love of God in you can be unleashed through earnest, heartfelt prayer to help set that person free from the deception that has led him or her into error.

Jude's use of the Greek word "compassion" — the Greek word *eleao* — lets us know that he was trying to graphically help us see and understand the serious plight of those who have embraced error or who have compromised their walk of faith. But because Jude used the word "compassion," he was also telling us that the spiritual condition of wayward believers and errant spiritual leaders is just as real and serious as the plight of a starving child, a dying man or woman, or a destitute family.

We need to understand the serious implications of error. When embraced, error infects and sickens a person spiritually and holds the potential of becoming spiritually lethal — a killer of ministries and destinies — unless the process of deception is arrested and the person truly repents.

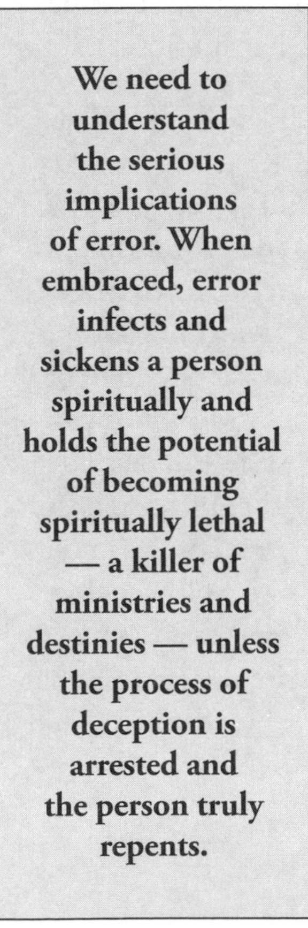

But as we allow the love of God to operate in us, compassion for these errant believers will begin to flow from us to them, and that stream of divine compassion will move us into prayer on their behalf and away from a judgmental attitude against them. God's compassion within us will compel us to do all we can to see these believers set free from the deception that has gripped them.

Concerning errant leaders, keep in mind that these individuals have ingested the poison of spiritual error and as a result have become sickened with spiritual toxins. They are spiritually ill people whose situations are grave. You may be upset with them for laying aside Scripture — and to be truthful, this *should* be upsetting. But harboring anger against those who have taken a wayward path won't remedy their spiritual condition — and it will harm *yours* for taking a wrong stance in your heart against those who err!

In such cases, we must learn to let the compassion of Christ flow from our hearts toward those who have become infected with spiritual error. Compassion is a mighty force that releases astonishing amounts of spiritual power. And as you allow His compassion to flow from you in prayer toward error-ridden people, that spiritual force goes to work to trigger the deliverance they so desperately need from the deceptive darkness that has grabbed hold to drag them into seduction. The powerful flow of God's power, released as you pray from His heart of compassion, has the ability to break the chains that came to gradually, bit by bit, bind their souls and their minds. Their condition may be so grave that only intervention by God will open their eyes and enable them to see their way out of the dark place they are in right now. This was the reason Jude urged, "And of some have *compassion....*"

If you know wayward believers or errant spiritual leaders, it is important to recognize their error and perhaps to even address it if appropriate. But becoming critical of those caught in deception will not help set them free, and it will negatively affect you. Address the error if needed, pray for them, and let the compassion of Jesus Christ flow from your heart toward them to help open their eyes and bring them back to where they need to be.

Never forget that divine compassion is a mighty force that reaches even into the flames of judgment to snatch people out of destruction, just as Abraham moved in prayer and compassion to intercede for Lot. We *must* open our hearts and become willing conduits of this supernatural flow of God's compassion toward those ensnared by deception in order to set their freedom in motion through the power of prayer.

Making a Difference — Distinguishing the Truth From a Lie

But then we come to the second point in Jude's exhortation, where he said, "And of some have compassion, *making a difference....*"

This phrase "making a difference" is translated from the Greek word *diakrinos*, which is a compound of the words *dia* and *krino*. The word *dia* carries the idea of *dividing* or *separating*, and *krino* means *to judge* or *to determine*. But when these two words are compounded into one word, in this verse, the new word pictures *an individual who has lost his ability to separate right from wrong*, and it can even depict *those who are unable to tell the difference between the truth and a lie*.

It is interesting that Jesus used this very word in Mark 11:23 when He said, "For verily I say unto you, That whosoever shall say unto this mountain, Be thou removed, and be thou cast into the sea; and shall not *doubt* in his heart, but shall believe that those things which he saith shall come to pass; he shall have whatsoever he saith."

In Mark 11:23, the word "doubt" is a translation of *diakrinos*, which is the same word translated "making a difference" in Jude 22. In Mark 11:23, the word *diakrinos* describes *chronic instability in what one believes and says.*

I find it significant that the Greek word *diakrinos* used in Jude 22 and translated as "making a difference" is the same word translated as "doubt" elsewhere. Believers or spiritual leaders who have gone astray develop a chronic instability in what they believe — and, ultimately, they begin to doubt God's Word altogether, even questioning the most basic fundamentals of scriptural truth. They sink deeper and deeper into deception and become so spiritually unstable that they begin to chronically question and doubt important Bible truths that they once believed and embraced. By using the word *diakrinos* — translated "making a difference" in Jude 22 — Jude informed us that individuals who are deceived are unable to reach accurate spiritual conclusions and therefore often embrace what they would have once deemed to be spiritual error or morally wrong.

Why Many Are Seduced

In Second Timothy 2:25, Paul told us that deceived believers and errant spiritual leaders need help to get back on track. He wrote, "In meekness instructing those that oppose themselves." The word "instructing" is key to understanding why many are seduced into doctrinal error. By using this word "instructing" in regard to helping errant spiritual leaders, Paul actually painted a picture and gave us the primary reason these individuals become so spiritually unstable and doctrinally veer off track.

The word "instructing" is a translation of the Greek word *paideuo*, which describes *the training, education, and instruction of a young, immature child*. Originally, the word *paideuo* denoted the act of enrolling a young child in his first classes at school where he would learn how to behave with other children and receive the elementary education needed to eventually progress to higher levels as he grew older.

Paul therefore sent a clear message by using this word pertaining to people who have gotten off base doctrinally. He was saying that these are misguided individuals who somehow missed spiritual kindergarten and never learned the basics — the foundational "ABCs" — of the Word of God. Having never had a solid foundation, they still try to advance to weightier levels, only to build a spiritual structure that is defective from the outset and destined to eventually collapse.

Just imagine the mess that would develop if a child never learned his ABCs, how to spell, or the basics of mathematics or science, yet he aspired to become a physicist. It's an understatement to say that such a person would inevitably make drastic errors leading to failure in his chosen profession. Regardless of how sincere he might be in his dream to become a physicist, this person would be unqualified because he lacks the prerequisite foundational knowledge required to advance to such a professional position.

These are misguided individuals who somehow missed spiritual kindergarten and never learned the basics — the foundational "ABCs" — of the Word of God. Having never had a solid foundation, they still try to advance to weightier levels, only to build a spiritual structure that is defective from the outset and destined to eventually collapse.

In Second Timothy 2:25, the apostle Paul made it clear that misguided believers and errant spiritual leaders go far afield because they were never educated in foundational teaching. Their knowledge of the Word of God is that of a babe, not a mature man, and since they lack the basics as part of their spiritual foundation, it is easier for these off-base Christians to be led astray by seducing spirits and doctrines of demons.

This is the image Paul had in mind when he told Timothy, "In meekness instructing those that oppose themselves...." The word *paideuo* indicates that to correct the doctrinal problems of those who have veered from the faith, someone must be able to "take them back to school" spiritually and begin to teach them the basic ABCs of God's Word that they missed along the way.

The problem is, by this time, pride has likely entered the picture. As a result, it is rare for a Christian who has fallen into error to be humble enough to receive instruction in the basics.

The truth is, if wayward believers had received a solid foundation in the Word of God earlier, they wouldn't likely be coming to the drastically wrong spiritual conclusions they're embracing at the point of their errancy. Their moral and doctrinal miscalculations are clear evidence that they "missed their ABCs." Consequently, they are being tossed to and fro on every wind of doctrine, constantly chasing one "new revelation" after another, because they have no firm foundation on which to build their spiritual lives.

This chronic spiritual instability is corrected only one way — by going back to the beginning and "learning the ABCs" of God's Word. Hebrews 5:14 tells us that this basic knowledge of God's Word gives people the ability to know what is right and wrong. That is why Paul told Timothy to "instruct" them. In other words, Paul was saying, "To get these people back on track, you need to 'take them back to elementary school' and give them a good education in the basics of the Bible."

This leads us back to Jude 22, where Jude declared, "And of some have compassion, *making a difference*…." In this statement, Jude was describing the illogical spiritual conclusions of errant believers and leaders. I remind you that the phrase "making a difference" — like doubt — has to do with one's inability to come to a final, stable, reliable conclusion about a matter. But rather than accuse these individuals of doing deliberate harm to the Church, Jude essentially stated, *"These people obviously never received a solid foundation for their spiritual lives, so it's no wonder they come to illogical spiritual conclusions. They don't even know their ABCs!"*

There's No Time To Lose

Jude continued by making this third point: "And others *save* with fear..." (v. 23). The word "save" comes from the Greek word *sodzo*. In this verse, it is used in the present active imperative tense, which means the Greek calls for immediate, fast, and continuous or steadfast action. Furthermore, this was not a suggestion from Jude; this was a *command.*

The word "fear" is from the word *phobos*, and it refers to *a fear that results from a threatening or alarming circumstance*. The fact that Jude would use this word indicates that the errant believers and spiritual leaders he was writing about were on the brink of some type of destruction. This would explain why Jude commanded his readers to act *fast* and *immediately*. These deceived saints were on the edge of imminent disaster, and if someone didn't act fast and do something to rescue them, they would suffer catastrophe.

This reminds me again of Lot — a man living on the brink of disaster who didn't understand the seriousness of his plight. However, because Abraham acted quickly to stand in the gap for his nephew and intercede for his deliverance, Lot's life was spared.

In the same way, Jude commanded his readers — and us — to be moved to action *immediately* because the circumstances of those who are in error are so serious. We must do everything we know to do to "save" these individuals as quickly as possible. A crucial ingredient of that saving process includes intercession, just as Abraham interceded for Lot.

As we pray and stay sensitive to the leading of the Holy Spirit, He will show us what other steps we might need to take to see deliverance come to those who have been led astray. The Holy

Spirit has the key to every person's heart, and He is ready to give us that key if we will hear Him speak to us.

Compassion That Reaches Into the Flames

Jude went on in verse 23 to state his fourth important point. When believers see other Christians headed down a dangerous path of spiritual deception, they must engage in "…pulling them out of the fire…."

Many scholars point out that Jude is a parallel book to Second Peter and that these two books of the Bible cover much of the same material. It is evident in these verses that Jude was putting before us the image of Lot escaping from Sodom and Gomorrah just before the fires of judgment fell, just as Peter described in Second Peter 2:6-9.

As we discussed in the previous chapter, Lot was "snatched" out of the raging fires of destruction by two angels God sent to investigate the sinfulness of Sodom and Gomorrah and to release judgment against those cities. We also saw that Lot was so spiritually calloused by living for an extended period of time in the midst of that negative environment that he didn't want to leave the condemned city, even when the angels informed him that judgment was coming. Genesis 19:16 tells us that the two angels had to nearly *drag* him out of Sodom before the fires fell upon the city to destroy it.

Using this example of Lot being rescued from Sodom by the two angels, Jude alerted us to *our* responsibility to help those who come across our path, caught in a web of deception. If their conscience is seared as was Lot's, they may not realize how serious their spiritual condition really is. In such cases, the Holy Spirit through Jude commands us to intervene. Just as the angels did for Lot, we are to do all we can in earnest, compassionate intercession to pull those people from the imminent fires of destruction.

The word "pulling" is from the Greek word *harpadzo* and conveys the picture of *laying hold of and snatching* someone out of a dangerous situation. We must obey this command by doing everything within our ability — through prayer empowered by divine compassion — *to lay hold of* and *to snatch* people out of their spiritually dangerous predicaments. Although wayward believers or leaders may not feel the heat of the fire or realize the seriousness of their spiritual condition, the Scriptures show that they *will* experience a negative consequence of some kind if intervention is not made on their behalf.

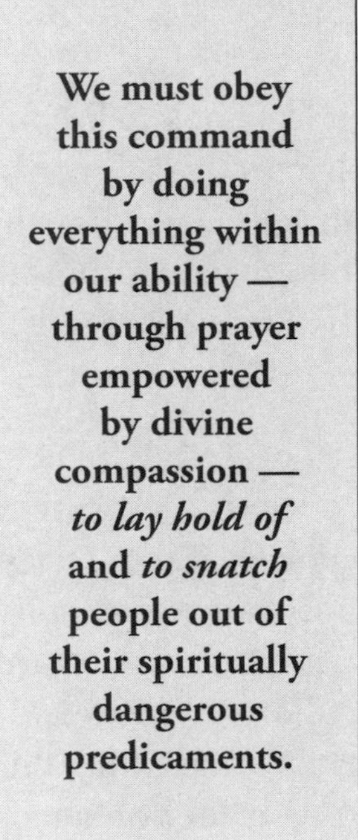
We must obey this command by doing everything within our ability — through prayer empowered by divine compassion — *to lay hold of* and *to snatch* people out of their spiritually dangerous predicaments.

We are not to just sit by and watch errant Christians sink deeper and deeper into deception. When we see people lured off track, we must pray and seek the guidance of the Holy Spirit. He will show us how to pray and whether we are to be further involved in helping them wake up to the reality of their situation so they can be delivered from the judgment they are about to bring upon themselves.

When Hate Is Right

For his fifth point, Jude wrote, "...Hating even the garment spotted by the flesh" (v. 23). The word "hate" is taken from the word *miseo.* It is one of the strongest words in the Greek language, and it means *to hate, to abhor*, or *to find utterly repulsive*. It describes a *deep-seated animosity* to something that one finds to be *completely objectionable*. A person experiencing this level of *miseo* not only *loathes* the object of his animosity, but he also *rejects* it entirely. This is not just a dislike; it is a case of *actual hatred*.

So when Jude told us to "hate" the garment spotted by the flesh, he was actually telling us that we should *loathe* this type of *fleshly contamination*. And notice Jude said that we are to hate the "garment." This is a Greek word that refers to a person's *undergarment*, not to the outer robe that a person wore in public.

Jude used this particular word meaning *undergarment* for "garment" to describe *moral contamination* that has gone beyond a mere surface contamination. This is moral decay that has begun to contaminate even the deepest part of this person's being. The filth Jude alluded to is not merely an outward problem like the outer cloak of a person's clothing. It symbolizes *a moral contamination that touches the deepest and most hidden parts of an individual's life and character*.

The implication is that at one time, this defilement may have been like loose soil on the outer robe of a man's clothing. But because the surface dirt was never washed away, the soil has now begun to permeate and penetrate all the way through to the undergarments — to the deepest level of a person's life.

Jude furthermore wrote that the hidden parts of such a person have been "spotted." The word translated "spotted" comes from a form of the Greek word *spilos*, which means *to stain*, *to defile*, or *to contaminate*. This defilement has spread throughout the person's entire being until deception has *spilled* into every area of his life. Realizing the seriousness of this condition, Jude says, "And of some have compassion, making a difference: others save with fear, pulling them out of the fire; hating even the garment spotted by the flesh."

**If you put all these Greek words together,
Jude 22 and 23 carry this idea:**

"You must have a compassionate attitude toward those so spiritually calloused that they no longer know the difference between right and wrong. The truth is that these unstable people are living right on the brink of disaster and are in real spiritual jeopardy. Their plight is so grave that it requires an immediate rescue plan to snatch them from the fires of destruction...."

In Conclusion

In the introduction to this book, I began by saying we are living in a historical moment about which the Holy Spirit had much to prophesy more than 2,000 years ago when the apostles were writing their epistles in the First Century. We are coming to the conclusion of that end-time period, and what the Holy Spirit long ago prophesied is coming to pass precisely as He so clearly predicted when the Scriptures were being written.

The Holy Spirit prophesied that there would be increased activity of seducing spirits and doctrines of demons at the end of this age. As the prophetic clock has continued to wind down toward the end, we have witnessed spirits of deception released full steam into the world. Their goal is to lure society into a mindset void of the voice of Scripture and to create a new world order divested of any absolute moral code. Isaiah prophesied that eventually people would call darkness light and light darkness (*see* Isaiah 5:20). That long-prophesied time has arrived. We are living in the midst of mind-boggling deception.

But as we have seen in this book, the Bible also prophesied that there would be a mighty outpouring of the Holy Spirit's power upon the Church as the age neared its conclusion that would result in a great last-days harvest of souls. We are in the middle of that great outpouring right now, and the Spirit of God is being mightily poured out with Heaven-sent power throughout the earth. Many are being gloriously swept into the Kingdom — and restored to soundness of spirit and mind — in every part of the globe.

In fact, many are entering the Church so quickly that they are bringing much of the world's erroneous thinking in with them. And as we have seen, there is a concerning trend as some leaders opt to modify doctrine to fit this confused mindset rather than correct the unscriptural beliefs that people bring with them when they come to Christ.

The Spirit of God is being mightily poured out with Heaven-sent power throughout the earth. Many are being gloriously swept into the Kingdom — and restored to soundness of spirit and mind — in every part of the globe.

We've seen that some leaders and pastors no longer emphasize the teaching of the Bible and its foundational doctrines as they once did. Consequently, the Church has become flooded with people who call Jesus "Lord," yet who don't know even the most basic Bible doctrines that are so vital to those living under the Lordship of Jesus Christ. Much of what is being communicated in pulpits and in Christian media is a reflection of pop culture more than a representation of the life-changing truths of the Bible. In the midst of it all, there has been the end-time invasion of seducing spirits into society *and into the Church* to lure people into ways of thinking that are demonically inspired and unscriptural.

As for our stance regarding wayward believers and spiritual leaders who have bought into modern-day lies and demonic distortions of truth — we are to intercede for them in their dire situation, motivated by the compassion of God. Our goal should always be to help effect their deliverance and restoration. Although it may be necessary to deal with their errors, we need never hold attitudes of anger or hostility against them. They themselves are victims of deception and need God's delivering power to set them free. Our part is to act as triggers in the process of their deliverance, releasing that divine power through the flow of God's compassion in intercessory prayer.

It's also the responsibility of every believer to help guard against further departures from the sound teaching of Scripture. Both believers and leaders must reinforce themselves in the doctrinal teachings of Scripture, for it is the bedrock of their faith.

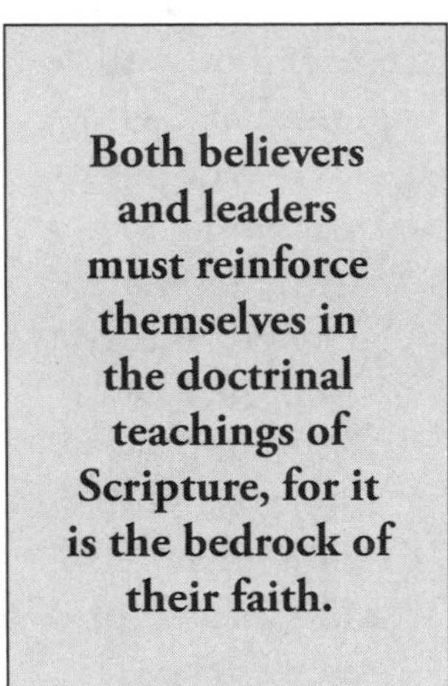

When it comes to these vital, foundational points, there is no room for negotiation or mitigation. To continue to be ignorant of what we believe and why we believe it — and therefore unable to defend it — is inexcusable. This is especially true for those who claim to be spiritually mature or who are numbered among those in spiritual leadership.

As I said in the Introduction, we must understand the times we're living in. These are the greatest of days and the most troublesome of times. Society is throwing off the authoritative voice of the Bible and seems bent on embracing ungodly behaviors and self-destructive ways of thinking. Many in the Church are doing the same or don't know how to respond to the doctrinal errors they see developing all around them. In a tumultuous time such as this, it is *imperative* that we keep our heads on straight in a world that seems to be going crazy.

We are called to be a light in darkness for a world that is sinking ever deeper into depravity. Society desperately needs the authoritative voice of God's Word held out as both a plumb line of truth and a lifeline for deliverance. We have absolutely no need to apologize for holding fast to His Word and its unchanging power.

The Bible alone has the power to liberate minds and free people from the deception that is raging across the globe in every stratum of society — and the devil knows it. The enemy is very aware that within the pages of the Bible lies the power to set men free. For this reason, Satan seeks to nullify the voice of Scripture and relegate the Bible to a dusty place on the bookshelf, an antiquated document that no longer has relevance for the present age.

We are called to be a light in darkness for a world that is sinking ever deeper into depravity. Society desperately needs the authoritative voice of God's Word held out as both a plumb line of truth and a lifeline for deliverance.

In Isaiah 60:1, Isaiah foretold that a day would come when gross darkness would come upon the peoples of the earth. However, he also triumphantly declared that it would also be the golden moment on God's timeline for His people to rise and shine the light of His glory to those who sit in darkness.

This is that prophetic hour. That's why the devil is presently so intent on derailing the Church from its predestined mission. This is why the enemy has so vigorously attacked the Church through deception to undermine the authority of the Bible.

For this reason, we who make up the Church must plant ourselves on the bedrock of Scripture and *refuse* to budge from the authority of God's holy Word. We must learn to partner with the

Holy Spirit to see the power of God released in the Church to drive back the forces of darkness in society and set people free. This truly is our greatest moment — but for that very reason, we must be more alert and watchful than ever.

Make no mistake — the devil *will* try to disrupt what God desires to do in this day. Satan will do his utmost to subtly lead God's people astray through doctrinal deception and moral compromise. But we have the victory through the name of Jesus, the blood of Jesus, and the power of His eternal Word! Our part is to use our minds wisely and to stay sensitive to the Holy Spirit as we learn to be led by Him with increasing accuracy.

We must learn to partner with the Holy Spirit to see the power of God released in the Church to drive back the forces of darkness in society and set people free. This truly is our greatest moment — but for that very reason, we must be more alert and watchful than ever.

It's a time to move forward with great wisdom and discernment as God's representatives on the earth. Although a confused mix of man's words and chaotic events may swirl around us, we must choose to hold fast to our faith in God's eternal truth. The devil will not stop trying to find his way into the midst of God's people. We may as well settle that in our hearts. But knowing that, we can stand fast in our place — *with heads on straight* — to help block every inroad and keep God's plan moving forward till the moment of His glorious return!

Think About It

1. God is a redemptive God. He proved Himself to be so when He gave His only Son to be the legal Sacrifice required to redeem mankind (*see* John 3:16). As Author, God created mankind, and as Finisher, He foreordained a redemptive way for fallen mankind to finish well.

   Nevertheless, it is still up to man to *choose* to finish well. And in the case of individuals who have been seduced to go in a wrong direction or pursue a wrong course, they must choose to repent and get back on track. As soon as they genuinely make that choice, they are washed clean of all wrong by the blood of Jesus (*see* 1 John 1:9). The call of God that is still on them will begin to develop and get stronger (*see* Romans 11:29). And as they put their trust in the Lord and humbly allow Him to do His full work in them, they will in time be ready to operate in the purity of that divine calling.

   In that divine redemptive process just described, you have a vital part! How would you explain the role you and other believers are to play in helping someone who veered off course get back on track? What are some of the vital spiritual keys that will ensure your effectiveness in that role?

2. Divine compassion is a spiritual force that sets the work of deliverance in motion when we open our hearts and fervently pray for those ensnared by error. We actually become living conduits of this supernatural flow of God's compassion toward those hurt by the destruction deception brings. We must simply yield to the Holy Spirit and release His power to set people free through prayer.

Have you ever experienced a time of prayer when a deep sense of God's compassion for whomever you were praying rose up in you as you interceded? Did you know whom you were praying for or what that person (or persons) was facing? Did you keep on praying till you sensed victory — even if you *didn't* know?

3. When people are caught in the snare of deception, their spiritual eyes must open so they can regain their ability to see the difference between the truth and a lie.

   Through heartfelt prayer, the veil is lifted from spiritual eyes (*see* 2 Corinthians 3:14). The entrance of God's Word brings light (*see* Psalm 119:130). The work of the Word through the power of prayer builds a rock-solid spiritual foundation needed to undergird each life.

   As you've read this last chapter, what has the Lord been speaking to your heart about *your* role in this crucial end-time hour? What does God want you to do in the days ahead to help further His redemptive process in other people's lives who are caught in some way in the snare of deception? How can you personally strengthen your foundation in the Word, deepen your prayer life, and "rise and shine" in the light of His glory to fulfill your part in His great plan before Jesus' return?

A PRAYER OF CONSECRATION

Father, after reading this book, I want to stop long enough to respond to these words that have challenged me in my walk with You. I thank You that You have strengthened my heart and are faithful to uphold me as I take a firm stand for the truth of Your Word. I purpose never to deviate from that stance. Regardless of popular opinion or current trends or what those around me choose to do, I have decided to stick with the immutable voice of the Bible and to remain anchored to its eternal truths.

Holy Spirit, I depend on You to empower me to remain firm in my commitment to Christ and to the Scriptures in these last days. As Christians become more unpopular, I thank You that You strengthen me and the believers around me so that we are able to remain strong and loving toward those who don't agree with our commitment.

Father, I pray for my family, friends, and for all believers who have made a similar decision to never veer from God's Word. We are living in troublesome times when pressure is being applied from nearly every direction to alter what we believe, so I pray for the power of Your Spirit to flood me and those who have made the decision to walk in the Bible's truths. I also ask You to fill our hearts with Your compassion for the Christians we know who have begun to veer off track. They need our love, not our judgment.

I pray for those who have already become wayward and have veered off track. I ask You to bring them back to where they need to be in the safe shelter of Your Word. The direction they are headed will ultimately lead to so many wrong choices with destructive results. Father, before they reap the consequences of their bad choices, I ask You to send voices to them that they will listen to — with just the right words to help them wake up, come to their spiritual senses, and be restored. I thank You that Your heart is for total restoration of everyone who has ears to hear what You are saying to them. Father, I ask You to open their spiritual ears and give them open hearts to receive and to act on what they hear.

I ask You to intervene in these wayward believers' lives — just as You intervened in Lot's life because of Abraham's intercession for him. Do it for me, Lord, because I am standing in the gap for them. I thank You that as I pray, You've already set in motion the process to snatch them out of destruction. They will be set back on a solid path that will make them a shining example of what Your power and grace can do in lives that have been restored.

I am concerned about what I see in society, in my nation, and even in the Church, so I pray for purity of ministry and for the precious Word of God to be awakened in our midst. Let a real revival of the Bible return to Your people, Father. I ask You to empower and anoint spiritual leaders on every level to speak as Your prophetic voice to this generation. Let courage flood their hearts so they rise up to speak truth even if it isn't politically correct in these times. Give pastors and spiritual leaders a burning desire to know You through Your eternal Word and then to impart the fullness of Your Word to Your people.

Last, I pray for the Church at large — as well as for my local church — to remain rooted in Scripture and to know and regularly experience the powerful demonstration of the Holy Spirit. I pray that the Church will be established both in the teaching of the Bible and in biblical teaching on the operations of the Holy Spirit. I pray that the gifts and power of the Holy Spirit will flow the way You long for Your people to know and experience them. Let Your Word and Your Spirit work together to bring us into the fullness of Christ as we approach the end of this age.

I pray all of this in Jesus' name!

ABOUT THE AUTHOR

RICK RENNER is a highly respected Bible teacher and leader in the international Christian community. Rick is the author of a long list of books, including the bestsellers *Dressed To Kill* and *Sparkling Gems From the Greek 1* and *2*, which have sold millions of copies in multiple languages worldwide. Rick's understanding of the Greek language and biblical history opens up the Scriptures in a unique way that enables readers to gain wisdom and insight while learning something brand new from the Word of God.

Rick is the founding pastor of the Moscow Good News Church. He also founded Media Mir, the first Christian television network in the former USSR that broadcasts the Gospel to countless Russian-speaking viewers around the world via multiple satellites and the Internet. He is the founder and president of RENNER Ministries, based in Tulsa, Oklahoma, and host to his TV program that is seen around the world in multiple languages. Rick leads this amazing work with his wife and lifelong ministry partner, Denise, along with the help of their sons and committed leadership team.

CONTACT RENNER MINISTRIES

For further information
about RENNER Ministries, please contact
the RENNER Ministries office nearest you,
or visit the ministry website at
www.renner.org.

**ALL USA
CORRESPONDENCE:**
RENNER Ministries
P. O. Box 702040
Tulsa, OK 74170-2040
(918) 496-3213
Or 1-800-RICK-593
Email: renner@renner.org
Website: www.renner.org

MOSCOW OFFICE:
RENNER Ministries
P. O. Box 789
101000, Russia, Moscow
+7 (495) 727-14-67
Email: partner@rickrenner.ru
Website: www.ignc.org

RIGA OFFICE:
RENNER Ministries
Unijas 99
Riga LV-1084, Latvia
+371 67802150
Email: info@goodnews.lv

KIEV OFFICE:
RENNER Ministries
P. O. Box 300
01001, Ukraine, Kiev
+38 (044) 451-8315
Email: partner@rickrenner.ru

OXFORD OFFICE:
RENNER Ministries
Box 7, 266 Banbury Road
Oxford OX2 7DL, England
+44 (0) 1865 355509
Email: europe@renner.org

BOOKS BY RICK RENNER

Chosen by God* (updated edition; formerly titled, *Say Yes!*)
Dream Thieves*
Dressed To Kill*
The Holy Spirit and You*
How To Keep Your Head on Straight in a World Gone Crazy
How To Receive Answers From Heaven!*
Insights to Successful Leadership
Life in the Combat Zone*
A Light in Darkness, Volume One,
Seven Messages to the Seven Churches series
The Love Test*
No Room for Compromise, Volume Two,
Seven Messages to the Seven Churches series
Paid in Full*
The Point of No Return*
Repentance*
Seducing Spirits and Doctrines of Demons
Signs You'll See Just Before Jesus Comes*
Sparkling Gems From the Greek Daily Devotional 1*
Sparkling Gems From the Greek Daily Devotional 2*
Spiritual Weapons To Defeat the Enemy*
Ten Guidelines To Help You Achieve Your Long-Awaited
Promotion!*
Turn Your God-Given Dreams Into Reality*
Why We Need the Gifts of the Spirit*
The Will of God — The Key to Your Success*
You Can Get Over It*

*Digital version available for Kindle, Nook, and iBook.
Note: Books by Rick Renner are available for purchase at:
www.renner.org

SPARKLING GEMS FROM THE GREEK 1

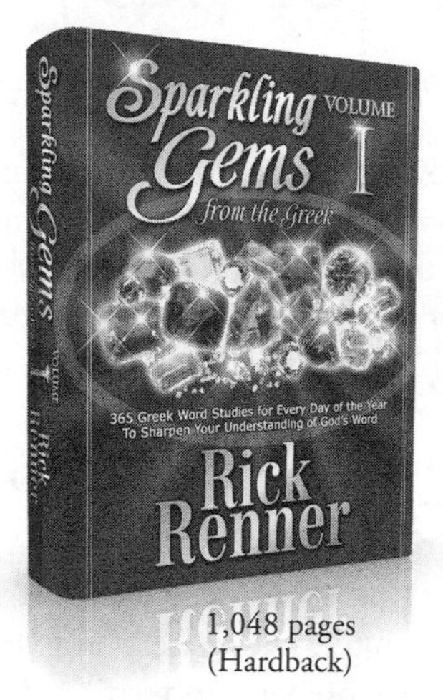

1,048 pages
(Hardback)

In 2003, Rick Renner's ***Sparkling Gems From the Greek 1*** quickly gained widespread recognition for its unique illumination of the New Testament through more than 1,000 Greek word studies in a 365-day devotional format. Today *Sparkling Gems 1* remains a beloved resource that has spiritually strengthened believers worldwide. As many have testified, the wealth of truths within its pages never grows old. Year after year, *Sparkling Gems 1* continues to deepen readers' understanding of the Bible.

To order, visit us online at: **www.renner.org**

Book Resellers: Contact Harrison House at 800-722-6774
or visit **www.HarrisonHouse.com** for quantity discounts.

SPARKLING GEMS FROM THE GREEK 2

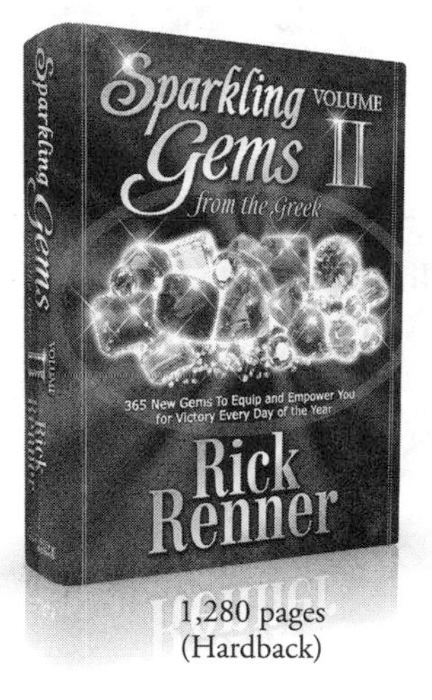

1,280 pages
(Hardback)

Now Rick infuses into ***Sparkling Gems From the Greek 2*** the added strength and richness of many more years of his own personal study and growth in God — expanding this devotional series to impact the reader's heart on a deeper level than ever before. This remarkable study tool helps unlock new hidden treasures from God's Word that will draw readers into an ever more passionate pursuit of Him.

To order, visit us online at: **www.renner.org**

Book Resellers: Contact Harrison House at 800-722-6774
or visit **www.HarrisonHouse.com** for quantity discounts.

SIGNS YOU'LL SEE JUST BEFORE JESUS COMES

208 pages
(Paperback)

As we advance toward the golden moment of Christ's return for His Church, there are signs on the road we're traveling to let us know where we are in time. Jesus Himself foretold the types of events that will surely take place as we watch for His return.

In his book ***Signs You'll See Just Before Jesus Comes***, Rick Renner explores the signs in Matthew 24:3-12, expounding on each one from the Greek text with his unique style of teaching. Each chapter is written to prepare and embolden a last-days generation of believers, not send them running for the hills!

The signs on the road are appearing closer together. We are on the precipice of something new. Soon we'll see the final sign at the edge of our destination as we enter the territory of the last days, hours, and minutes *just before Jesus comes*.

To order, visit us online at: **www.renner.org**

Book Resellers: Contact Harrison House at 800-722-6774
or visit **www.HarrisonHouse.com** for quantity discounts.

NO ROOM FOR COMPROMISE
VOLUME TWO

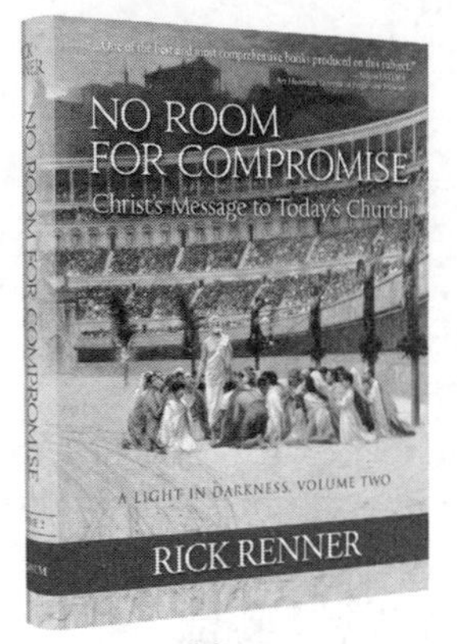

448 pages
(Hardback)

No Room for Compromise: Jesus' Message to Today's Church is *Volume Two* of the *Seven Messages to the Seven Churches* series. It presents an engaging exploration of the pagan culture of the First Century Church, with an emphasis on the city of Pergamum. Against this historical backdrop, Rick Renner highlights Jesus' message to the church of Pergamum when He appeared in a vision during the apostle John's imprisonment on the island of Patmos.

With superb photographs, many of which were shot on location in Turkey, Rick guides readers through a fascinating, detailed explanation of Jesus' message to the Pergamene church as he prophetically declares the critical significance of this message to the Church in these last days before Jesus returns. Rick also gives the reader a larger context within which to frame the pivotal moment when Jesus appeared to John on that isolated island. Rick takes the reader through a revealing overview of the first three centuries AD in which the infant Church grew amidst much opposition within a pagan world, demonstrating that darkness can never overcome the light, life, and power that the truth of Jesus Christ offers all those who believe.

Volume Two is a comprehensive, completely indexed reference book and provides:

- In-depth scriptural teaching that makes the New Testament come alive.
- Over 400 pages, including 330 beautifully designed, full-color pages.
- Nearly 400 images — including over 100 shot on location — classic artwork, artifacts, illustrations, and maps.

To order, visit us online at: **www.renner.org**

Book Resellers: Contact Harrison House at 800-722-6774 or visit **www.HarrisonHouse.com** for quantity discounts.

DRESSED TO KILL
A Biblical Approach to Spiritual Warfare and Armor

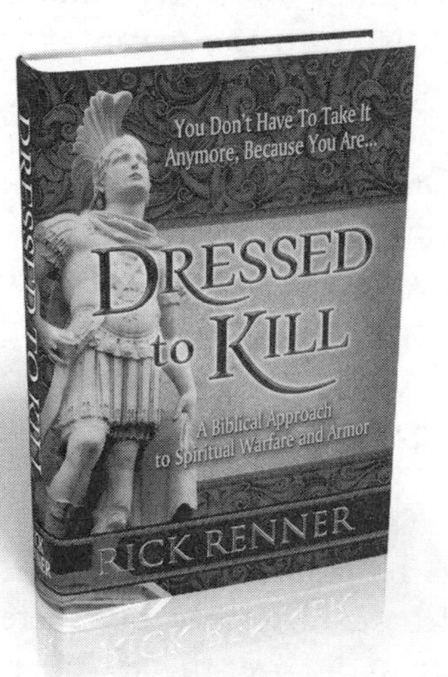

Rick Renner's book ***Dressed To Kill*** is considered by many to be a true classic on the subject of spiritual warfare. The original version, which sold more than 400,000 copies, is a curriculum staple in Bible schools worldwide. In this beautiful volume, you will find:

- 504 pages of reedited text
- 16 pages of full-color illustrations
- Questions at the end of each chapter to guide you into deeper study

In ***Dressed To Kill***, Rick explains with exacting detail the purpose and function of each piece of Roman armor. In the process, he describes the significance of our *spiritual* armor not only to withstand the onslaughts of the enemy, but also to overturn the tendencies of the carnal mind. Furthermore, Rick delivers a clear, scriptural presentation on the biblical definition of spiritual warfare — what it is and what it is not.

When you walk with God in deliberate, continual fellowship, He will enrobe you with Himself. Armed with the knowledge of who you are in Him, you will be dressed and dangerous to the works of darkness, unflinching in the face of conflict, and fully equipped to take the offensive and gain mastery over any opposition from your spiritual foe. You don't have to accept defeat anymore once you are *dressed to kill*!

To order, visit us online at: **www.renner.org**

Book Resellers: Contact Harrison House at 800-722-6774
or visit **www.HarrisonHouse.com** for quantity discounts.

LIFE IN THE COMBAT ZONE

272 pages (Paperback)

The battle lines are drawn. A collision course is set. In the coming battle, will you rush the front lines or shrink from the conflict? Although the risk is great, the rewards for engaging in the fight are sure.

In ***Life in the Combat Zone***, author Rick Renner encourages you to *fight* like a Roman soldier, *train* like a Greek athlete, and *work* like a farmer — all to become that unwavering warrior who hears God's voice, surrenders to His call, and willingly enters the combat zone poised to win.

Spiritual conflicts are real and unavoidable. There are no shortcuts to victory, but there *can* be an inevitable outcome. Rick will help you discover the key qualities you'll need to withstand the heat of the battle so you can emerge triumphant and receive the victor's crown.

To order, visit us online at: **www.renner.org**

Book Resellers: Contact Harrison House at 800-722-6774 or visit **www.HarrisonHouse.com** for quantity discounts.

The Harrison House Vision

Proclaiming the truth and the power
of the Gospel of Jesus Christ with excellence.
Challenging Christians
to live victoriously,
grow spiritually,
know God intimately.